Advanced Networking Concepts

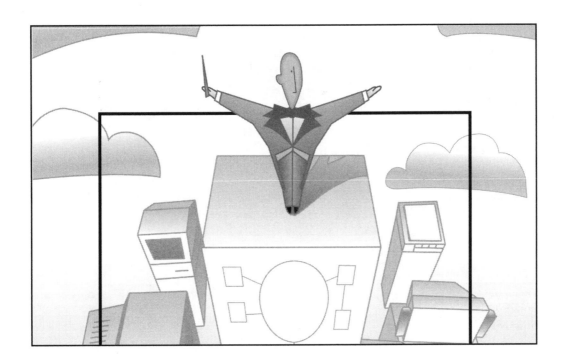

Michael J. Palmer
Robert Bruce Sinclair

COURSE
TECHNOLOGY

ONE MAIN STREET, CAMBRIDGE, MA 02142

an International Thomson Publishing company I(T)P®

Cambridge • Albany • Bonn • Boston • Cincinnati • London • Madrid • Melbourne • Mexico City
New York • Paris • San Francisco • Singapore • Tokyo • Toronto • Washington

Advanced Networking Concepts is published by Course Technology.

Managing Editor:	Wendy Welch Gordon
Product Manager:	Richard Keaveny
Associate Product Manager:	Susan Roche
Production Editor:	Nancy Shea
Marketing Manager:	Tracy Wells
Manufacturing Supervisor:	Susannah Lean
Copy Editor:	Susan Altman
Composition House:	GEX, Inc.
Cover Designer:	Doug Goodman
Text Designer:	David Reed

© 1997 by Course Technology—I(T)P®

For more information contact:

Course Technology
One Main Street
Cambridge, MA 02142

International Thomson Editores
Campos Eliseos 385, Piso 7
Col. Polanco
11560 Mexico D.F. Mexico

International Thomson Publishing Europe
Berkshire House 168-173
High Holborn
London WCIV 7AA
England

International Thomson Publishing GmbH
Königswinterer Strasse 418
53227 Bonn
Germany

Thomas Nelson Australia
102 Dodds Street
South Melbourne, 3205
Victoria, Australia

International Thomson Publishing Asia
211 Henderson Road
#05-10 Henderson Building
Singapore 0315

Nelson Canada
1120 Birchmount Road
Scarborough, Ontario
Canada M1K 5G4

International Thomson Publishing
Hirakawacho Kyowa Building, 3F
2-2-1 Hirakawacho
Chiyoda-ku, Tokyo 102
Japan

Trademarks

Course Technology and the open book logo are registered trademarks of Course Technology.
I(T)P® The ITP logo is a registered trademark of International Thomson Publishing.
Some of the product names and company names used in this book have been used for identification purposes only and may be trademarks or registered trademarks of their respective manufacturers and sellers.

Disclaimer

Course Technology reserves the right to revise this publication and make changes from time to time in its content without notice.

0-7895-0195-3

Printed in the United States of America

10 9 8 7 6 5 4 3 2 1

RELATED TITLES IN THE NETWORKING SERIES

Networking Concepts

Guide to Networking, Second Edition, by Alan M. Cohen

Introductory Network Management, by Richard Burke *(forthcoming)*

Windows NT

Hands-On Microsoft 4.0 Workstation for Server and Network Administrators, by Michael J. Palmer

Hands-On Microsoft NT 4.0 Server with Projects, by Michael J. Palmer

Microsoft NT 4.0: Network Administrator, by Michael J. Palmer *(forthcoming)*

Novell

Hands-On NetWare: A Guide to Novell NetWare 3.11/3.12 with Projects, by Ted L. Simpson

NetWare 3.11/3.12: Network Administrator, by Ted L. Simpson

Hands-On NetWare: A Guide to NetWare 4.1 with Projects, by Ted L. Simpson

NetWare 4.1: Network Administrator, by Ted L. Simpson, David Auer, and Mark Ciampa

Local Area Networks with Novell, by H. Rene Baca, Christopher M. Zager, Margaret A. Zinky

Local Area Networking With Novell Software, 2nd, by Alvin L. Rains, Michael J. Palmer

Introduction

A few years ago most networks were simple runs of wire used to join a handful of people. They were in offices with ten or fifteen computers connected to Novell, Microsoft, or Banyan file servers. The applications shared on the early networks included word processors, spreadsheets, and rudimentary databases.

The first local area networks (LANs) were a great success, leading to a push for even more connectivity. Soon equipment became available to join LANs together so that several hundred users could share applications and files. Software and hardware were developed to enable common access to printers, modems, fax machines, and other computer equipment. Host systems such as IBM mainframes, DEC minicomputers, and SUN workstations also were adapted for network access.

Today, networks have become the life blood of most organizations that rely on computing resources. We are in a second wave of networking, where network connectivity is as important as an MVS, NetWare, UNIX, or Microsoft NT operating system. An effective design of a network is as complex as programming an integrated payroll, accounting, and sales management system.

The challenge of designing a sound network is similar to designing a highway system. Like super highways, networks are filled with traffic soon after installation, and the associated problems of congestion are not far behind. Increased demands such as electronic mail, client/server applications, and enterprise-wide networking all have contributed to the growth in network traffic.

Many of today's networks have several hundred to several thousand users. Configuring the network equipment that links users and hosts is as difficult as configuring a Microsoft NT file server or a DEC alpha computer.

This book, *Advanced Networking Concepts,* combines a range of timely and complex networking subjects in one place to provide students and instructors with a single learning resource for their advanced Networking courses.

Approach

Advanced Networking Concepts sets itself apart from other networking books through its unique hands-on approach and its orientation to real-world situations and problem solving. Unlike other advanced networking concept texts that cover a narrow range of topics in excessive detail, *Advanced Networking Concepts* unites many complex networking subjects in one place so professors are able to assign one book for their students to read.

Each chapter in *Advanced Networking Concepts* includes chapter objectives, a summary of the chapter, definitions of key terms, and student exercises. Chapters 1 and 2 review networking basics. Chapter 3 discusses the network transport systems such as Ethernet, token ring, FDDI, and ATM. Chapter 4 describes protocols, including TCP/IP, IPX, X.25, ISDN, and Frame Relay. Chapter 5 describes a range of network equipment, such as repeaters, bridges, routers, hubs, and switches. Equipment examples are drawn from key vendors — Bay Networks, Cisco, 3COM, and Cabletron. Chapter 6 introduces students to network design and reinforces the concepts with real-life examples, including many network drawings. Chapter 7 focuses on advanced network design with examples drawn from educational and business campuses. All examples in this book are supplemented with detailed network drawings. Chapters 8 and 9 stress network management including network security, network management software, network load, and growth issues. Chapter 10 shows students how to troubleshoot network problems such as high-volume traffic, equipment failure, and interface card problems. A variety of network troubleshooting equipment are illustrated with examples from actual troubleshooting situations. Chapter 11 concludes the book by examining future networking directions for ATM, ISDN, imaging, electronic data interchange, and other technologies.

Features

To ensure that students comprehend the concepts discussed in this book and how they are applied in real business organizations, this text incorporates the following features:

Extensive illustrations that reflect real-life examples. To help students fully understand the material being explained, each chapter contains numerous illustrations that reflect situations students might encounter in a real-life situation.

Chapter Objectives. Each chapter begins with a detailed list of objectives that allow students to see at a glance what topics will be covered in the chapter. The objective list also provides students with a useful review and study aid.

Chapter Summary. Reflecting the authors' commitment to helping students gain a comprehensive knowledge of the subject matter, following each chapter is a summary that recaps the topics learned in the chapter.

Key Term Review. Throughout each chapter key terms are clearly introduced in bold type and defined when they are first used. At the end of each chapter, a Key Term Review List provides students with a useful review and study tool.

Review Exercises. To help students assess their comprehension of the material, each chapter concludes with a series of questions that ask students to apply the material in a real-life situation. Instructors have the flexibility to ask students to submit their answers for grading.

The Supplements

All of the supplements available with this book are provided to the instructor on a single CD-ROM.

Instructor's Manual. The Instructor's Manual that accompanies this textbook was written by the author and has been quality-assurance tested. It includes:

- Additional instructional material to help for class preparation

- PowerPoint Slides for classroom presentations, including HP Open View to view the slides without the PowerPoint Software

- Solutions for all end of chapter materials

Course Test Manager 1.1. Accompanying this book is a powerful assessment tool known as the Course Test Manager. Designed by Course Technology, this cutting-edge Windows-based testing software helps instructors design and administer tests and pre-tests. In addition to being able to generate tests that can be printed and administered, this full-featured program also has an online testing component that allows students to take tests at the computer and have their exams automatically graded.

Acknowledgments

Writing a book is a wonderful opportunity to bring together ideas, experiences, and people for the benefit of readers. The ideas and concepts associated with networking have long been exciting for us as we have grown with the technology from the days of thick net installations to modern fiber optics. This is a rewarding field that is making information more available to people of all walks of life.

Networking concepts have come alive for us through many experiences in many places with wire, connectors, file servers, and all kinds of network equipment. They also have come alive through sharing and teaching to pass along information to others.

Most importantly, creating a book brings people together with the common goal of tying words into concrete understanding. Many people have played an instrumental role in making this book possible. We want to thank the people at Course Technology for their confidence in this book and for all the work that has gone into the project. This particularly includes Wendy Welch Gordon, Joe Dougherty, and John Connelly for their efforts and interest in the project. We also want to thank Richard Keaveny for his tireless role in linking all of the pieces into a finished product. Susan Altman, our copy editor, has made significant improvements throughout the book. We also want to thank CTI staff members Susan Roche, Nancy Shea, Larry Goldstein, Greg Bigelow, Lyle Korytkowski, Tracy Wells, and Susannah Lean for their work. Further, we did not have the opportunity to learn the names of the four reviewers of the book, but we are extremely grateful for their comments and advice. Finally, a special thanks goes to our families for their constant support and patience.

Dedication

To my brother, Ed Palmer, a scholar and a friend — MJP

To my family, Marilyn, Aaron, and Sarah — RBS

TABLE OF CONTENTS

ADVANCED NETWORKING CONCEPTS

AN INTRODUCTION TO NETWORKS

At no point in history have communication opportunities been as great as they are today. Today a marketing representative in Hong Kong can send electronic mail (e-mail) to a business associate in New York City and have a reply within minutes. A professor at Boston College can access a computer in Sweden for instantaneous information about a colleague's Internet address. A minister in Wyoming can use his or her computer to discuss next Sunday's sermon with another minister in Minnesota.

These communications are made possible by networks. Networks link computers in organizations of all sizes. They link grade school students to their peers across the country, while their college counterparts collaborate on a history research paper in a school computer lab.

As network technology continues to mature, information specialists are scrambling to keep pace. Every day there are demands to connect more people to networks. Recent publicity about the Internet has caused even more people to consider tapping into the "information superhighway."

> ### AFTER READING THIS
> ### CHAPTER YOU WILL BE ABLE TO:
>
> - EXPLAIN COMPUTER NETWORKING BASICS AND NETWORKING TERMINOLOGY
> - DEFINE THE COMMON ELEMENTS OF NETWORKING
> - DESCRIBE THE TYPES OF NETWORKS
> - EXPLAIN NETWORK CAPABILITIES AND SHOW HOW THEY ARE LINKED TO USER PRODUCTIVITY

Demand for networks has made networking technology the foundation for access and exchange of information. Finding ways to make the technology widely available has come at the cost of complexity. Networking computer equipment is exacting work that requires a high level of understanding.

Also, because networks are intricately joined, stability of systems is necessary. Critical business functions and strategies depend on networks.

NETWORK BASICS

A **network** is a communication system that enables computer users to share computer equipment, application software, data, and voice and video transmissions. Networks can link users who are across the room or across the world. Network information is transmitted by wire or through radio waves, such as microwaves. There are two primary reasons for having a network. First, by sharing software and equipment, network owners are able to save expenses on resources. One printer can be used for an entire office, saving the cost of attaching a printer to each computer. Second, networks make people more productive. People are able to share information without leaving their offices or homes.

A simple network consists of personal computers connected to one another by a single "run" of wire. An example of a simple network is five computers in the same office area connected by one segment of cable. Communication between the computers occurs peer-to-peer. In **peer-to-peer communication**, each computer is able to "talk" directly with any of the other computers on the network. Files and network drives can be shared among the networked computers. Figure 1-1 illustrates a simple network.

Figure 1-1

A simple
peer-to-peer
network

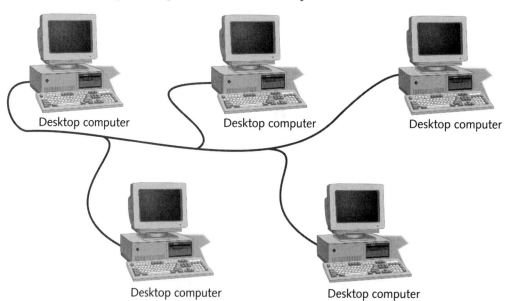

Desktop computer   Desktop computer   Desktop computer

Desktop computer   Desktop computer

More advanced networks share **file servers**, such as Novell NetWare and Microsoft NT servers. A file server is a computer with an operating system that allows multiple users on a network to access software applications and data files. Also it may provide services such as network printer management and fax service management.

To the network, a file server is a **host** machine. Examples of hosts are IBM mainframe computers, Sun UNIX computers, and DEC Alpha minicomputers. Hosts are computers that have operating systems designed to allow several users to access them at the same time. Processing of data may occur on the host, as is the case with an IBM mainframe. Processing also may occur on the host's client, as is true for a NetWare file server.

A **client** is any computer that can access a host. Personal computers are the most typical kind of client. Another client might be a Sun Microsystem workstation. The workstation may fill two roles, one as a host to other computers and one as a client of another host. A **workstation** is a computer with its own CPU. Processing by the CPU enables users to perform mathematical computations, create a spreadsheet, compile a computer program, or write a term paper. A personal computer (PC), such as an 80486 or Pentium computer, is a typical workstation. The Sun UNIX computer is an even more powerful workstation.

Advanced networks can have a combination of host and client computers. They also can have attached peripherals, such as printers, fax machines, and other computer equipment. Figure 1-2 illustrates an advanced network.

NETWORKING ELEMENTS

Today's networks have several common elements. These are listed in Table 1-1.

Each connection on a network is a **node**. Hosts, clients, workstations, and printers are all nodes. The concept of a node is important to a network, because the network can experience problems if too many nodes are attached to one segment.

To share network resources, nodes must be linked together physically. **Cabling** is the most common way to join network nodes. This method involves running communication cable between each node. The cable provides a physical medium for transmitting an signal. The signal contains data that are used by workstations, hosts, and printers. Most nodes have a **network interface card (NIC)** that can capture the signal and translate it for use by the node. Figure 1-3 (on page 5) is an example of a network interface card.

Besides cabling, nodes can be linked by transmitting data on radio frequencies. Amateur radio operators were among the first users of this technology. They have established a network of electronic bulletin boards where nodes communicate through packet radio. Wireless commercial networks that use **spread spectrum technology (SST)** are also emerging. This technology takes advantage of high-frequency communications where the data-carrying signal is transmitted from one location to another by low-power transmission. Wireless networks are less common than cabled networks, but this technology is growing at a rapid pace.

All networks have a physical layout that determines how the data signal goes from one node to the next. The physical layout is the **topology** of the network. The topology is most easily represented by drawing the connections between network nodes. Nodes can be connected in star patterns, in circles, or in a straight line pattern. As later chapters will show, network topology influences how efficiently a network operates and how easily problems can be repaired.

Figure 1-2

An example of an advanced network

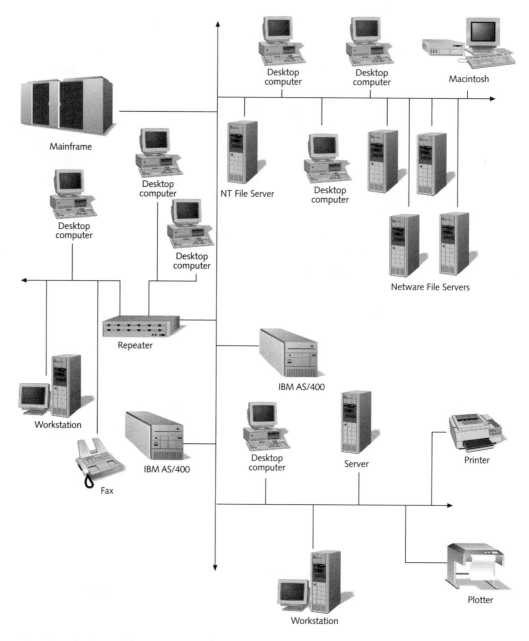

Nodes
Cabling
Topology
Data Packets
Addressing
Communication Software
Data Transmission Rate

Table 1-1

Common network elements

Figure 1-3

A network
interface card
(NIC)

The signal that goes between network nodes is called a **data packet**. The communication software on each node packages data into small units of information to be transported by the electrical signal. It takes many packets of data to print a single page of text on a network printer.

The form of the packet is determined by the type of communication software used on the network. Most packets also contain information about which node sent the packet, which node is to receive the packet, the type of data to be transmitted, the size of the packet, and a means of detecting damaged packets.

Network topologies and cabling influence the speed at which packets are able to travel. The **transmission rate** of packets many be as low as 1 megabits per second (Mbps) or over 100 times that speed. Cabling and radio transmission technologies are constantly evolving to increase packet transmission rates.

Packets find their way from one node to another by means of **addressing**. Each node on a network must have a unique "address." Each individual network also has its own address. The target and source addresses are critical to the construction of a packet and its ability to find its destination. Figure 1-4 shows an example of addresses in a network.

Figure 1-4

Network nodes
with unique
addresses

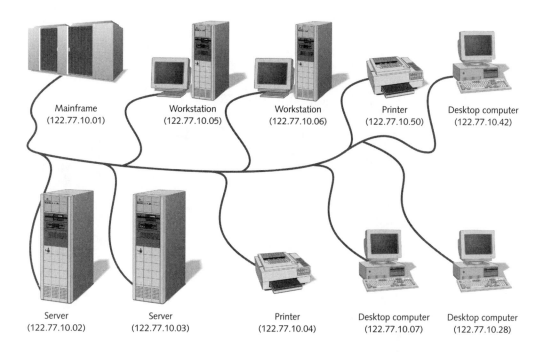

Mainframe
(122.77.10.01)

Workstation
(122.77.10.05)

Workstation
(122.77.10.06)

Printer
(122.77.10.50)

Desktop computer
(122.77.10.42)

Server
(122.77.10.02)

Server
(122.77.10.03)

Printer
(122.77.10.04)

Desktop computer
(122.77.10.07)

Desktop computer
(122.77.10.28)

The heart of any network is the communication software used to guide data along their way. All networks use one or more software **protocols** that enable data packaging and transmission. Protocols define the rules for handling and interpreting transmitted data. Each data packet is constructed according to the rules of the network protocol. For example, many college campuses use the **Transmission Control Protocol/Internet Protocol (TCP/IP)** to transmit data. Novell NetWare networks use the **Internetwork Packet Exchange (IPX)** and the **Sequenced Packet Exchange (SPX)** protocols. These protocols can be transmitted on a single network as long as workstations can recognize the protocols. (Chapter 4 presents a detailed explanation of these protocols.)

TYPES OF NETWORKS

Before networking, connecting computers to one another was accomplished by making direct connections to a mainframe or minicomputer. For example, a workstation could be connected to a mainframe to reduce the number of computing resources needed, such as terminals. On a single workstation, users could perform word processing and spreadsheet tasks, or run software to access a mainframe like a terminal.

Modems also have been used to connect computers over long and short distances by telephone wire. Unfortunately modems offer very limited resource sharing, because host printers and other devices are not within close proximity.

Networks have opened resource-sharing possibilities that were not possible through modems or by directly connecting computers. On a network, laser printers, color printers, graphics machines, fax machines, plotters, CD-ROM drives, and central disk storage all can be shared by large numbers of users.

Early networks connected users in close proximity, such as in the same office area or floor of a building. These were truly **local area networks (LANs)** with a limited area of service. Once LANs became a reality, the push was on to find ways to connect one LAN to another—for instance to connect a LAN in one building with a LAN in an adjacent building. Connecting multiple LANs has created **metropolitan area networks (MANs)**. A large business campus might have LANs used for administrative processing connected to LANs used for scientific research. A state university in one city can have a MAN that links its research centers and other facilities throughout the same city.

The reach of networks has grown to extend across continents and oceans. These **wide area networks (WANs)** give college students at the University of Oregon the ability to use supercomputers housed at the University of Illinois. A commercial vendor in Rochester, New York, can send software application updates to clients in Colorado and in London, England, via network connections.

Network technology is pervasive and has blurred the distinctions between LANs, MANs, and WANs. It is now difficult to define where a LAN ends and a WAN begins. The distinctions are growing more vague as television cable companies partner with telephone companies to bring networking into every home.

NETWORK CAPABILITIES

In the last 30 years the emphasis in computing has moved from a focus on the needs of hosts to a focus on the needs of the computer user. IBM mainframe computers, NetWare and NT file servers, and other hosts are no longer the center of computing strategy. Networking to meet the needs of users has become the infrastructure of computing. The information available to users is massive and growing daily. Movement today is toward high-performance networks with unlimited connectivity.

Present user-oriented network capabilities include the following:

- File and print services
- Fax services
- Modem services
- Host access
- Client/server software
- Information networks (such as the Internet)

E-MAIL

Electronic mail has become a critical application on networks. Many organizations rely on their e-mail services to communicate about projects, to discuss sales strategies, and to prepare for meetings. College professors are contacted by their students via e-mail for help on tests and assignments. Many software vendors provide assistance to their customers by e-mail. Even television viewers can contact their favorite news organizations through e-mail.

A major advantage of e-mail is that it is fast and convenient. Another advantage is that mail distribution lists can be built so that many people at different locations can receive the same message. Also, many networked organizations are offering calendar and appointment software to complement e-mail. For example, Microsoft's Schedule+ enables a user to view appointments on another person's calendar and send an invitation for a new appointment by Microsoft Mail or Microsoft Exchange.

FILE AND PRINT SERVICES

Networks that have file servers can offer a range of file and print services. The network user can have an account on a file server for the purpose of storing work files, such as a database. He or she also can make the database available to other people within a department workgroup, eliminating the need to transfer a floppy disk from person to person.

Another advantage of file sharing is the ability to run software applications on multiple workstations. A site license can be purchased to place one copy of a word processor on the network file server to be shared by 200 users. When a software upgrade is released, only the version on the server needs to be replaced, rather than having to upgrade all 200 computers that access the server.

Network print services make a variety of printers available to users. Laser printers, color printers, and plotters all can be shared by a workgroup on the network. For example, your office partner can print a report on a laser printer from a NetWare server while you are printing an architectural drawing on a plotter from your DEC workstation.

FAX SERVERS

Network fax servers reduce the need to purchase a fax machine for every department in an organization. From anywhere on the network, a user can prepare a document with graphics and send it to a fax server. Some fax servers have interfaces to popular e-mail packages. When a fax comes in, it is sent to the user's electronic mailbox. Other interfaces are similar to print servers, where incoming faxes are automatically printed on a designated printer.

ACCESS SERVERS

Access servers enable users to dial into a network from home or while traveling. Novell offers the Network Access Server (NAS), which enables users to log onto a NetWare server through modems. The NAS is a single network computer with software to make it act like several individual remote computers that log onto a NetWare file server.

A full range of host computers can exist on the same network to offer many kinds of processing options. For example, a college campus network may have five Microsoft NT servers, eight Novell NetWare servers, an IBM mainframe computer, an IBM RISC 6000 computer, two Digital (DEC) Alpha computers, and 40 Sun workstations. A single user on the network can access one or all of these computers, given the proper security authorizations. And that user can print on the same Hewlett-Packard plotter from the IBM mainframe or from the NT server.

CLIENT/SERVER APPLICATIONS

A major push for networking services today is the drive to implement new **client/server applications**. Client/server applications involve computing that is performed on the client side (e.g., individual workstations) as well as on the server side. This represents a shift from host-based computing, in which all processing occurs on the host computer, such as a mainframe. It also is a shift from server-based computing, such as NetWare, in which files are loaded from the server onto the workstation for processing at the workstation.

An example of a client/server application might be a payroll system designed to use both the server and the workstation. The payroll system's computations, such as the payroll benefit and deduction calculations, would be performed at the workstation to relieve the CPU load on the server. Large complex reports would be processed by the server's database through a custom-built data view, and then transmitted to the workstation for viewing.

There are efforts throughout industry to "re-engineer" how companies are organized. Many organizations and consultants are working with client/server applications to place more information in the hands of computer users and make it easier to use. This is possible only with extensive networking capabilities.

INTERNET

The Internet is the broadest example of networking capabilities. It is a vast collection of thousands of networks connected worldwide. Millions of computer users are attached to these networks in every part of the United States and in countries all over the world. The Internet brings together government, educational, business, and research organizations. Internet participants share in discussion groups, work on leading-edge technological developments, conduct business, publish news stories, and access weather information.

NETWORKS IN INDUSTRY, GOVERNMENT, AND EDUCATION

The business edge for companies is closely tied in with their ability to use computer resources effectively. In the 1980s, many companies discovered that their costs to support mainframe technology were high when compared to the benefits of the technology. They began "downsizing" applications to run on smaller computers, such as IBM's RS/6000. Many companies also implemented applications on PC-based file servers, such as NetWare. Companies also have installed large cable "plants" to network PCs and to provide greater connectivity to the decentralized computers and file servers. Today's emphasis on client/server development makes networking even more central to competitive business strategies.

Networks have become the center of computing as more data are moved off mainframe computers. Most business, government and educational users will eventually connect to a network.

Business users will not find cost savings in the move to client/server computing and networks. Instead, future benefits will be focused on productivity. Systems will be designed around the way offices conduct business, so the benefits will be in placing more information at the fingertips of those who need it.

Many companies already are taking advantage of the opportunities. For example, mainframe reporting systems have traditionally been difficult to use, except for expert users and programmers. Newer reporting capabilities available through tools such as Microsoft Access, Crystal Reports, and other reporting tools are giving users control over the reports they create. Relational databases such as Oracle, Sybase, and Microsoft's SQL Server are making data more accessible to users through small computer systems.

Electronic mail systems also have contributed to productivity by their ability to send data objects such as voice messages, spreadsheets, bar graphs, reports, and pictures. Mail can be sent across the room or across the world.

Maturing **graphical user interfaces (GUI)** also are making users more productive. This interface uses pictures and graphics to represent operations on the computer. For example, Windows is a GUI interface designed to make using a computer intuitive. GUI applications written in development tools such as PowerBuilder, Visual Basic, and CA-Realia have a fast development cycle. And the results of these tools are software applications that are very intuitive to use. Less user training is needed and documentation can be written in GUI formats, such as Microsoft Help.

Central to increasing productivity is the ability to share resources through networking. Figure 1-5 lists some of the productivity gains related to networking.

Figure 1-5

Productivity gains from networking

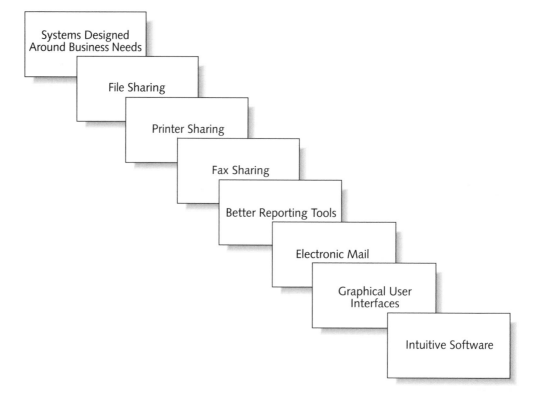

Besides industry, educators and government have made large strides in productivity. For example, the University Corporation for Atmospheric Research offers a range of software services through the Internet. College library consortiums make information available on library holdings, serials, periodicals, and other services. Without walking to the campus library, a student can determine if one of the consortium libraries has a particular book needed for a research project.

On many college campuses, students can connect to the school network from their dorm rooms. They have access to word processing software, compilers, spreadsheets, CAD software, library resources, e-mail, and a range of other services. If the student does not own a computer, he or she can go to a lab. Computer labs provide UNIX workstations, PCs, printers, plotters, and other services students need.

If a student is working on an assignment late at night, he or she can send e-mail containing a question to his or her professor. The student also may send a query out to other students in the class, or to students at another campus.

SUMMARY

Networks have become the central computing resource for many companies, schools, and government agencies. Today's networks range from simple network designs with peer-to-peer communications in a small office or department to advanced networks with file servers, mainframes, workstations, and printers which reach throughout a large business campus.

Networks consist of elements such as nodes, cabling, network topology, data packets, addressing, communication software, and established data transmission speeds. As networking technology advances, there will be more wireless network options, which will give networks even greater reach than is available through cabled networks.

Advances in networking already have blurred distinctions between LANs, MANs, and WANs. These distinctions will continue to be less important as the Internet reaches more people and as private vendors bring networking into homes, just as cable TV is a common presence today.

Existing networks have given computer users high expectations for gains in productivity. Network capabilities such as e-mail, file services, print services, fax services, access to the Internet, client/server applications, and dial-in services have become important to user productivity. These capabilities are now central to how organizations conduct their activities.

KEY TERMS

Term/Acronym	Definition
Addressing	Network equipment is identified by means of a unique "address." No two network computers, printers, or other network equipment will have the same address assigned to them.
Cabling	The communication wire used to connect equipment in a network. The cable provides a medium for the electrical signal that carries information from one networked computer to another.
Client	A computer that is used to access a file server, mainframe, mini-computer, or other computer that allows access to multiple users. The client may use the accessed computer (host) in order to process data. Other software and data may be transferred from the main computer to the client for processing.

Client/Server Applications	Many software applications are being written based on networking capabilities. In client/server systems, processing of data may occur at the workstation (client) or at the host or server.
Data Packet	The unit of information that is sent from one network node to the next. A computer on the network forms data into small distinct units. The data-filled units are sent one at a time to the receiving computer.
File Server	A computer with an operating system that enables multiple users to access it and share software applications and data files.
Graphical User Interface (GUI)	Interface that uses pictures and graphics to represent operations on the computer.
Host	This type of computer has an operating system that allows multiple computers to access it at the same time. Programs and information may be processed at the host, or they may be downloaded to the accessing computer (client) for processing.
Internetwork Packet Exchange (IPX)	This protocol is used by Novell NetWare and provides best-effort delivery of data packets. This protocol uses a variation of the data transfer algorithm known as routing information protocol.
Local Area Network (LAN)	A series of interconnected computers, printers, and other computer equipment that share hardware and software resources. The service area is usually limited to a given floor, office area, or building.
Metropolitan Area Network (MAN)	This is a network that reaches throughout a large area, such as a city or a large college campus.
Network	A communication system that enables many users to share computer resources such as personal computers, application software, data/voice/video information, host computers, printers, and fax capabilities.
Network Interface Card (NIC)	This electrical circuit board is used by computers, printers, and other equipment so they are able to connect to a network and transfer data.
Node	Any device or entity connected to a network is a node. Network-connected personal computers, file servers, printers, and mainframes are individual nodes.
Peer-to-Peer Communication	In this type of communication, any computer can communicate with other computers on an equal or peer-like basis.
Protocol	An established guideline that determines how networked data are formatted into a packet, how they are transmitted, and how they are interpreted at the receiving end.
Sequenced Packet Exchange (SPX)	This protocol is packet-oriented and relies on sequence numbers or acknowledgments (provided by the packet) for data transmission.
Spread Spectrum Technology (SST)	This technology is used by wireless networks in place of cable to allow network nodes to communicate. Network data are transmitted by means of high-frequency radio signals.

Transmission Control Protocol/Internet Protocol (TCP/IP)	Two combined protocols. TCP is a reliable connection-oriented data transfer method that uses connectionless routing, which is provided by IP.
Topology	The layout or physical design of a network is its topology. Networks are built with different physical designs, including a star shape, a circle, and a straight line.
Transmission Rate	The speed at which data are transported on a network. On some networks the speed may be as low as 1 megabits per second (Mbps), and on others it may be over 100 Mbps.
Wide Area Network (WAN)	A far reaching system of networks. WANs can extend across state lines and across continents. They make it possible for thousands of users to send data to one another.
Workstation	Any computer that has its own CPU. The workstation may be used as a stand-alone computer for word processing, spreadsheet creation, or other software applications. It also may be used to access another computer such as a file server or a mainframe computer.

REVIEW EXERCISES

1. Trace the development of networking technology over the past ten years. What new capabilities do you predict for the next five years?

2. Explain how research and development activities in private industry can be advanced through use of the "information highway."

3. Why is it becoming more difficult to distinguish between LANs, MANs, and WANs? Will there continue to be a need for the term LAN?

4. Describe five capabilities of the Internet. Access the Internet and describe how you would locate the Internet addresses of professors or researchers at four U.S. universities and two European universities.

5. What are the essential components of a network? Research how these components are used at your school.

6. Why is a reliable e-mail server important? Describe five common uses of e-mail. What would happen if e-mail was not available on your campus?

7. How many file servers are in use at your campus? How many are on the campus network? How are the file servers on the network used?

8. _____ enables data packets to go to the intended destination.

9. What are some examples of resources that can be shared on a network?

10. Describe the process used to send data on a network.

11. Data transmission rates are measured in _____.

NETWORK TOPOLOGY AND STANDARDS

Every network is created to address particular computing needs. Some networks house vital business functions, while others may support scientific research. There are several ways to design a network to accommodate the needs of those who will be using it. Once a network is in place and fulfilling user needs, a significant investment has been made. This investment includes cabling, network equipment, file servers, workstations, and hosts. Network design and protecting the user's investment in a network are two interrelated concerns. The network design impacts the life of the investment in the network. Some designs are low in cost, but expensive to maintain or upgrade. Other designs are easy to maintain and offer simple upgrade paths. This chapter discusses basic design issues, beginning with a description of network topologies and their strengths and weaknesses.

Then network standards organizations and the standards they have created are discussed. These standards represent an effort to protect the user's investment by encouraging vendors to adopt common design and communication models. These common models enable the user to leverage existing equipment to take advantage of present and emerging technologies.

AFTER READING THIS CHAPTER YOU WILL BE ABLE TO:

- DEFINE NETWORK TOPOLOGY
- DESCRIBE HOW NETWORK APPLICATIONS INFLUENCE THE TOPOLOGY SELECTED FOR A NETWORK
- DESCRIBE THE NETWORK STANDARDS ORGANIZATIONS
- EXPLAIN NETWORK LAYER ARCHITECTURE
- EXPLAIN THE OSI NETWORK MODEL

TOPOLOGY

The design layout of a network is its topology. Before a network is installed, it is critical to select a topology that is appropriate to the intended use for the network. Some networks are used primarily to access word processing applications. Others focus on critical administrative applications such as accounting and payroll functions, and reliability is important. Still others are intended for scientific and engineering applications that require transmission of large computer-aided design (CAD) and drawing files.

Selecting the best topology for an installation requires the network designer to be a systems analyst. The systems analyst's job is to work with the proposed network computer users to inventory their immediate and future computing needs. Several factors must to be examined in the analysis stage. These include finding answers to the following questions:

- What applications will be used on the network?
- What types of hosts and file servers are to be connected?
- Will the network be connected to other networks?
- Will the network have mission critical applications?
- Is data transmission speed important?
- What network security is needed?
- What is the anticipated growth in the use of the network?

The applications intended to be used in a network influence the number and frequency of packets to be transmitted, which is known as **network traffic**. If the network users are primarily accessing word processing software, the network traffic will be relatively low, and most of the work will be performed at workstations, rather than on the network. Client/server applications generate a medium to high level of network traffic, depending on the client/server software design. Networks on which there is frequent exchange of database information, such as Microsoft Access files, have medium to high network traffic. CAD applications generate high levels of traffic because they involve extremely large data files.

The influence on a network of hosts and file servers is closely linked to the type of software applications that are used. For example, some colleges use networked file server systems to verify the students' meal plans, athletic gym privileges, and privileges to attend entertainment events. These systems use plastic ID cards that are read by magnetic bar coding devices. The bar code readers are connected to the file server through the network. This type of file server generates a high volume of network traffic because it is designed to constantly poll the bar code readers for activity.

Whether other networks will be connected to the new network also affects the topology used. The network topology for a small business that will never use more than four computers will be different from the topology required by an industrial campus. The small business is unlikely to connect to additional networks. The industrial campus may consist of several interconnected networks, such as a network to control machines in the plant, a network for the business systems, and a network for the research scientists. Some topologies permit better network **connectivity** than other topologies.

Another question that the systems analyst should ask is whether the applications on the network are "mission-critical." If the network is used for a company's payroll, then it is mission-critical. This type of network topology will need to include **system redundancy**. That is, the network must include alternate routes for data transmission, so that failure of one part of the network does not prevent the payroll from running. This is called fail-safe technology.

Some networks, such as those on which large files are transmitted, need high-speed data transmission capabilities. The **network speed** is important to the productivity of the users. High-speed capability is particularly needed when images, graphics, and other large files need to be transported over long distances.

Security is another issue that influences network design. **Security** is protection of data so that only authorized individuals have access to confidential information. Security involves network designs that permit **data encryption** and controlling who has access to given hosts. Data encryption uses algorithms to encode data packets before they are transmitted, and decoding by the computer at the receiving end. The process of limiting access to hosts is most effective when the network equipment is set up to ensure that only designated workstations are able to communicate with a particular host.

Network topology directly influences the potential for *growth*. College campus networks and large industrial networks must be designed to permit growth. In these situations, new hosts, additional workstations, and more peripherals are constantly being added. For example, a scientific department may determine there is a need to connect their isolated LAN to the broader network for communication with administrative departments. Or two business units may decide to merge and thus will require additional network capability.

BUS TOPOLOGY

The **bus** topology is one of the most common network designs (Figure 2-1). It consists of a single cable, with multiple nodes attached to it. The logic behind the design layout is a linear segment of cable that is terminated at each end. The terminators are 50-ohm electrical resistors.

Data are transmitted to all nodes, each of which must determine if it is the target destination.

The bus topology has a relatively low implementation cost. The management costs, though, are high. For example, it is difficult to isolate a single malfunctioning node, and one defective node can take down the entire network (although the design advances presented in later chapters make this less likely).

RING TOPOLOGY

The **ring** topology has no endpoint or terminators. The layout is a continuous loop of cable to which the network nodes are attached (Figure 2-2).

Figure 2-1

Bus topology

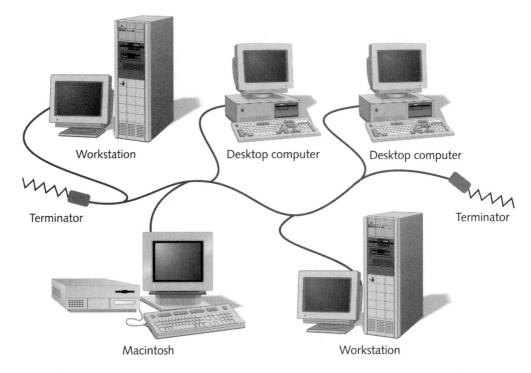

Figure 2-2

Ring topology

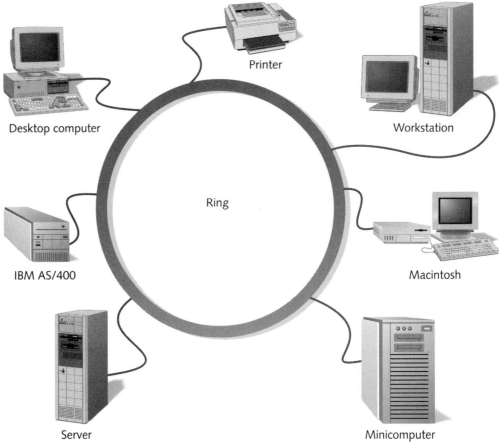

They pass the transmitted signal from node to node. When it was first developed, the ring topology permitted data to go in one direction only, stopping at the node that originated the transmission. New high-speed ring technologies consist of two loops for redundant data transmission in opposite directions. Figure 2-3 shows a high-speed dual ring topology.

Figure 2-3

High-speed
dual ring

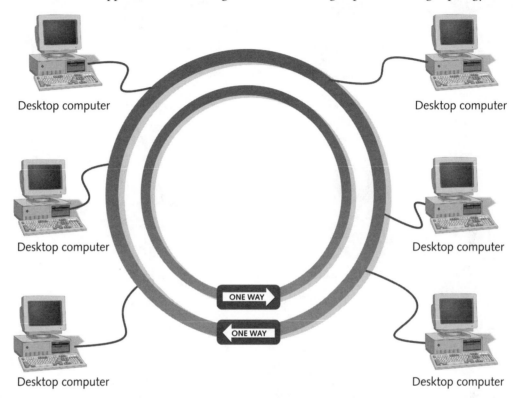

Desktop computer   Desktop computer

Desktop computer   Desktop computer

ONE WAY

ONE WAY

Desktop computer   Desktop computer

The ring topology is relatively expensive to implement, but it is easier to manage than the bus topology. The network equipment used to build the ring makes it easy to locate a defective node. This topology is well suited for transmitting signals over long distances, and it handles high-volume network traffic better than the bus topology.

STAR TOPOLOGY

The oldest topology is the **star**, which was introduced with digital and analog switching devices used in telephone systems. The physical layout of the star topology consists of multiple nodes attached to a central hub (Figure 2-4). Single wire segments radiate from the hub like a star.

The start-up costs of the star topology are greater than for a bus network and comparable to those of the ring network. This is because the star topology requires a wiring hub and more cabling than the bus topology. Like the ring topology, however, the star is easier to manage, because malfunctioning nodes can be identified quickly. If a node or a cable run is damaged, it is easily isolated from the network, and service to the other nodes is not affected.

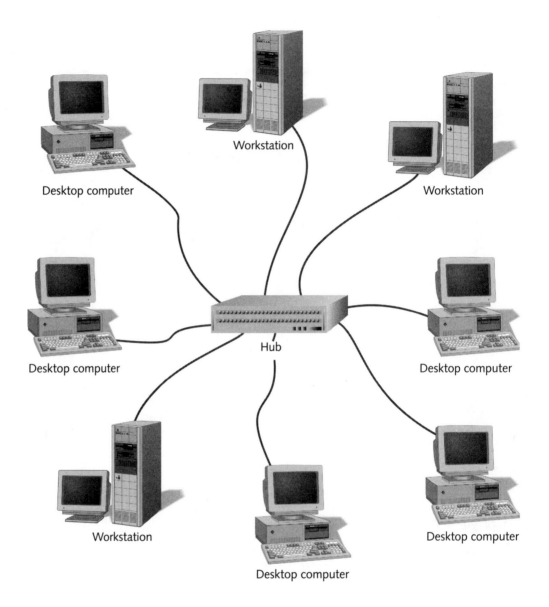

Figure 2-4

Star topology

STANDARDS ORGANIZATIONS

Network design and topology require standards to guide equipment vendors and network personnel. The standards provide common ground for transmitting data, manufacturing generic network equipment, and designing operating systems for use on a network. Network standards define the maximum time a packet has to travel from one node to another before it is determined that the packet did not reach its destination. They define what to do when a packet is sent with only partial information, and they establish how to prevent confusion when too many packets are sent at once.

Several different standards organizations have established networking guidelines. These organizations exist to help protect the consumer's investment in networking equipment. In the absence of standards, vendors are likely to develop proprietary equipment that locks consumers into each vendor's line of products. Pressure from consumers has led to support of the standards organizations and has motivated vendors to follow the established standards. For example, equipment purchased for one token ring network will work on another because of standards, and different LANs can be interconnected because standards exist.

A basic rule when purchasing network equipment is to *purchase network equipment that follows common network standards or that follows proposed standards, and to avoid proprietary equipment supported by a single vendor.*

AMERICAN NATIONAL STANDARDS INSTITUTE

One standards organization that has impacted many areas of technology is the American National Standards Institute (ANSI). This group has set standards ranging from screen display attributes to guidelines for fiber optic cable transmissions. ANSI serves as the United States' representative to the International Standards Organization.

INSTITUTE OF ELECTRICAL AND ELECTRONICS ENGINEERS

An influential international organization that establishes communication standards is the Institute of Electrical and Electronics Engineers (IEEE). The Computer Society Local Network Committee of the IEEE has developed many LAN standards in use today. The IEEE also sets standards for integrated voice and data networks.

CONSULTATIVE COMMITTEE ON INTERNATIONAL TELEGRAPH AND TELEPHONE

A third international standards organization is the Consultative Committee on International Telegraph and Telephone (CCITT). Based in Geneva, Switzerland, this branch of the International Telecommunications Union (ITU) sets standards for modems, e-mail, and digital telephone systems.

The CCITT addresses e-mail through its X.400 standard and the emerging X.500 recommendations. The X.400 standard contains guidelines for placing mail messages in an envelope so that receiving units, or gateways, are able to receive and translate incoming mail. For example, Microsoft Mail's gateway can receive mail from cc:Mail's gateway successfully because both are X.400 compliant.

The X.400 standard also contains guidelines for mailing video, voice, and graphics files. This enables a Microsoft Excel spreadsheet or a Crystal Services database report to be sent from a Microsoft Mail gateway to any X.400 mail gateway.

The X.400 recommended standards address the areas listed below:

- Mail service and user interface elements
- Guidelines for encoding and decoding mail objects
- Syntax for mail transfer
- Methods to ensure reliable mail transfer
- Guidelines for a message transfer layer
- Messaging protocol for telex

The CCITT is currently developing X.500 standards to complement X.400. The X.500 guidelines enable users of different mail packages to more effectively look up other mail users and address e-mail to them. The X.500 standards encourage the creation of universal directories, similar to the telephone system's white pages for private customers and yellow pages for commercial customers. For example, the X.400 and X.500 standards enable Lars Svenson in Stockholm, Sweden to send an economics report with associated bar graphs and database reports to Sally Martin in Chicago, Illinois. The X.500-compliant mail package at Lars's computer searches the naming service directory to find Sally's network e-mail address. The e-mail address is encoded along with the text and graphics by the mail gateway at Lars's site, per the X.400 guidelines. It is then routed to the gateway that processes Sally's mail. The gateway strips off the X.400 encoding and forwards the mail to Sally's electronic post office box, so it is available to read as soon as Sally turns on her computer.

E-mail vendors have not fully applied the X.400 and X.500 standards, but most are committed to this direction.

INTERNATIONAL STANDARDS ORGANIZATION

The International Standards Organization (ISO) is based in Geneva, Switzerland. Each nation has an option to participate in this organization. The ISO and ANSI have developed the seven-layer network communications model known as Open Systems Interconnect (OSI). The OSI model was developed in 1974 in an effort to standardize network architecture. The goal was to encourage vendors to develop network equipment that would avoid proprietary design. For example, this means that routers made by any of several vendors can all work on the same network.

The OSI model consists of seven distinct modules (Figure 2-5). Although each module performs a specific function, together the modules provide for integrated network services and communication, and enable software communication between all layers of the model.

Figure 2-5

OSI seven-
layer model

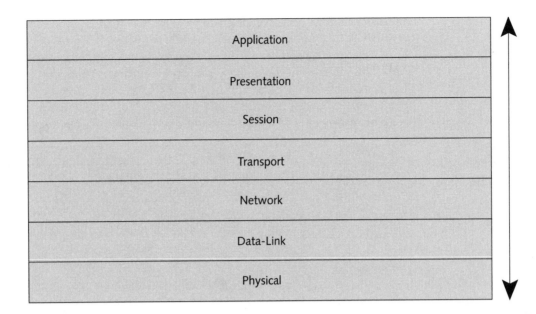

OSI LAYERED ARCHITECTURE

The OSI model is an example of **layered architecture**. Each layer is a module performing one primary type of function and has its own format of communication instructions,
called protocols. The protocols used to communicate between functions within the same
layer are called **peer protocols** (Figure 2-6). Each layer will be discussed in detail in the
following pages.

Figure 2-6

OSI model
peer protocols

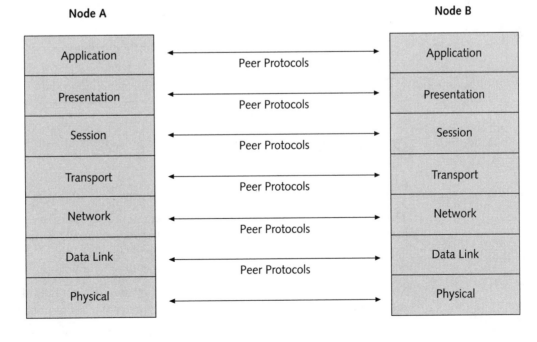

Information from one layer is transferred to the next by means of commands called **primitives**. The information that is transferred is called a protocol data unit (PDU). As the information progresses to the next layer, new control information is added to the PDU. This information is known as protocol control information (PCI). The PDU is user data combined with PCI data. When the PDU is ready to be passed to the next layer, instructions needed to transfer it to that layer are added. These are called interface control information (ICI). At this point, the unit becomes the interface data unit (IDU).

OSI LAYER	DESCRIPTION
Physical Layer	This layer is the data transmission medium for network communications and is responsible for monitoring data error rates.
Data-Link Layer	Data packets are encoded and decoded into electrical signals at this layer. Transmissions are synchronized so that frames are sent in the same sequence as received.
Network Layer	This layer creates the logical paths, known as virtual circuits, for transmitting data from node to node. Routing data is a function of this layer.
Transport Layer	The successful node–to–node transportation of data is managed by this layer. Packet errors, packet order, and other critical transport issues are handled.
Session Layer	The transmission link between two nodes is maintained by this layer to ensure that point–to–point transmissions are established and remain uninterrupted.
Presentation Layer	This layer formats and encrypts data to be sent across a network.
Application Layer	Application services are provided by this layer for file transfers, e-mail, and other network software services.

Once the IDU is received by the next layer, the ICI is stripped out. The resulting packet is called the service data unit (SDU). (See Figure 2-7 for an example of these layered communications.) As the SDU travels from one layer to the next, each layer adds its own information. Thus, the packet grows larger as it travels through the layers.

OSI LAYERS

Physical layer

The lowest layer of the OSI model is the physical layer. This layer is the data transfer medium. Protocols used within the physical layer are responsible for generating and detecting voltage in order to transmit and receive signals carrying data. The cabling and equipment that link the nodes to one another all form the physical layer.

The physical layer handles the data transmission rate and monitors data error rates. It is affected by physical network problems, such as a defective bus terminator.

The protocols developed by standards committees are built into the physical layer. These include the IEEE 802 protocols for Ethernet and token ring network communications (see Chapter 3). Cable specifications also are incorporated into the physical layer.

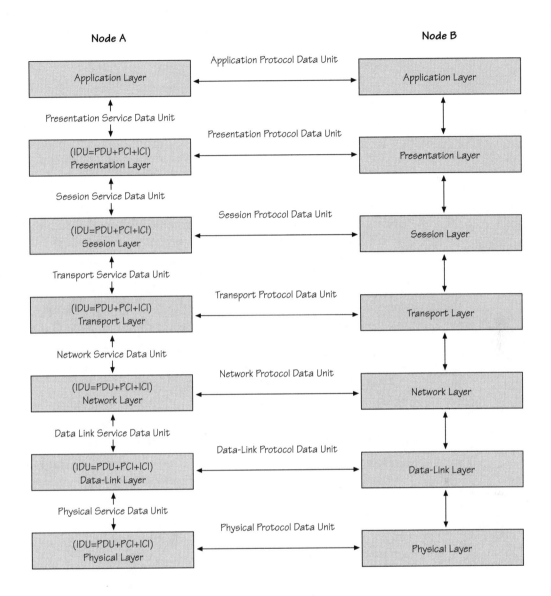

Figure 2-7

Layered communications in the OSI model

Data-Link Layer

The construction of data packets is accomplished at this level. Each packet is formatted in a specified way, so that data transmissions are synchronized. This level enables the data to be encoded in an electrical signal by the transmitting node, decoded by the receiving node, and checked for errors. The data-link layer also creates the formatting that allows packets to contain node addressing.

Once communication is established between two nodes, their data-link layers are connected physically (through the physical layer) and logically (through peer protocols). The communication is first established by transmission of a small set of signals. As soon as the link has been made, the receiving data-link layer decodes the signal into "packets" or "frames." It removes the PCI from the transmitting data-link layer and attaches its own PCI information for the next OSI layer. The data-link layer checks incoming signals for duplicate, incorrect, or partially received data. If an error is detected, it requests a retransmission of the data. As the data-link layer transfers frames up to the next layer, it ensures that frames are sent in the same order as received.

On IEEE 802–compliant LANs, the data-link layer incorporates the logical link control (LLC) protocol. This is an example of a peer protocol. It enables two communicating data-link layers on separate nodes to have common guidelines for flow control, error handling, and data retransmission requests.

Network layer

The third layer up is the network layer. This layer controls the passage of packets along the network. All networks consist of physical routes (cable paths) and logical routes (software paths). Packets are sent along the most expedient routes, physical and logical, for efficient transmissions. This layer also permits packets to be sent from one network to another, through routers. Routers are physical devices that contain software to enable packets formatted on one network to reach a different network in a format that the second network understands. By controlling the passage of packets, the network layer acts like a switching station, routing packets along the most efficient of several different paths.

The network layer is able to route data on different paths by creating **virtual** (logical) **circuits**. Virtual circuits are logical communication paths set up to send and receive data. The virtual circuits are known only to the network layer.

Since the network layer manages data along several virtual circuits, the data can arrive in the wrong sequence. The network layer is responsible for tracking this situation and resequencing the packets before they are transported to the next layer.

Similar to the data-link layer, the network layer reads PCI information from the sending layer and attaches its own control information to the packets. The network layer also addresses packets and resizes them to match the requirements of the receiving network. (Chapter 3 discusses packet formats used on different networks.)

Finally, the network layer ensures that packets are not sent on faster than the receiving layer can manage.

Transport layer

This layer ensures that data are sent reliably from the point of origin to the destination node. For example, the transport layer ensures that the data are sent and received in the same order. It establishes the level of packet error checking, with the highest level guaranteeing that data are sent without error, and within an acceptable amount of time.

The peer protocols used within the transport layer employ several reliability measures. Class 0 is the simplest protocol. It performs no error checking or flow control, relying on the network layer to perform these functions. The Class 1 protocol monitors for packet transmission errors. If an error is detected, it requests the sending node's transport layer to re-send the packet. The Class 2 protocol monitors for transmission errors and provides flow control between the transport layer and the session layer. The Class 3 protocol provides the functions of Classes 1 and 2, and it adds the option to recover lost packets in certain situations. Last, Class 4 performs the same functions as Class 3, but adds more extensive error monitoring and recovery.

Session layer

The session layer is responsible for the continuity of the communications link between two nodes. It establishes the link and ensures that the link is maintained for the duration of the communication session. The session layer also provides for orderly communication between nodes. For example, it establishes which node will transmit first. It determines how long a node can transmit and how to recover from transmission errors.

This layer also links each unique address to a given node, just as ZIP codes allow mail to be associated with the appropriate postal region.

Once the communication session is finished, this layer "performs a disconnect" between the nodes.

Presentation layer

This layer takes care of data formatting. Each type of network uses a particular formatting scheme, which is accomplished by the presentation layer.

In one sense, the presentation layer is like a syntax checker. It ensures that numbers and text are sent so they can be read by the presentation layer at the receiving node.

This layer also is responsible for data encryption. Encrypting data involves scrambling the data so they cannot be read by unauthorized users who attempt to intercept them. Data encryption is presently used by many software systems for passwords, but it is rarely used for any other type of transmitted data.

Application Layer

The application layer is the highest level of the OSI model. This layer provides services for application software, such as databases. Some of the services provided include file transfer, file management, message handling for electronic mail, and terminal emulation.

CURRENT MODEL STATUS

The OSI model still is in the articulation stage and so has not been fully implemented by vendors. For example, **file transfer protocol (FTP)** is software used by many to transfer files to a network, but it does not conform to the OSI model.

SUMMARY

There are three main topologies in use today: bus, ring, and star. These topologies each have different advantages. For example, the bus topology is generally less expensive to implement than the ring or star, but problems are easier to trace on ring and star networks than on bus networks.

As demand for networks has evolved, standards organizations have worked to ensure the compatibility of networks and networking equipment. The ANSI, IEEE, CCITT, and ISO have worked nationally and internationally to encourage vendors to follow common guidelines for networking.

The OSI model of network communications in particular has provided a basis for nodes to communicate within the same network, and for networks to communicate with other networks using different architectures.

KEY TERMS

Term/Acronym	Definition
Bus Topology	This type of network is configured so that nodes are connected to a segment of cable in the logical shape of a line, with a terminator at each end.
Connectivity	The ability to connect a variety of devices to a network. Network connectivity is based on factors such as the network protocol, the type of cabling, and the speed of the network.
Data Encryption	The process of creating computer algorithms that encode and decode data so that they are protected from interception by others.
File Transfer Protocol (FTP)	Software designed to transfer data files from one computer system to another, such as from an MVS system to a UNIX system.
Layered Architecture	In the network model, this means that data packets travel up and down defined communication levels, such as those described in the OSI model. Each level or layer adds information to or extracts information from the data packet.
Network Speed	The speed at which network architecture permits packets to travel on the cable.
Network Traffic	The amount and frequency of data transported over a network. Many network monitoring tools measure network traffic in terms of a percentage of full use of the network bandwidth.
Peer Protocol	In the OSI model, this is used by nodes to communicate within one layer.
Primitive	A command used by a layer in the OSI model to communicate with an adjacent layer.
Ring Topology	The configuration of a network in the shape of a continuous ring or circle, with nodes connected around the ring.
Security	The ability to protect data from unauthorized access, such as tapping into network traffic.
Star Topology	In this topology, a network is configured with a central hub and cable segments radiating from the hub to the nodes.
System Redundancy	A network system that has built-in measures to prevent failure is said to be redundant. System redundancy might include alternate network paths, fail-safe network equipment, and algorithms to handle network errors.
Virtual Circuit	A logical communication path established by the OSI network layer for sending and receiving data.

REVIEW EXERCISES

1. You are consulting for a company that wishes to install a network. What questions would you ask before making your recommendations for the network design?

2. Explain how the OSI model implements fail-safe procedures to assure that data arrive at their destination accurately.

3. On a particular bus network, there are many PC workstations, an IBM mainframe, network printers, and two UNIX workstations. Each afternoon, some of the workstations lose their connection for unknown reasons. It is not the same workstations that lose connection each time. Why is this type of problem difficult to diagnose? What might be causing the problem?

4. Find the CCITT's X.500 guidelines on the Internet, and summarize them.

5. Draw a simple network topology for a statistics computer lab on your campus. Why do you think the topology you selected is the best choice for the lab?

6. Why is a layered network architecture an advantage?

7. Research what voltage levels are most commonly used in the physical layer of the OSI model. Why are these levels used?

8. The terminator on a bus network is _____ ohms.

9. What are the X.400 guidelines used for?

10. Why do you need to have the skills of a systems analyst when you design a network?

11. What is the IEEE? How does this organization influence networking?

12. What is a peer protocol? Why is it important?

13. Network cabling is part of the _____ OSI layer.

14. How many terminators are used in a ring topology?

15. A _____ is the central point of a star network.

CHAPTER THREE

NETWORK TRANSPORT SYSTEMS

The history of networking advancements has parallels to the history of automobile transportation. Automobiles and roadways are part of a transport system that symbolizes the evolution of our emphasis on speed. The first autos were slow and dependent on travel over bumpy dirt roads. Early transportation was often unreliable and limited to relatively short distances. Today automobile technology and paved roads have evolved into a fast, reliable way to travel.

Like automobile travel, network transport systems (the systems used to move data on a network) have evolved now stressing speed and reliability. Early networks had transport speeds of 4 and 10 Mbps, and although networks were fairly reliable, they had few fail-safe mechanisms. Network speeds today can run in the range of a billion bytes per second (Gbps), 100 times faster than the early networks. And newer technologies offer better error checking plus built-in fail-safe features.

AFTER READING THIS
CHAPTER YOU WILL BE ABLE TO:

- EXPLAIN THE NETWORK ACCESS METHODS FOR ETHERNET, TOKEN RING, ARCNET, FDDI, AND ATM
- DESCRIBE HOW DATA PACKETS ARE FORMATTED
- EXPLAIN PACKET ENCODING TECHNIQUES
- EXPLAIN COAXIAL, TWISTED-PAIR, AND FIBER OPTIC CABLING TECHNOLOGIES

This chapter describes the network transport systems in use today such as Ethernet, token ring, and FDDI. It also describes emerging technologies such as ATM and HIPPI. The structure of the data packets used by each of these transport systems is presented to illustrate network addressing, how the data are packaged, network communications, and error checking.

Cabling is discussed in this chapter to show the importance of the highway or physical medium used in data transport. Advances in cabling have proven to be just as significant to networks as advances in highway construction have been to auto transportation. The new fiber optic cables are a giant step from the thick coaxial cables originally used in many networks.

ETHERNET

A common transport system for networks is **Ethernet**. Work on Ethernet was started by the Xerox Corporation in the early 1970s. Xerox's original experiment was so successful that the Intel and Digital Equipment Corporations joined Xerox to add enhancements to Ethernet.

There now are two nearly identical Ethernet guidelines. One, established by the IEEE, is known as the 802.3 standard. The other, developed from a joint venture by Digital, Intel, and Xerox, is the DIX version of Ethernet. Both standards relate to the OSI data-link layer.

The differences between these Ethernet standards affect two important networking elements: the media type and frame structure. The IEEE 802.3 standard for media type applies to coaxial cable only. DIX Ethernet is designed for coaxial, twisted-pair, and fiber optic cable media.

In terms of frame structure, the differences between IEEE 802.3 and DIX Ethernet are minor but are important in terms of network communication. These differences are described in the sections that follow.

ETHERNET COMMUNICATIONS

The Ethernet communications control mechanism is known as Carrier Sense Multiple Access with Collision Detection (CSMA/CD). CSMA/CD is an algorithm that transmits and decodes formatted data packets. The algorithm detects node addresses and monitors for transmission errors.

There are several characteristics of Ethernet communications over a single cable run. These characteristics include the following:

- There is no central control that governs data transmission.
- The network is multi-access (accessed from many points) and all nodes have equal ability to transmit on the network.
- Data units are transmitted as encapsulated packets.
- Each transmitted packet contains addresses of the sending and receiving nodes.
- Packet addressing includes the ability to specify one node, multiple nodes, or all nodes on the network.

- The packets reach every network node.

- It is the responsibility of the receiving or "target" node to recognize and accept packets with its address as the destination.

- Data transmission is relatively fast (10 or 100 Mbps).

- Efficient error detection reduces transmission delays to a minimum.

- The communication specification discourages the implementing of special features that might lead to incompatible network variations.

When data are transmitted in Ethernet communications, they are encapsulated in packets or *frames*. Each packet is composed of predefined parts. The first part is the *preamble*, which is 56 bits in length. The preamble synchronizes packet transmission and consists of an alternating pattern of 0s and 1s. The next field is the 8-bit *start frame delimiter*. The start frame delimiter bit pattern is 10101011. Following the start frame, there are two address fields—*destination address* and *source address*. Under IEEE 802.3 guidelines, the address fields can be either 16 or 48 bits. Next, a 16-bit field specifies the *packet length*.

The *data* portion of the packet comes after the length field. The length of the encapsulated data must be a multiple of 8 bits. A *pad* field is included in case the data length is not a multiple of 8 bits. The end portion of the packet is a *frame check sequence* (FCS) field, which is 32 bits long. This field uses a cyclic redundancy check (CRC) value to enable error detection. The value is calculated from the other fields in the packet at the time of encapsulation. It is recalculated when the packet is received by the destination node. If the recalculation does not match the original calculated value, an error condition is generated.

Figure 3-1 illustrates the fields that compose an 802.3 packet.

Figure 3-1

IEEE 802.3 packet

Preamble 56	S F D 8	Dest. Address 16 or 48	Source Address 16 or 48	Length 16	Data and Pad 576-12208	FCS 32

The packet configuration for DIX Ethernet varies slightly from that defined by the IEEE. The DIX preamble contains the start delimiter and is 64 bits in length and includes the start of frame (SOF) delimiter. Destination and source addresses under DIX are strictly 48 bits. See Figure 3-2 for an example of a DIX packet.

Figure 3-2

Ethernet (DIX) packet

Preamble 56	S O F 8	Dest. Address 48	Source Address 48	Type 16	Data 576-12208	FCS 32

DIX Ethernet does not use a length field, but uses a 16-bit *type* field instead. This field is for upper-level network communications. The data field is encapsulated without a pad field and is between 576 and 12,208 bits in length. Minimum and maximum field sizes are used to improve packet collision detection and to ensure that the network is not occupied too long by a large packet.

The last field in the DIX frame is the 32-bit long *frame check sequence* field. This field performs a CRC in the same way as the 802.3 standard.

ENCODING SCHEME

DIX and IEEE 802.3 Ethernet both use the *Manchester encoding scheme* to encapsulate data (Figure 3-3). In this scheme, the signal is changed within each bit. The binary 0 bit goes from high, such as 0 volts, to low, such as negative 2 volts. The binary 1 bit switches in the opposite direction. It goes from low (negative 2 volts) to high (0 volts). The signal switching serves two important functions. One is that it ensures the transmission of each bit is clocked. The second function is that it helps guarantee that the carrier signal is detected on the cable.

Figure 3-3

Manchester
encoding
scheme

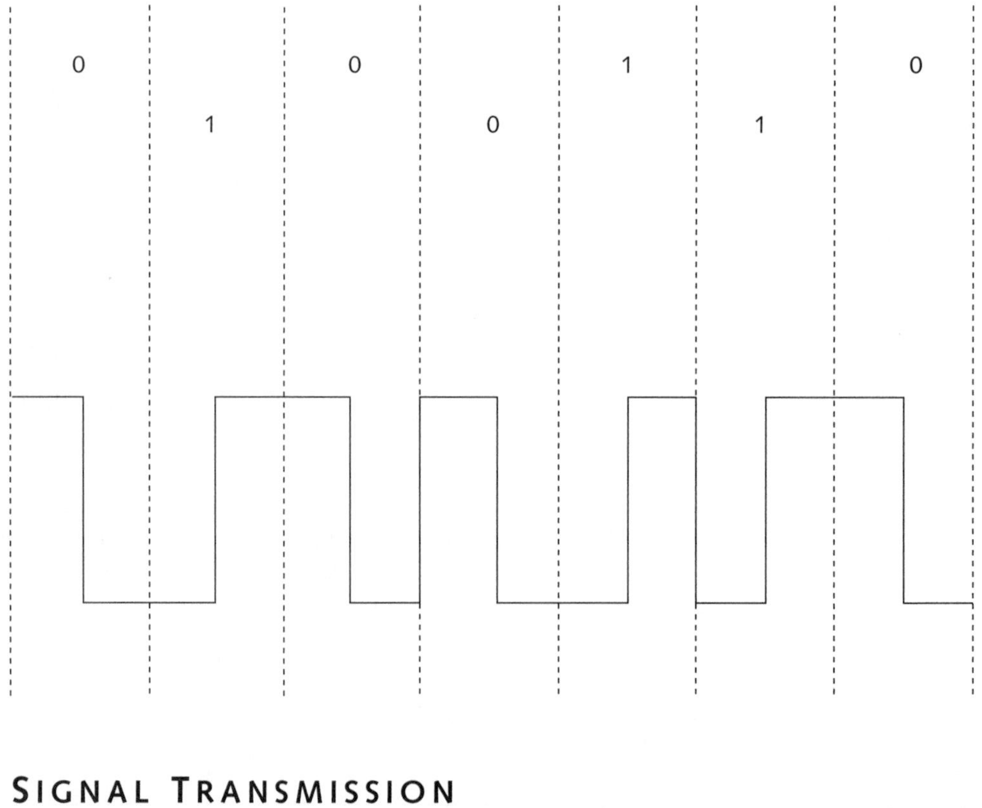

SIGNAL TRANSMISSION

The sending node encapsulates the packet to prepare it for transmission. All nodes that wish to transmit a packet on the cable are in contention with one another. No single node has priority over another node. The nodes listen for any packet traffic on the cable. If a packet is detected, the non-sending nodes go into a "defer" mode. The Ethernet protocol permits only one node to transmit at a time. Signal transmission is accomplished by carrier sense.

When no signal traffic is detected for a given amount of time, any node is eligible to transmit. Figure 3-4 illustrates an 802.3 network where one node is transmitting and the others are in defer mode.

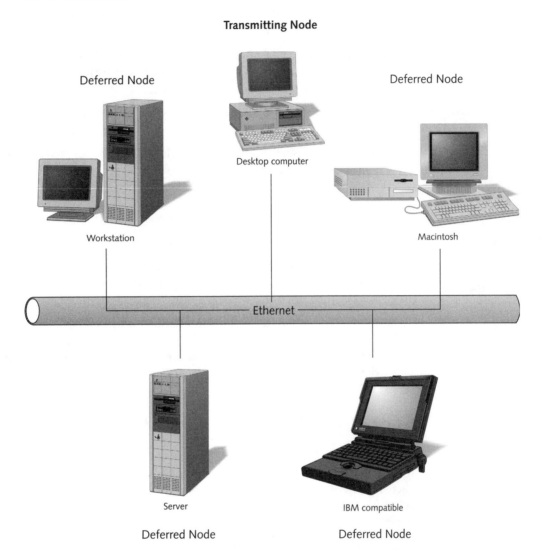

Transmitting Node

Deferred Node

Desktop computer

Deferred Node

Workstation

Macintosh

Ethernet

Server

IBM compatible

Deferred Node

Deferred Node

Figure 3-4

Ethernet network with one node transmitting at a time

Occasionally, more than one node will transmit at the same time. This is called a **collision**. The transmitting node detects a collision by measuring the signal strength. A collision will have occurred if the signal is at least twice the normal strength.

A transmitting node uses the collision detection algorithm to recover from packet collisions. This algorithm causes the stations that have transmitted to continue their transmission for 32 to 48 bytes. The continued transmission is a jam signal that enables all listening nodes to determine a collision has occurred. The software at each node generates a random number that is used as the interval to wait until transmitting. This ensures that no two nodes will attempt to transmit again at the same time.

NETWORK ADDRESSING

Network addressing is accomplished through the OSI data-link layer subset known as **media access control** (**MAC**). The MAC subset uses network addressing to direct encapsulated data to the data-link layer of the receiving node.

Every network node has a physical MAC address that is "burned" into a Programmable Read Only Memory chip (PROM) in the node's network controller, which attaches the node to the network cable.

Each vendor has a range of addresses that they use to burn into the PROM. All controller vendors are registered with the IEEE so they can receive a range of permitted addresses.

Physical MAC addresses are 48 bits long, with the first 24 bits used to identify the vendor. Some examples of vendor IDs include the following:

- 02608C is assigned to the 3Com Corporation
- 080020 is assigned to Sun Microsystems
- 0000A2 is assigned to Wellfleet Communications

The last 24 bits in the MAC address are assigned by the vendor. Some vendors use an assignment code to show that the network controller is for particular types of equipment, such as workstation controllers, router controllers, bridge controllers, and so on.

To prevent confusion on the network, it is important that no two controllers have the same address. If this should happen and both controllers are active, network communications become unreliable. It is difficult for the network to determine if packets are being sent or received by a single, distinguishable node.

ETHERNET PHYSICAL CONNECTIVITY

The data encapsulation and decapsulation of Ethernet are performed at the physical level by a controller board at the node. For example, personal computer workstations are connected to the network through a **network interface card** (**NIC**). This device is a transceiver (transmitter and receiver) and provides channel access to coaxial, twisted-pair, or fiber optic cable.

The controller board contains the logic that encapsulates the data with the preamble, start delimiter, addressing information, length or type field, data/pad field, and frame check sequence. The controller board also contains the algorithms for decapsulation, transmit and defer activity, collision detection, and collision response.

The software algorithms that perform these functions are compiled into programs and related files that are called network drivers. Every NIC requires specific network drivers suited for the network access method, data encapsulation format, cabling type, and physical MAC addressing. The software drivers interface with the logical portion of the physical and data-link layers.

ETHERNET CABLING

The IEEE 802.3 standards specify the maximum cable length as 500 meters using baseband transmission (refer to the section on coaxial cabling later in this chapter for an explanation of baseband transmission). The maximum transmission rate is 10 Mbps.

Originally most 802.3 implementations used thick-wire coaxial cable, which is wide in diameter and inflexible for desktop connections. Now thin-wire coaxial cable is more commonly used. Thin-wire cable is much smaller in diameter, cheaper, and has the flexibility to be connected directly to the desktop computer. With the implementation of DIX, Ethernet cable plants also can accommodate twisted-pair and fiber optic cable. A **cable plant** is the total amount of cabling used to build a network.

Ethernet cabling is part of the physical makeup of a network. It is an example of the implementation of the physical layer specified in the OSI model.

FAST ETHERNET

Several manufacturers have united to bring 100 Mbps Ethernet to the market. Due to their efforts, the IEEE is working to standardize this technology, which is also known as "fast Ethernet." Currently, two fast Ethernet standards are evolving, because the vendors have formed two "camps." One camp, represented by Hewlett-Packard, has led the way in developing the IEEE 802.12 standard. The other camp has pushed the IEEE 802.13 emerging standard and is represented by vendors including Bay Networks, Sun Microsystems, and 3Com. These systems are described below.

100BASE-VG

The IEEE 802.12 version of fast Ethernet has acquired the name 100BASE-VG or 100VG-AnyLAN. This approach abandons the CSMA/CD transmission technique for one called Demand Priority.

Demand Priority ensures that the transmitted signal travels in only one direction. It is used in star networks, where workstations are linked by a central hub. In this scheme, each node sends the hub a request to transmit. Requests are granted one by one. Incoming packets are examined for their destination address and sent directly to the recipient node on the star. Due to the physical star configuration, none of the other nodes will see the packet, since it never travels past other nodes. Each packet is moved from the transmitting node through the hub directly to the recipient node.

Demand Priority allows packets to travel up to 100 Mbps by eliminating the possibility of collisions. Besides fast transmission, Demand Priority has two important benefits. One is security. Since only the receiving node sees the transmitted packet, data cannot be viewed and decoded at any other node. No other transmission mode can guarantee this type of network security. The other benefit is the ability of Demand Priority to handle multimedia and time-sensitive transmissions. The highest priority can be given to these transmissions, so that voice and video are transmitted within appropriate time sequences to prevent interruptions.

100BASE-X

The IEEE 802.13 form of fast Ethernet is known as 100BASE-X. This version of fast Ethernet uses the CSMA/CD media access method for transmission of signals. Unlike 100BASE-VG, the signal is propagated in more than one direction on the network. Signal transmission is on UTP or fiber optic cable.

In order to accomplish fast Ethernet, the 100BASE-X algorithm requires that the total length of the network be limited to 250 meters, and the signal cannot go through more than two repeaters. (repeaters are discussed in Chapter 5).

TOKEN RING

The **token ring** access method was developed by IBM in the 1970s and remains IBM's primary LAN technology. Today token ring is defined by IEEE's 802.5 standard.

Logically, a token ring network is configured as a continuous ring with no starting point or end point. A *token* is continuously transmitted on the ring to coordinate when a node can send a packet. The token is 24 bits in length, with three 8-bit fields. The fields are the *starting delimiter* (SD), *access control* (AC), and the *ending delimiter* (ED).

The starting delimiter is a signal pattern unlike any other on the network. This prevents it from being interpreted as anything else. Manchester encoding is used to be certain that the data signal is not a 0 or a 1. Instead, it is constructed as a non–data signal. This unique combination of 8 bits is only recognized as a start of frame identifier.

The 8-bit access control field indicates whether an encapsulated data packet is attached to the token. That is, it indicates whether the token is busy carrying data or free to be used by a node.

The ending delimiter is a unique Manchester-encoded non-data signal. These 8 bits compose a signal that is not confused with the starting delimiter and that cannot be interpreted as data. This portion of the token shows whether more contiguous packets are to be transmitted by a node (a last frame identifier). It also carries information about any error conditions detected by other stations.

USING TOKENS IN TRANSMISSION

There is only one token available on the ring. When a node wishes to transmit, it must capture the token. Then, no other node can capture the token and transmit until the active node is finished. The station that captures the token builds a packet with the starting delimiter and the access control field at the beginning of the packet. The ending delimiter is placed at the end of the packet. The packet is sent around the ring until it is read by the target node. It continues around the ring until the original transmitting station picks it up and checks the token to determine if it was received. The transmitting station then encapsulates the next packet of data with the token, or it builds a token without data to return to the ring so a different station will grab it.

Figure 3-5

IEEE 802.5 token ring frame

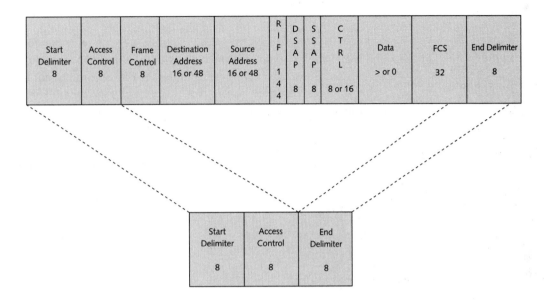

Data/Command Frame

Token Frame

Figure 3-5 illustrates a token ring packet with the token fields attached to the data fields. The first 16 bits are the starting delimiter and the access control fields. Following these fields is the *frame control* field. This field identifies the packet as a data frame or as a frame used for network management, such as reporting network errors.

The next two fields are either 16 bits or 48 bits in length and are used for addressing. The first contains the *destination node address*, and the second holds the *source node address*.

Following the addressing fields is the *routing information field* (RIF). This field is 144 bits or less in length. The RIF contains source routing information

The next three fields enable the data-link layer to manage packets and communicate with higher layers of the OSI model. These fields are the *destination service access point* (DSAP), the *source service access point* (SSAP), and the *control* fields. The DSAP and SSAP are each 8 bits long. Service access points enable the network layer to determine which network process should accept a packet. The DSAP specifies the access point to use to deliver data to the target node. The SSAP is the network layer access point that sent the data. The control field is used to indicate the function of the frame, such as whether it holds data or error reporting information.

The control field is either 8 bits or 16 bits long.

The *data* field comes after the control field. It contains data to be sent to a node or error reporting information to be used for network management. The data field has no determined size.

The 32-bit *frame check sequence* field is used to check the accuracy of the full packet. Similar to an Ethernet packet, it uses a cyclical redundancy check algorithm to ensure that the information is sent and received as intended. The CRC value in the frame received must match the value that was sent.

The final portion of the token, the ending delimiter, comes after the frame check sequence field. This frame contains information to show the receiving node that the end of the packet has been reached. It also indicates whether another packet is to be sent from the same node or whether this is the last packet from that node. Finally, it may contain information showing that another station has found an error in the packet and that the packet will be retransmitted. If the packet has an error, it is **stripped** or removed from the network by the sending node.

One more field is contained in a token ring packet after the ending delimiter. That field is the *frame status* field. It is an 8-bit field. Two of these bits are of particular importance to the transmitting node: The *address-recognized bit* shows that the target node recognized its address as formatted in the packet. The other bit is the *frame-copied bit*. This bit shows whether or not the target node successfully copied the packet as sent.

BEACONING

Each token ring network designates one node as the *active monitor*. Usually this is the first station to be recognized when the network is brought up. The active monitor is responsible for packet timing on the network and for issuing new packets if problems occur. Every few seconds, the active monitor broadcasts a MAC level frame to show it is functioning properly. The other workstation nodes are *standby monitors*. Periodically, they broadcast *standby monitor present* frames to show they are working normally.

If no broadcasts are detected from the active monitor or one of the standby monitors, the ring goes into a *beaconing* condition. Beaconing starts when a node sends a *beacon frame* to indicate that it has detected a problem. The ring will try to self-correct the problem, such as assigning a new standby monitor if the original has gone out of action. When beaconing occurs, no data tokens are transmitted until the problem is resolved.

TOKEN RING PHYSICAL CONNECTIVITY

The token ring controller has a transceiver that can be connected to coaxial or twisted-pair cabling. The controller functions in one of three modes: repeat, transmit, and copy. In the *repeat mode*, the node has no data to be transmitted. The node's controller simply reads the token and passes it to the next node. In the *transmit mode*, the node wishes to transmit data. The node's controller reads the token each time it circulates around the ring, until the token is not busy or reserved by another node. The controller captures the token and formats a packet with the token and accompanying data. Other nodes on the ring are unable to transmit because the token is not available.

When a node transmits a packet, it is transmitted to every other node for examination. The bits after the starting delimiter are read by each node to determine if the packet is intended for that node. If not, the node retransmits the uncopied packet for the next node to read. If the packet is intended for the receiving node, then that node's controller enters the *copy mode*. The receiving node will copy the packet and return it to the ring with the information that the packet was successfully addressed and read.

The node that originated the packet will receive it last and *strip* it (remove it) from the network. Only the sending node is able to strip the packet from the ring. If the sending node has more data to transmit, it will place another formatted packet on the ring. When it is finished sending data, the node constructs a 24-bit token to place on the ring for another node to capture.

Originally, token ring networks transmitted at a rate of 4 Mbps. Today the transmission rate is 16 Mbps. Nodes equipped to send at 4 Mbps cannot be intermixed with those equipped to send at 16 Mbps, and vice versa.

The token ring access method is well suited for large networks housing hundreds of nodes. One advantage of token ring networks over Ethernet networks is that broadcast storms and workstation interference are very rare. Broadcast storms sometimes occur on Ethernet networks when a large number of nodes attempt to transmit at once, or when nodes persist in transmitting repeatedly. Network interference also occurs on Ethernet networks when a damaged NIC continues to broadcast transmissions regardless of whether the network is busy. These problems are rare on token ring networks, since only one node is able to transmit at a time. Damaged NICs also are easier to trace on token ring networks, since the node with the token is easy to identify.

PHYSICAL TOPOLOGY

Although a token ring network uses a logical ring topology, the physical topology is a star pattern. Each station on a token ring network is connected to a multistation access unit (MAU). The MAU acts as a central hub to pass tokens from one station to the next.

ARCNET

ARCNET is not a standardized media access method, but is worth noting since it is used at some locations. Standard Microsystems Corporation supplies equipment for ARCNET networks. These networks use a form of token passing on a ring topology. The format for the token and packet is similar to that used by IEEE's 802.5 standard. Unlike standard token ring, which transmits at 4 or 16 Mbps, ARCNET operates at a much slower 2 Mbps. ARCNET networks are used in limited areas, such as within the same office or floor. ARCNET networks can extend up to 20 kilofeet in total ring length.

Software and drivers for these networks also are supplied by Standard Microsystems. Each workstation is equipped with Vianet software. ARCNET commands are linked to the workstation's operating system, so they are relatively transparent.

ARCNET software services include the following:

- Naming and network identification services
- Control of access to ARCNET resources
- Configuration utilities
- An interface with Novell software

The interface with Novell enables ARCNET to take advantage of file locking, record locking, disk quotas, file sharing, and file distribution.

FDDI

The **Fiber Distributed Data Interface (FDDI)** standard was developed in the mid-1980s to provide higher-speed data communications than offered by Ethernet or token ring. This standard is defined by the ANSI X3T9.5 standards committee and provides an access method to enable significant data throughput on busy networks. At a data throughput rate of 100 Mbps, FDDI is truly an advancement over Ethernet and token ring. For example, the complete Encyclopedia Britannica can be sent over an FDDI network segment in just over 20 seconds.

FDDI supports up to 500 nodes on a single fiber optic cable segment. The ultimate performance capability is transmission speed of 450,000 packets per second. This is 30 times the capacity of Ethernet, which has a 15,000 packet-per-second maximum. Data traffic consisting of voice, video, and real-time applications all are supported by FDDI.

ACCESS METHOD

FDDI is similar to the token ring access method in that it uses token passing for network communications. It differs from standard token ring in that a timed token access method is used. An FDDI token travels along the network ring from node to node. If a node does not need to transmit data, it picks up the token and sends it to the next node. If the node possessing the token does need to transmit, it is allowed to send as many frames as desired for a fixed amount of time, called the target token rotation time (TTRT). Because FDDI uses a timed token method, it is possible for several frames from several nodes to be on the network at a given time. This capability enables FDDI to be a "high-throughput architecture."

Once a node transmits a frame, the frame goes to the next node on the network ring. Each node determines if the frame is intended for it, and each node checks the frame for errors. If the node is the intended target, it marks the frame as having been read. Also, if any node detects an error, it marks a status bit in the frame to indicate an error condition. When the frame arrives back at the originating node, it is read to determine whether or not it was received by the target node. The frame also is checked for errors. If an error is detected, the frame is retransmitted. If no errors are found, the frame is removed from the ring by the originating node. Figure 3-6 illustrates the FDDI timed token access method.

Two types of packets can be sent by FDDI: synchronous and asynchronous. Synchronous transmissions are used for time-sensitive transmissions, such as voice, video, and real-time traffic (applications that require continuous transmission). Asynchronous transmissions are used for normal data traffic (which does not have to be sent in continuous bursts). On a given network, the TTRT equals the total time needed for a node's synchronous transmissions plus the time it takes for the largest frame to travel around the ring.

FDDI PACKET FORMAT

FDDI's frame format is similar but not identical to that used by standard token ring. Figure 3-7 shows the packet frame format of FDDI.

Figure 3-6

Timed token access method

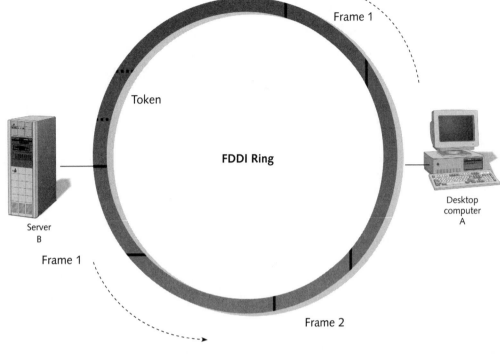

Figure 3-7

FDDI frame format

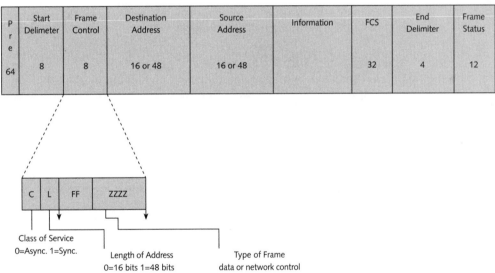

The beginning field in the packet is the *preamble*. It exists to synchronize how each station clocks transmission of the packet. The synchronization is important because, unlike token ring, FDDI permits more than one token on the network at a given moment. The preamble holds 64 bits that have no intrinsic purpose other than as clocking signals.

The *start delimiter* is part of the FDDI token and is 8 bits long. As with standard token ring, this field signifies the start of the token.

The next field is called the *frame control*. This 8-bit field shows the type of frame being transmitted. For example, the frame control indicates whether the frame is synchronous or asynchronous. It also shows if the address lengths are 16 bits or 48 bits, and it specifies if the frame carries data or network control information.

As described in the frame control, an FDDI address can be 16 or 48 bits. The first address field contains the *destination address*. The next address field has the *source address*.

Following the address fields is the *information field*, which contains data for the receiving station or information about the network status. There is no specific size associated with this field.

Similar to Ethernet and token ring, FDDI has a *frame check sequence* that uses a CRC value. The CRC value calculated by the destination node must be the same as the corresponding value sent by the source node. If not, an error condition is generated. The CRC value is calculated from information in the frame control, address, and information fields. This field is 32 bits in length.

The *end delimiter* shows that the end of the frame has been reached. Like the start delimiter, this is part of the FDDI token. The end delimiter is 4 bits long.

Last in the FDDI packet frame is the *frame status field*. It enables further error checking by showing whether or not the destination address was recognized by the target node (the address-recognized code is an A). It also shows whether or not the packet was copied by the target node (as designated by the code F). The field also may contain information on whether an error has occurred (coded as an E), such as if a packet is received malformed and needs to be retransmitted. The frame status field is 12 bits long.

An FDDI token consists of the preamble, start delimiter, frame control, and end delimiter.

FDDI ERROR MANAGEMENT

FDDI nodes monitor for two types of network error situations: long periods of no activity, and long periods where the token is not present. In the first instance, the token is presumed to be lost; in the second instance, a node is assumed to be transmitting continuously.

If either error condition is present, the node that detects the error sends a stream of specialized frames called *claim frames*. The claim frames contain a proposed TTRT value. The first node stops transmitting, and the next node on the ring compares its proposed TTRT value with the value sent by the previous node. After the comparison, it sends the lower of the TTRT values in its claim frames to the next node. By the time the last node is reached, the smallest TTRT value has been selected. At this point the ring is initialized by transmitting the token and the new TTRT value to each node, until the last node is reached.

FDDI PHYSICAL CONNECTIVITY

FDDI is used with single-mode or multi-mode fiber optic cable. A mode is like a bundle of light entering the fiber at a particular angle. Single-mode cable allows one bundle of light to enter the fiber, whereas multi-mode cable allows many bundles of light to enter at a given time.

Single-mode fiber is used for network "backbones" (primary run of cable to join networks) where data must travel over long distances. Multi-mode fiber is used for desktop workgroup applications that involve shorter transmission distances.

FDDI networks have data transmission redundancy, which gives them high reliability. Redundancy is accomplished by using two network rings. One ring is defined as the primary cable run for information transmission. The secondary ring provides a backup route for transmitted information, should the primary ring be broken. Data on the secondary ring travel in the opposite direction as data on the primary ring. Figure 3-8 is an illustration of the dual FDDI rings.

Figure 3-8

High-speed
dual ring

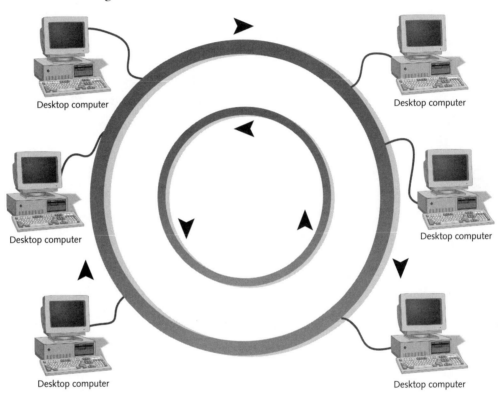

Desktop computer

Desktop computer

Desktop computer

Desktop computer

Desktop computer

Desktop computer

If there is a failure in the FDDI primary ring, the logic of the cable architecture provides *wrapping*. This means that the signal is directed onto the cable route so it doubles back to become a single ring. Fault-tolerant wrapping is shown in Figure 3.9.

Two classes of nodes connect to FDDI. Class A nodes are attached to both network rings. Class A nodes consist of network equipment, such as concentrators (concentrators are discussed more in Chapter 5). Class A nodes have the ability to reconfigure the ring to enable wrapping in the event of a network failure. Class B nodes connect to the FDDI network through Class A devices. They attach to the primary ring only. Class B nodes are servers or workstations, such as personal computers (see Figure 3-10 and Figure 3-10A).

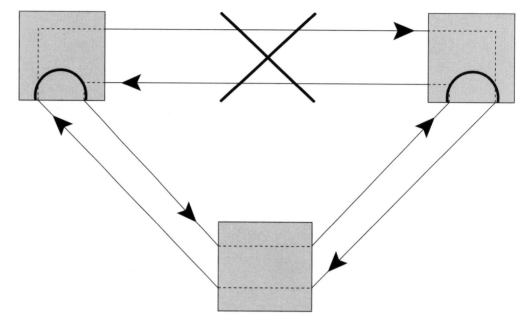

Figure 3-9

Fault-tolerant
wrapping

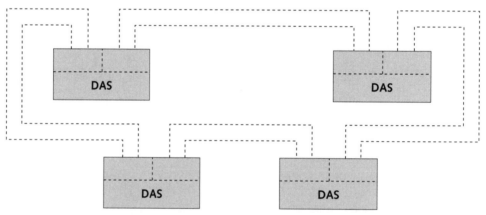

Figure 3-10

Class A (DAS)
dual attached
stations

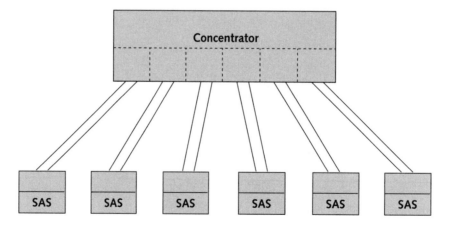

Figure 3-10A

Class B (SAS)
single
attached
stations

ATM

The existence of multiple communication standards, such as Ethernet, token ring, and FDDI, has pointed out the need for an international standard. **Asynchronous Transfer Mode (ATM)**, developed by CCITT, is such a standard and has gained wide acceptance for network interoperability. The acceptance of ATM is related to three factors:

- It is designed to handle data, voice, and video transmissions.

- It can be used for LAN and WAN communications, since there is flexibility in geographic distance.

- It can accommodate high-speed communications.

Many networks must use separate media for voice, video, and data, because the transmission characteristics are different for each. Voice and video transmissions tend to be continuous streams of signals along the cable, and video signals can occupy large bandwidths. Data signals need less bandwidth but are transmitted in bursts. Because ATM can handle voice, video, and data on a single network medium, it represents a large potential savings in network resources. ATM can be used for both LAN and WAN communications, which eliminates the need for separate short- and long-distance networks.

Connectivity between local, metropolitan, and worldwide networks would be greatly simplified if all users implemented a single networking system such as ATM. ATM is particularly gaining attention in the networking industry because it can handle transmission speeds in the gigabyte range. This offers greater flexibility as more organizations begin to tax network data throughput with object-oriented, multimedia, and client/server applications.

ATM CELLS

An ATM formatted packet is called a **cell**. The cell has a fixed length format and contains two primary sections. The first section, the header, is 40 bits long. The second section, the payload, consists of 384 bits. Figure 3-11 and Figure 3-11A show the ATM cell format.

Figure 3-11

ATM cell format

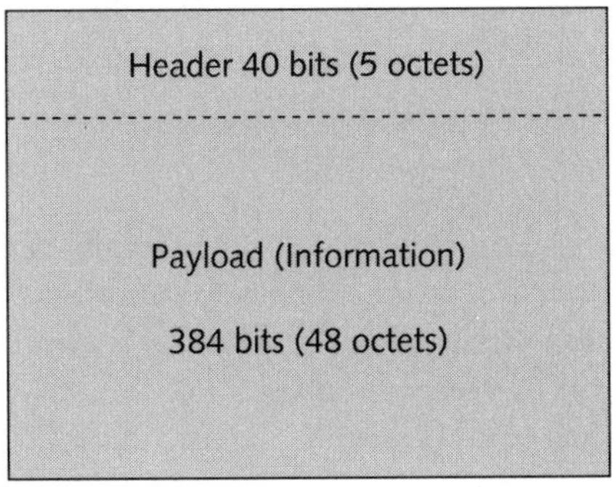

Header 40 bits (5 octets)

Payload (Information)

384 bits (48 octets)

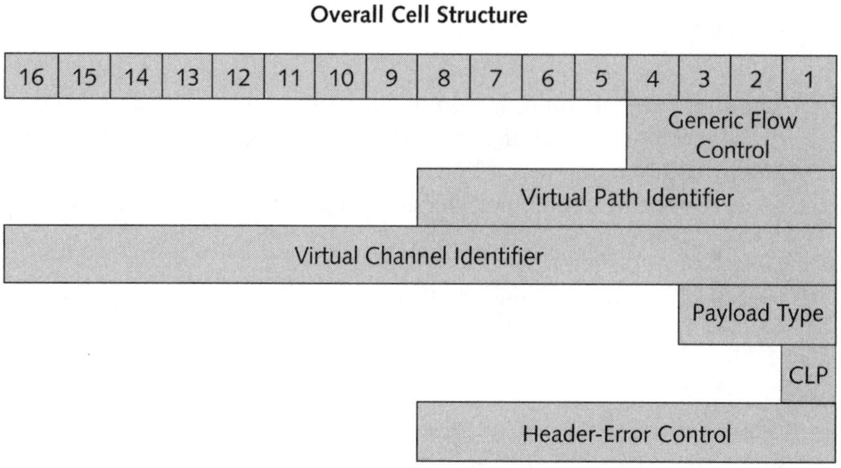

Figure 3-11A

ATM header
subfields

Overall Cell Structure

| 16 | 15 | 14 | 13 | 12 | 11 | 10 | 9 | 8 | 7 | 6 | 5 | 4 | 3 | 2 | 1 |

Generic Flow Control

Virtual Path Identifier

Virtual Channel Identifier

Payload Type

CLP

Header-Error Control

As Figure 3-11A indicates, the header contains six fields.

The beginning of the header contains flow control information for the ATM cell. This is the *generic flow control* (GFC) portion of the field, which is 4 bits in length. The next two fields are the *virtual path identifier* (VPI) and the *virtual channel identifier* (VCI). These contain management information for the physical layer about the communication channel in use, and address information. VPI and VCI are simply references to the network equipment (such as a switch or concentrator) that the cell travels through to its destination. The VPI field is 8 bits long and the VCI field is 16 bits in length.

The next field in the header specifies the *payload type* (PT). This 3-bit field shows whether the cell payload contains user information or connection management information. It also indicates whether or not the cell encountered network congestion during transmission.

The 1-bit *cell loss priority* (CLP) *field* follows the PT field. The CLP field indicates whether or not the cell should be transmitted by network equipment when there is high network traffic. A 0 value means the cell has a high priority. A 1 means that the cell can be dropped if there is network congestion.

The last header field is the *header-error control* (HEC). This 8-bit field contains information to indicate if an error has occurred during the transmission of the packet.

The payload portion of the ATM cell is always the same length and contains voice, video, or data transmissions.

ATM is a layered communications system. The *physical layer* consists of the electrical transport interface, which conducts the cell as a signal. ATM cells can be transported over coaxial, twisted-pair, and fiber optic cable systems. The next layer up is the *ATM layer*. This layer constructs the cell header and adds it to the payload data. The *adaptation layer* (AAL) is the third layer. This layer takes voice, video, and data, and it constructs the cell payload.

ACCESS METHOD

ATM connectivity is accomplished through a network switch, which dictates the path a cell can take from source to destination (see Figure 3-12). When a node is prepared to transmit data, it "negotiates" with the switch for an open path to the destination node. In the negotiation, the sending node indicates the type of data to be sent, the transmission speed needed, and other information about the requested transmission. This information determines the type of transmission channel to be made available to the node. For example, continuous stream data, such as voice, may require a higher-speed channel than nonvoice data sent in bursts. Voice data will also need a channel with more bandwidth than nonvoice data.

Figure 3-12

Path negotiation

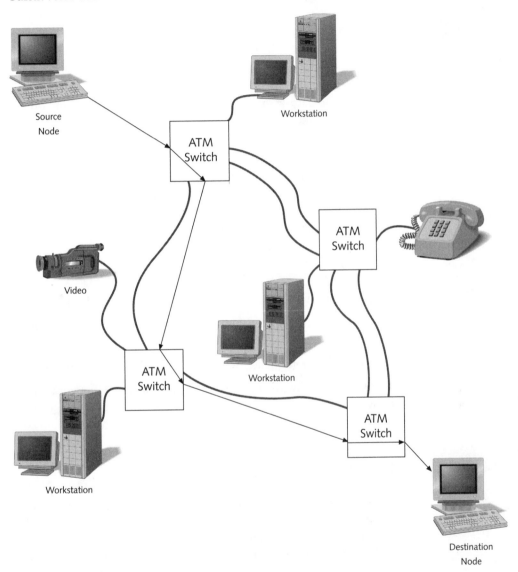

The switching technology permits the network to handle many types of data transfer needs. The advantages of ATM switching compared to shared bus technologies are summarized by the following list:

- ATM switching enables data to be transmitted at access speeds appropriate to the type of data sent.
- ATM permits use of higher bandwidths.

- Each ATM connection (communication session) has its own dedicated bandwidth.

- Connection processes are more clearly defined with ATM, since they are handled by the switch from point to point.

HIPPI

High Performance Parallel Interface (HIPPI) is a new high-speed standard developed in the early 1990s. This standard originally grew out of work performed at the Los Alamos National Laboratory in New Mexico. The HIPPI standards now fall under the ANSI X3T9.3 Committee.

This standard addresses the need to develop high-speed channel communications for applications such as supercomputers. Part of the development effort has been driven by the requirement for better scientific video capabilities. Scientists often work with visual images that require high resolution. Sending such images requires high bandwidth and large data frames. For example, the ability to support a resolution of 1024 by 1280 pixels requires a data frame in the range of 4 MB, transmitted at 24 frames per second.

The advantages of HIPPI include the following:

- Data throughput rates of 800 Mbps and 1.6 Gbps.

- A standardized generic interface easily utilized by a large range of vendors.

- Interface with common network architectures for attaching peripherals to host channels.

- Future applicability for digital HDTV, image data streams, and digitized voice.

HIPPI is used primarily to connect peripherals to the network, such as disk and tape controllers. The network connectivity is achieved through high-speed switches that operate at full bandwidth per channel. Figure 3-13 shows an example of a HIPPI network.

NETWORK ACCESS

When a node is ready to send on a HIPPI network segment, it can hold the switched connection for the amount of time required to send 68 bursts of data. There is no limit to the number of packets that can be sent in one session, other than the number that can be sent within the 68 burst limit. The transmission speed is based on the capacity of the source and destination nodes (within the 800 Mbps or 1.6 Gbps limit).

HIPPI uses flow control to prevent the source node from overrunning the destination node with data faster than it can be handled. This ensures that the destination node does not issue a disconnect message because its capacity has been exceeded.

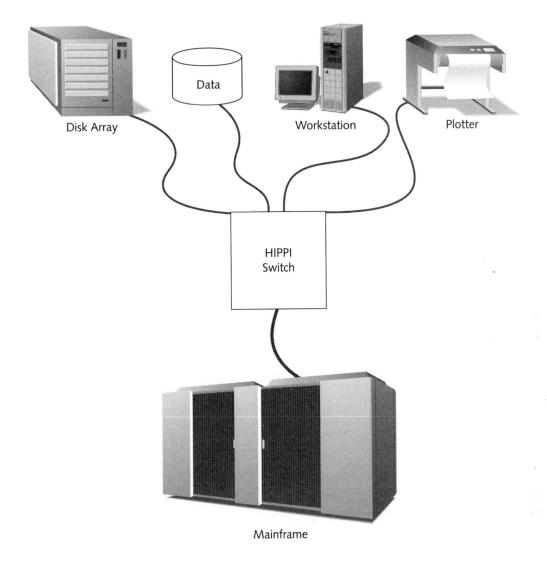

Figure 3-13

HIPPI network

Disk Array

Data

Workstation

Plotter

HIPPI
Switch

Mainframe

HIPPI transmissions go into error status only when there is a parity mismatch between the source and destination nodes, or when the source packet contains support for 1.6 Gbps transmission in a situation where the destination node does not support this speed.

HIPPI PACKET FORMAT

The first field in the HIPPI packet is the 64-bit long *header*. The next two fields contain the *destination-switch address* and the *source-switch address*. These fields are each 32 bits long.

Following the switch addresses are the *destination* and *source node addresses*, which are each 64 bits long. The next field contains information used by the *LLC* network layer and is 64 bits long. The *data* section of the packet can be any length to accommodate the number of bursts sent. The last field contains "filler" and indicates the *end of the frame*. Although HIPPI frames can vary in length, they must always be a multiple of eight octets (64 bits) in length. The filler is used to ensure there is an even number of 32-bit words in the frame. Figure 3-14 illustrates the HIPPI frame format.

Figure 3-14

HIPPI frame
format

Header	Dest. Swch	Src. Swch	Dest. Addr.	Source Addr.	LLC	Data	EOF (filler)
64	32	32	64	64	64		

WIRING

The foundation for any network is based on the type of wiring selected. This is because the wiring system is the physical or bottom layer of the OSI model. Each access method, Ethernet to HIPPI, is influenced by the wiring system or *cable plant*.

The ease of network management and the reliability of the network depend on what wiring system is used. Some wiring systems deliver high-speed transmissions but are difficult to repair. Other wiring systems, such as telephone wire, may already be installed in a building. Some wiring is more susceptible to **radio frequency interference** (**RFI**) and to **electro-magnetic interference** (**EMI**) than others.

Three types of wiring systems are used in networks: coaxial, twisted pair, and fiber optic.

COAXIAL CABLE

Coaxial cable is used extensively in Ethernet networks. Standards for coaxial cable were set in 1980 by the IEEE. There are two types of coaxial cable: thick and thin.

Thick coaxial cable

Thick coaxial cable (Figure 3-15) was the first type of cable used for Ethernet applications. A copper or copper-clad aluminum conductor is the core. The conductor has a relatively large diameter, as compared with thin coaxial cable. The conductor is surrounded by insulation, and an aluminum sleeve is wrapped around the outside of the insulation. A polyvinyl jacket covers the aluminum sleeve.

The cable jacket is marked every 2.5 meters to show where a network device can be attached. If devices are attached more closely than this, network errors may result. This type of cable is also called RG-8 cable (RG means radio grade). The impedance of the cable is 50 ohms, and cable segments are terminated by a 50-ohm resistor.

Thick coaxial cable is difficult to bend because of the large diameter of the copper conductor. On the plus side, this cabling has better EMI/RFI immunity than thin coaxial because of the large-diameter conductor and aluminum shielding.

Thick coaxial cable works on bus networks using transmission speeds of 10 Mbps. According to IEEE standards, the maximum cable length or "run" is 500 meters. The shorthand for these specifications is 10BASE5. The *10* indicates the cable transmission rate is 10 Mbps. *BASE* means that baseband transmission is used. The *5* indicates 5 x 100 meters for the longest cable run.

Figure 3-15

Thick coaxial
cable (10BASE5)

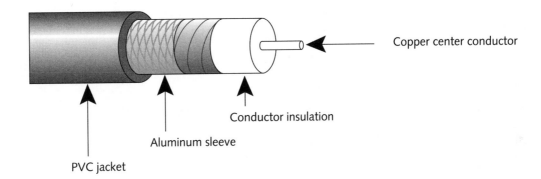

Copper center conductor

Conductor insulation

Aluminum sleeve

PVC jacket

According to the IEEE specifications, the maximum cable length (including repeaters) is 2500 meters, which will support up to 100 nodes.

Thick coaxial cable can be used for baseband or broadband transmissions. The **baseband** mode of transmission is used on Ethernet networks and supports the CSMA/CD access method. This type of transmission is performed by amplitude, frequency, or phase modulation. Baseband Ethernet packets travel at a percentage of the speed of light, known as the **propagation velocity (Vp)**. Vp is defined as a percentage of c where $c = 3 \times 10^8$ ms. 10BASE5 cable has a minimum Vp of .77c. For Ethernet topologies, this type of cable also has Maximum Medium Delay per segment restrictions. The Maximum Medium Delay is determined by the media type, Vp, the number of MAUs, and the segment length. For thick coaxial cable, the Maximum Medium Delay per segment is 2165 nanoseconds (ns).

The **broadband** mode consists of a set of distinct channels. Each channel operates at a unique frequency. The broadband mode was designed to support diverse signal transmissions such as cable TV, data, and other information services.

Thick coaxial is not as popular as other cabling due to its diameter and the difficulty in manipulating it.

The following list summarizes the characeristics of thick coaxial cable for Ethernet:

- Device attachments possible every 2.5 meters
- Maximum cable length is 500 meters
- Maximum cable length with repeaters is 2500 meters

- Transmission speed on the cable equals 10 Mbps

- Up to 100 nodes can be attached per segment

- Supports baseband transmissions

- Minimum Vp of .77c

- Maximum Medium Delay per segment is 2165 ns

- Cable type is RG-8

- Uses 50-ohm terminators

Thin coaxial cable

Thin coaxial cable is also known as RG-58. The IEEE standards for this type of cable were established in 1985. This is baseband cable that supports a data rate of 10 Mbps on Ethernet bus topologies. The maximum cable segment length is 185 meters, with up to 30 nodes per segment (shorthand notation is 10BASE2). The impedance of the cable is 50 ohms, and segment terminators are 50-ohm resistors. It has a Vp of .65c and a Maximum Medium Delay per segment of 950 ns.

The physical construction of thin coaxial cable is similar to that of thick coaxial, except for the diameter of the cable. A copper conductor is at the center of the cable, and the diameter of the conductor is significantly smaller than that of thick coaxial. The conductor is surrounded by insulation, and the insulation is surrounded by a woven mesh outer conductor. The cable is surrounded by a polyvinyl jacket that is usually gray or black in color.

Thin coaxial cable has slightly less immunity to EMI/RFI than thick coaxial. Its thin diameter and flexibility make it suitable to run through walls and on cable runs. It is very easily brought to the desktop for connection to a workstation's NIC by means of a BNC connector. The following is a summary of the characteristics of thin coaxial cable:

- Device attachments possible every 0.5 meters

- Maximum cable length is 185 meters

- Transmission speed on the cable equals 10 Mbps

- Up to 30 nodes can be attached per segment

- Supports baseband transmissions

- Minimum Vp of .65c

- Maximum Medium Delay per segment is 950 ns

- Cable type is RG-58

- Uses 50-ohm terminators

TWISTED-PAIR CABLE

Unshielded twisted-pair cable

Unshielded twisted-pair (UTP) cable is telephone wire. Since it was formalized for networking by the IEEE in 1990, it has become the most popular Ethernet cabling medium. It is flexible to install, economical, and permits the use of existing telephone cable. Cable that is already installed can be used, so long as it was installed within the last 5-10 years. The IEEE shorthand for UTP cable is 10BASET.

UTP consists of four strands of wire. The ends of each cable run are attached to RJ-45 connectors. The individual strands in UTP have several twists per foot of cabling. The twists help ensure that the electrical signal is not attenuated.

This cable is used in Ethernet and token ring applications. No matter the application, UTP always has a physical star topology. This means that the cabling is installed point to point, from the workstation's NIC to a central communications hub that functions as a repeater (see Figure 3.16). The hub is a Multistation Access Unit (for token ring applications) or a concentrator (for Ethernet applications). A network with 10BASET wire can logically function as a ring or a bus by means of the software within the hub.

Ethernet twisted-pair cable

For Ethernet bus applications there is no external terminator, since the cable is terminated within the hub and the NIC. The maximum segment length from the hub to the workstation is 100 meters. The minimum Vp for 10BASET is .59c, and the Maximum Medium Delay per Segment is 1000 ns.

Communication problems that occur in 10BASET installations are easier to trace than in thick or thin coaxial cable installations. The physical star configuration, with one node per segment, makes it easy to trace a bad node or wire run.

The availability of UTP for Ethernet networks has opened the way for vendors to develop 100 Mbps Ethernet communication rates. The IEEE endorses using 100BASE-VG to accommodate the higher speed.

Token ring applications of UTP do not have the same specifications as Ethernet. The following is a summary of Ethernet twisted pair characteristics:

- Physical star configuration
- Maximum cable length is 100 meters
- Transmission speed on the cable equals 10–100 Mbps
- Nodes connected via concentrator
- Supports baseband transmissions
- Minimum Vp of .59c
- Maximum Medium Delay per segment is 1000 ns
- No external terminators

Figure 3-16

Central
communica-
tions hub
(MAU)

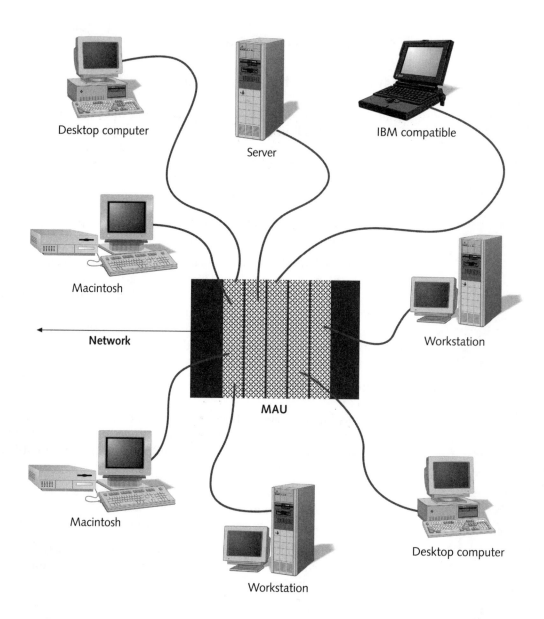

Desktop computer

Server

IBM compatible

Macintosh

Network

Workstation

MAU

Macintosh

Workstation

Desktop computer

Token ring applications of twisted-pair cable

Token ring networks can use shielded or unshielded twisted-pair cable. Shielded twisted-pair has shielding around the strands of cable to help reduce EMI/RFI. Three types of wire are normally used for token ring. Type 1 wire is shielded twisted-pair, which consists of two solid wires surrounded by shielding. Braided shielding is used for indoor applications, and corrugated metallic shielding is used for outdoor applications. If only one MAU is present, the maximum cable segment is 300 meters for type 1 wire. Where multiple MAUs are installed, the maximum cable segment is 100 meters.

Type 2 wire has two solid twisted-pair cables in the middle, shielding over the middle wires, and four solid twisted-pair cables around the shield. There are indoor and outdoor versions of type 2 wire, depending on whether the shielding is braided or corrugated metallic.

Two types of connectors are used with type 1 and 2 wire on token ring networks. A DB-9 connector is used at the workstation or node end of the cable. At the MAU end, a hermaphroditic connector is used. This comes in a black connector shell, and is a non-gender–specific type of cable.

Type 3 wire involves using the existing unshielded telephone cable plant in a building. When type 3 wiring is used, a **media filter** is placed at each network node to filter out "noise" or undesired signals on the wire. The maximum cable segment for type 2 and 3 wire is 100 meters. Type 3 wire uses regular RJ-11 and RJ-45 connectors. These are small plug-in type telephone connectors.

The list below summarizes twisted-pair cable on token ring applications:

- Physical star configuration
- Uses type 1, 2, or 3 wire
- Maximum cable length is 100 meters (or 300 meters for type 1 wire if only 1 MAU is used)
- Transmission speed on the cable equals 4–16 Mbps
- Nodes connected via MAUs
- Media filter is used for type 3 cable

FIBER OPTIC CABLE

Fiber optic cable is composed of a central glass cylinder that is encased in a glass tube, called *cladding*. The central core and cladding are surrounded by a polyvinyl cover (see Figure 3.17).

There are three fiber cable sizes. The size is measured in microns and has two components, the core diameter and the cladding diameter. For example, 50/125 micron (mu) fiber cable has a core diameter of 50 microns and a cladding diameter of 125 microns. The other two commonly used sizes are 62.5/125 micron fiber cable and 100/140 micron cable. All three types of cable have multi-mode transmission capability; this means that multiple light waves can be transmitted on the cable at once.

The cable core carries optical energy as transmitted by laser or light emitting diode (LED) devices. The glass cladding is designed to reflect light back into the core.

Fiber optic cable is well suited for FDDI, Fast Ethernet, and ATM networks because it is capable of propagating the transmitted light wave at high speeds. Another advantage is that fiber optic cable has high bandwidth with low attenuation over long distances. Since the data travel by means of optical power, there are no EMI/RFI problems associated with this type of cable. It also is very difficult for someone to place unauthorized taps into the cable, since cable installation requires a high level of expertise. A disadvantage of this cable is that it is very fragile.

Figure 3-17

Fiber optic
cable

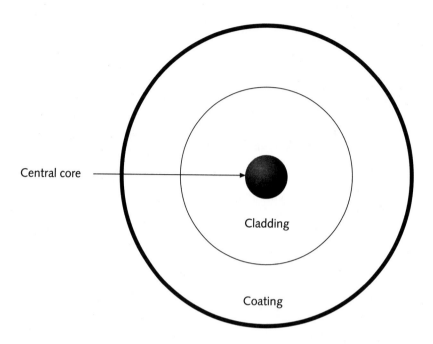

The success of transmitting data by light waves is related to the wavelength of the light. Some wavelengths travel through optical fiber more efficiently than others. Light wavelength is measured in nanometers (nm). Visible light, in the range of 400–700, does not travel through fiber optic cable with enough efficiency for data transfer. Infrared light in the range of 700–1600 nm travels with the necessary efficiency for data transmission.

Optical communications occur through three ideal wavelengths or windows: 850 nm, 1300 nm, and 1550 nm. FDDI transmissions use the 1300-nm window.

Power loss on fiber optic cable is measured in decibels (dB). Loss of optical power is directly related to the length of the cable. There also is power loss as the wave passes through connectors and splices. The maximum attenuation for FDDI applications is 1.5 dB/Km.

The wave must leave the transmitting device with a minimum level of power so it is accurately translated at the receiving end. The minimum power level is called the **power budget**. For FDDI communications, the power budget must be 11 dB.

Fiber optic cable has a minimum Vp of .66c. The maximum segment length is 1000 meters, and the Maximum Medium Delay per segment is 5000 ns. The characteristics of fiber optic cable in FDDI applications are the following:

- Dual ring configuration
- Single-mode and multi-mode cable types
- Transmission rate of 100 Mbps
- Power budget of 11 dB needed
- Maximum attenuation of 1.5 dB/Km

- Minimum Vp of .66c
- Maximum Medium Delay per segment is 5000 ns

SINGLE-MODE AND MULTI-MODE FIBER OPTIC CABLE

Fiber optic cable comes in two modes: single-mode and multi-mode. Single-mode cable is used mainly for long-distance communications. The central core diameter is much smaller than for multi-mode cable. Only one light wave is transmitted on the cable at a given time. Laser light is the communication source for single-mode cable. The laser light source, coupled with a relatively large bandwidth, enables long-distance transmissions at high speeds (such as for FDDI). The intensity of the light makes it hazardous to look into the cable; severe eye injury can result.

Multi-mode cable can support simultaneous transmission of multiple light waves. The transmission distance is not as great as for single-mode cable, because the available bandwidth is smaller and the light source is weaker. The transmission source for multi-mode cable is a light emitting diode.

SUMMARY

This chapter has explored a full range of network transport systems. Ethernet, token ring, and ARCNET are early systems that continue to have widespread use. Each system has a unique access method to transport data, such as CSMA/CD used by Ethernet, and token passing used by token ring. Each system also performs error checking to ensure packets reach their destination node intact.

FDDI, ATM, and HIPPI are newer, high-speed transmission technologies. They usher in video and voice transport capabilities to accompany the more traditional data transport systems. FDDI adds fail-safe options with its dual-ring and wrapping architecture.

At the physical layer, network cabling is an important complement to these data-access systems. Fiber optic cable offers high-speed communications possibilities in contrast to coaxial cable. Twisted-pair cable is proving to be a flexible cabling alternative as new options are developed for Ethernet, FDDI, and ATM implementations.

KEY TERMS

Term/Acronym	Definition
ARCNET	This proprietary transport method is similar to token ring. ARCNET has a limited geographic range and transmits data at much slower speeds than token ring.
Asynchronous Transfer Mode (ATM)	ATM is a transport method that uses multiple channels and switching to send voice, video, and data transmissions on the same network. ATM data transfer stresses efficient, high-speed data throughput.
Baseband	A network cable with only one channel to transmit data.

Broadband	This type of cable has several channels for transmitting data simultaneously.
Cable Plant	All the combined cable wire that runs in a building or on a campus.
Cell	ATM data are encoded into units called cells for transmission on the network.
Collision	At times packets collide on an Ethernet network, particularly when network traffic is high. A packet collision serves as an indication that broadcasting should stop until the collision situation has passed.
Electro–Magnetic Interference (EMI)	Magnetic force fields are generated by many electrical devices. These force fields can cause interference with electric signals in nearby computer cabling.
Ethernet	This network transport system uses the CSMA/CD access method for packet transmission in LAN applications. Ethernet is typically implemented in a bus or star topology.
Fiber Distributed Data Interface (FDDI)	FDDI is a transport system that uses token passing to implement high-speed data transfer. FDDI networks can support voice and video transmissions in addition to data.
High Performance Parallel Interface (HIPPI)	This transport method is designed for use with peripherals that need very high data speeds, such as supercomputer disk drives. HIPPI is capable of transmitting very large data packets along a single channel.
Media Access Control (MAC)	A sublayer of the OSI data-link layer. It uses addressing for transmitting and receiving data. It also schedules transmissions on shared access mediums, such as Ethernet.
Media Filter	Electronic interference is eliminated on twisted-pair cabling by using a media filter.
Network Interface Card (NIC)	Workstations connect to a network through a circuit board that functions as a transceiver (transmitter/receiver) for data.
Propagation Velocity (Vp)	One means to show how fast data packets travel is to express their speed in terms of a percentage of the speed of light, which is the propagation velocity.
Power Budget	The minimum power level required to transmit a light wave successfully along fiber optic cable.
Radio Frequency Interference (RFI)	Electronic devices operate at frequencies that cause them to emit radio waves. These radio waves can cause interference on computer cabling and other communication equipment.
Stripping	In this process, data are removed from a token ring or FDDI network by the sending node.
Token Ring	This network transport method passes a token from node to node. The token is used to coordinate transmission of data, because only the node possessing the token can send data.

REVIEW EXERCISES

1. Explain Manchester encoding and how it is used.

2. Research the information transfer needs on your campus. What network transport method would best meet the campus's needs? How would you wire the buildings?

3. Why are problems on an Ethernet network difficult to trace?

4. Compare the transmission characteristics of coaxial, twisted-pair, and fiber optic cable. Which cabling method is best suited for data transfer needs within a building? Which is best suited for data transfer between buildings?

5. What cabling method is best suited for high-speed communications?

6. Compare the access methods that use CSMA/CD to those that use token passing. What are the advantages and disadvantages of each?

7. What is a DIX packet? What is its format?

8. Diagram how HIPPI is used.

9. What network speed is possible on FDDI?

10. What network transmission speed is possible on ATM?

11. How are data transmitted on fiber optic cable?

12. _____ and _____ are forms of interference experienced on network cabling.

13. What are the advantages of thin coaxial compared to thick coaxial?

14. What is MAC?

15. Which media access method provides the best security? Why?

16. How is single-mode fiber optic cable used?

17. Error checking in frames is accomplished by _____.

18. Explain how token transmission in FDDI is different from token transmission in token ring communications.

19. What is the transmission speed of ARCNET?

20. Explain what happens on an Ethernet network when a collision is experienced.

CHAPTER FOUR

PROTOCOLS

Millions of people are accessing the Internet for research, discussion forums, hobby groups, business information, and personal interest. The thousands of different kinds of computers they connect to are made by vendors such as IBM, Sequent, DEC, and Sun. Even though these computers use different operating systems, they are able to communicate because of a common language available through protocols (as we discussed in chapter 1, a protocol is a set of rules determining how data are formatted and transmitted). This chapter presents commonly used and emerging protocols. These include TCP/IP, IPX, X.25, ISDN, and frame relay. Each of these protocols is discussed in relation to the OSI model.

AFTER READING THIS CHAPTER YOU WILL BE ABLE TO:

- EXPLAIN CURRENT AND EMERGING NETWORKING PROTOCOLS
- LINK PROTOCOLS WITH THE OSI MODEL
- DISCUSS HIGH-SPEED DATA TRANSMISSION TECHNOLOGIES
- EXPLORE HOW PACKET SWITCHING IS USED IN NETWORKING

TCP/IP

In the late 1960s it became clear that computers with different operating systems needed to be able to communicate with one another. The Department of Defense launched an initiative through its Advanced Research Projects Agency (ARPA) to enable research universities to link their computers through a network (ARPAnet). Universities, such as Stanford and University College in London, responded by developing a network protocol to enable DEC, VAX, and IBM mainframes to communicate. The protocol was called *Transmission Control Protocol/Internet Protocol* (TCP/IP). Once TCP/IP was implemented, it was soon incorporated into the popular Berkeley UNIX operating system.

Since its creation in the early 1970s, TCP/IP has become widespread on networks throughout the United States. It is available for PCs, UNIX workstations, minicomputers, Macintosh computers, and mainframes. TCP/IP has enabled several thousand public and commercial networks to connect to the Internet for access by millions of users.

TCP/IP involves a layered set of protocols similar to the OSI protocol layers. (The relationship between TCP/IP and OSI is explained later in this chapter.) TCP/IP consists of nearly 100 nonproprietary protocols that interconnect computer systems at a low cost. Essential protocols within TCP/IP include the following:

- Transmission Control Protocol (TCP)
- User Datagram Protocol (UDP)
- Internet Protocol (IP)

Complementing the main protocols are four application services provided through TCP/IP:

- File Transfer Protocol (FTP)
- TELNET Protocol
- Simple Mail Transfer Protocol (SMTP)
- Domain Name Service (DNS)

These protocols and services are described in the following pages.

TCP

Transmission Control Protocol (TCP) is a transport protocol that establishes communication sessions between software application processes initiated by users on the network. TCP provides for end-to-end delivery of data by controlling data flow. Nodes agree upon a "window" for data transmission that includes the number of bytes that will be sent. The transmission window is constantly adjusted to account for existing network traffic. The essential TCP functions are to monitor for session requests, to establish sessions with other TCP nodes, to transmit and receive data, and to close transmission sessions.

As it transmits data, TCP breaks the data into streams called **datagrams**. The datagrams are formed, transmitted, and reassembled through a set of algorithms that follow the **User Datagram Protocol (UDP)**. If datagrams are received out of order, UDP enables the receiving node to wait for the missing datagrams and reassemble them in the same order as they were sent.

Each TCP datagram consists of a header followed by data. The header defines the following attributes:

- Source and destination addresses

- Sequence number of the datagram (this enables the receiving node to put the datagrams in the correct order)

- Acknowledgment of transmission (TCP retransmits the datagram if acknowledgment is not received)

- Size of the header (TCP headers may vary in size)

- Reserved field, (currently not used)

- "Flags," which signal the beginning or end of a transmission session

- Transmission window size, showing how many bytes of data a node has agreed to receive

- Checksum for error detection (a comparison of the sum of bits sent to the sum of bits received)

- Location in the stream where data ends

- Options field for node-to-node communications

IP

A network, such as the Internet, may consist of a series of autonomous networks. These **subnets** may include Ethernet, token ring, X.25, and other networks. The *Internet Protocol* (IP) defines how the subnetworks can be interconnected (see Figure 4–1).

Figure 4-1

IP subnetworks

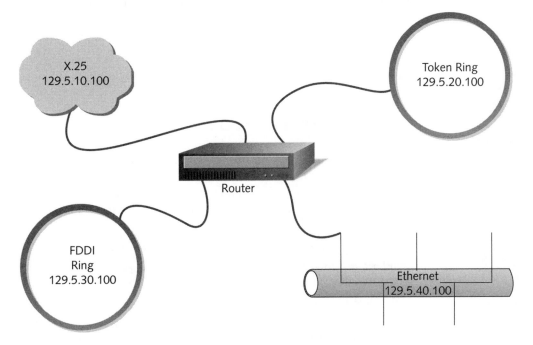

The basic functions of IP are to provide for data transfer, packet addressing, packet routing, fragmentation, and detection of transmission errors. Successful data transfer and routing to the correct subnet are made possible by IP addressing conventions. Each network node has a 32-bit IP address. The address identifies a given network as well as a specific node on the network. The most common IP address format is called the **dotted decimal notation system**. An example IP address is the following: 129.5.10.100. The 129.5 portion of the address signifies the network number. The last part of the address, 10.100, is the host number.

The IP protocol adds its own header information to the TCP datagram. For example, the source and destination addresses are included for packet delivery and routing. A "checksum" is in the IP header for error detection. The header also contains a time-to-live (TTL) field, which determines how long a TCP/IP packet may travel undelivered on the network before it is removed. Every time the packet goes through a gateway, the TTL field is decreased by 1. If the value in the field reaches 0, the packet is removed by the next gateway it encounters. The TTL field helps keep network congestion from undelivered packets to a minimum.

Since the data are sent in streams, the IP header keeps track of how they are fragmented. A fragmentation control field enables the IP protocol to ensure data packets are reassembled correctly.

TELNET

TELNET is an application protocol within TCP/IP. TELNET provides support for terminal emulation, such as for an IBM 3270 terminal or a DEC VT220 terminal. (Unlike a workstation, a terminal has no CPU for local processing). TELNET enables a user to connect to a host computer so that the host responds as though it were connected to a terminal. For example, TELNET with a 3270 emulator can connect to an IBM ES9000 mainframe like a terminal. The ES9000 requires a login ID and password, just as though it were directly connected to a terminal.

TELNET runs in the TCP/IP network layer that is equivalent to the OSI session layer (see Figure 4-2).

FILE TRANSFER PROTOCOL

As another TCP/IP application protocol, the file transfer protocol (FTP) is an algorithm that enables the transfer of data from one remote device to another, using TCP and TELNET protocols. Through FTP, a user in Maine can log on to a host computer in California and download one or more data files from the host. (The user first must have an authorized user ID and password on the host.)

FTP is designed to transfer entire files only in bulk. It does not provide the capability to transfer a portion of a file or records within a file. The FTP transmission is composed of a single stream of data concluded by an end-of-file delimiter. FTP can transfer binary files and ASCII text files.

A popular alternative to FTP is the **Network File System (NFS)** software offered by Sun Microsystems. NFS sends data in record streams instead of in bulk file streams.

SIMPLE MAIL TRANSFER PROTOCOL

Simple Mail Transfer Protocol (SMTP) is designed for the exchange of electronic mail between networked systems. UNIX, MVS, VMS, and other computers can exchange messages if they have TCP/IP accompanied by SMTP.

SMTP provides an alternative to FTP for sending a file from one computer system to another. This is handy since SMTP does not require use of a login ID and password for the remote system. All that is needed is an e-mail address for the receiving end. SMTP is limited to sending text files, so files in other formats must be converted to text before they are placed in an SMTP message.

Messages sent through SMTP have two parts: an address header and the message text. The address header can be very long, because it contains the address of every SMTP node through which it has traveled and a date stamp for every transfer point. If the receiving node is unavailable, SMTP can "bounce" the mail back to the sender.

SMTP is not an X.400 protocol, but it does establish rules for how the sending and receiving computers need to format and exchange mail. One method employed by SMTP is to create a queue in a file directory. The queue serves as a "post office" for local users on the machine where it resides. If the queue contains messages for another computer system, it notifies the SMTP application on that system and forwards the message.

DOMAIN NAME SERVICE

The TCP/IP protocol suite includes a Domain Name Service (DNS), which provides a name for every node in an organization. For example, a research organization might have four computers, each with its own address and machine name. The names might be ACCT, ENG1, ENG2, and HOME. The addresses for the computers might be 129.70.5.100, 129.70.5.101, 129.70.5.102, and 129.70.5.103 respectively. The "domain" for all of these computers might be BUS.COM (with BUS representing the business name and COM designating a business on the Internet).

In this example, the DNS software would be running on one of the computers in the domain, such as the HOME computer, maintaining a translation table of machine name to IP address. This makes HOME the domain server, and ACCT, ENG1, ENG2 and HOME members of the domain. When a message, such as an e-mail, is sent to ENG1@BUS.COM, the DNS algorithms translate the address into 129.70.5.101 for use on the TCP/IP network. The domain server can translate messages sent from machines within the domain and from machines on the outside, such as from the Internet.

See Table 4-1 for an example of machine names, IP addresses, and domain names. Some examples of Internet domain names are listed in Tables 4-2 and 4-3.

Table 4-1

Machine name, IP address, and domain name examples for four computers at a company and four computers at a university

Machine Name	IP Address	Domain Name
ENG	122.40.2.101	engin.com
ACCT	122.40.2.10	engin.com
SALES	122.40.3.02	engin.com
R&D	122.40.3.01	engin.com
BIO	124.78.5.01	univ.edu
ADMIN	124.78.4.02	univ.edu
REG	124.78.4.01	univ.edu
GEOLOGY	124.78.7.01	univ.edu

Table 4-2

Internet domain conventions by type of organization

Type of Organization	Domain Representation
Educational	edu
Commercial	com
Government	gov
Military	mil

Table 4-3

Internet domain conventions for countries

Country	Domain Representation
Australia	au
Finland	fi
Hungary	hu
Italy	it
Japan	jp
Poland	po
Sweden	se
United States	us

Figure 4-2

TCP/IP–OSI relationships

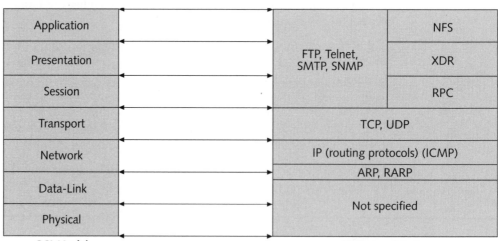

OSI Model / IP Protocol Suite

RELATIONSHIPS BETWEEN TCP/IP AND OSI

Each of the TCP/IP components we have discussed so far has a correspondence to the OSI layered model (Figure 4-2). As TCP/IP has grown in acceptance, portions of TCP/IP have moved closer in adherence to OSI. For example, the physical and data-link levels of TCP/IP are compatible with Ethernet, token ring, token bus, FDDI, and ATM. At the physical level, TCP/IP supports coaxial, twisted-pair, and fiber optic cable mediums. And, at the data-link level, it is compatible with the IEEE 802.2 logical link control standard and MAC addressing.

The network layer equivalent in TCP/IP is the Internet Protocol (the IP portion of TCP/IP). The next layer of compatibility is the transport layer. The transmission control protocol (TCP) operates at this level, as does the user datagram protocol (UDP).

The upper layers of the OSI model are represented by the TCP/IP applications protocols. For instance, TELNET operates at the equivalent of the session layer. The presentation and application layers are represented by SMTP and FTP.

IPX

Novell adapted one of the early LAN protocols, the **Xerox Network System (XNS)** protocol, for use with its **NetWare** operating system. XNS was introduced by the Xerox Corporation as a means to communicate over Ethernet. In the early 1980s, several vendors implemented their own versions of XNS. Novell's adaptation is called the Internet Packet Exchange (IPX) protocol for use with NetWare.

NetWare is an operating system that enables microcomputers and minicomputers to function as file servers. Executable files, such as WordPerfect or Microsoft Word, are stored on the file server. When the server receives a request from a workstation, the executable file is sent to the workstation to be loaded in its memory. It is then run from the workstation.

NetWare also stores data files for workstations. The data files can be shared by one or more workstations, with NetWare providing security to determine what access is granted to each workstation. For example, a word processing file might be shared by a NetWare workgroup. Anyone within the designated group would be able to access the file and read or modify it. The file would be loaded into the workstation's memory, modified, and rewritten in the shared NetWare directory. NetWare's print servers provide a means to print the file on a network printer.

Novell file servers use software drivers that compose the **NetWare Core Protocol (NCP)**. The Novell NCP communicates with software drivers called the **network shell**, which are installed at each workstation. IPX is the communication protocol used to transfer information between the NCP and the network shell. IPX controls how each frame of data is formatted for transmission. It also determines how data are routed on a Novell network.

IPX DATA FORMATTING

IPX formats data packets similarly to the IEEE 802.3 standard. IPX packets contain destination, source, and length fields at the start of each packet, and the last field is a frame check sequence field for error checking.

The difference between 802.3 and IPX is the so-called proprietary portion—the information after the length field and before the frame check sequence field (see Figure 4-3). The proprietary portion of IPX includes the following:

- A checksum field, which performs an action similar to a parity check

- A field that shows the length of the IPX packet

- The transport control field, showing the number of routers through which the packet has traveled

- A field to indicate what type of packet is being sent, such as a packet with routing information or an NCP packet

- A destination network address to show which network is "home" to the receiving node

- The host address of the node or workstation that will receive the packet

- A field that shows the network number of the node that sent the packet

- The network address of the sending node

- A "socket address" so the packet will be sent to the correct software process level at the receiving node

The data transport methods supported by Novell's IPX include Ethernet, IEEE 802.3, token ring, and ARCNET.

Figure 4-3

IPX proprietary packet format

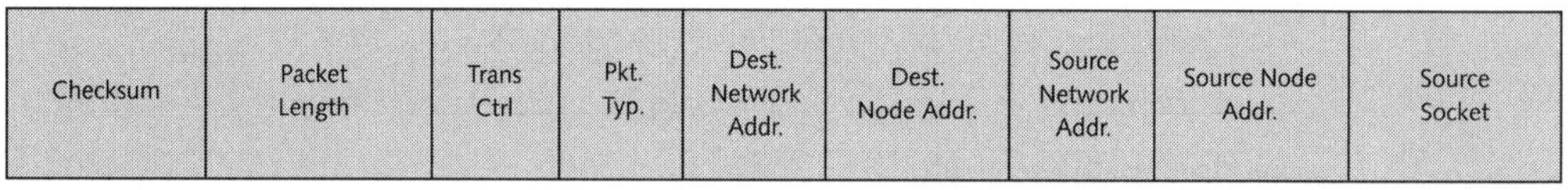

Checksum	Packet Length	Trans Ctrl	Pkt. Typ.	Dest. Network Addr.	Dest. Node Addr.	Source Network Addr.	Source Node Addr.	Source Socket

IPX ROUTING

Novell implemented IPX with routing capabilities, so it would be able to transport data over multiple networks. IPX routing is made possible by the source and destination network information contained in the IPX packet. This information is used by network routers to deliver the IPX packet to the correct network and the correct node on that network.

Novell uses both internal and external routers, as shown in Figure 4-4. (Novell at one time referred to these as "bridges.") An internal router is a file server equipped with interface cards for more than one type of network. For example, the file server might have an Ethernet NIC and a token ring NIC. Data sent to an Ethernet workstation travel through the file server's Ethernet NIC. Data intended for a token ring workstation are routed through the server's token ring NIC.

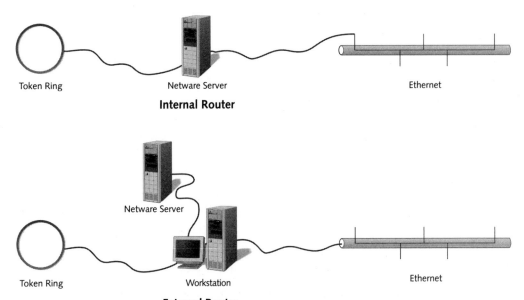

Figure 4-4

Novell internal and external routers

A Novell external router is a workstation equipped with multiple NICs, such as Ethernet, ARCNET, and token ring NICs. The external router uses software that maintains routing tables, so that data are sent to the network specified in the destination network number of the IPX packet.

Each network that houses a Novell file server is given a unique network number. The network number might be likened to the street name on a letter, and the node address would be similar to the number of the house on that street. The combination of the network number and node address ensures that data are delivered to the correct node.

Each router maintains an IPX routing table. The routing table contains the number of each network, the address of each forwarding router, and information about how many routers (or **hops**) a packet must travel through to reach its destination. The routing table enables the router to transfer a packet to the right network.

SPX

Novell developed Sequence Packet Exchange (SPX) after IPX was developed. SPX enables the rapid exchange of application-specific data. One use of SPX is for exchange of database data on the network. Novell's RCONSOLE utility also takes advantage of SPX. This utility enables a workstation to display the same information that appears on a NetWare file server monitor. With RCONSOLE loaded, the workstation user can execute file server console commands without having to be at the file server keyboard.

X.25

The X.25 protocol is a packet-switching protocol developed by the CCITT to ensure reliable data communications, even over networks with low-quality transmission equipment.

The X.25 protocol is used internationally for public data networks. It is particularly common in the European community, and thus it is used in the United States to communicate with European networks. X.25 interconnects remote LANs, PCs, and host computers.

An X.25 network can transmit data packets according to three modes: switched virtual circuits, permanent virtual circuits, and datagrams. A switched virtual circuit is a two-way path or "channel" established from station to station, through an X.25 switch. The circuit is a logical connection that is established only for the duration of the data transmission. Once the transmission is completed, the channel can be made available to other nodes.

Permanent virtual circuits are logical communication channels that remain connected at all times. The connection remains in place even when data transmission stops.

Datagrams are packaged data sent without establishing a communication channel. The packets are addressed to a given destination and may arrive at different times, depending on which path is selected. Datagrams are not used on international networks, but were included in the CCITT specifications for the Internet. The X.25 Internet datagram encapsulates the IP layer on top of the X.25 packet, so that the IP is not aware of the X.25 component. The IP network number is simply mapped to the X.25 destination address.

PACKET SWITCHING

The X.25 standard defines communications between two types of entities: **data terminal equipment** and **data communications equipment**. Data terminal equipment (DTE) can be a terminal, a PC, or a host computer. Data communications equipment (DCE) is network equipment that functions as a packet-switching node.

In the most common configuration, the DTE is attached to a packet assembler/disassembler (PAD). The PAD translates data from the DTE into X.25 format. It also translates the received X.25 formatted data into a format understood by the DTE. Software at the PAD formats the data and provides extensive error checking. PADs also can send out data from several DTEs at the same time. They do this through **packet switching.**

Packet switching involves transmitting messages using a "store-and-forward" technique. The data messages are broken into packets by the DTE and sent to the PAD. The PAD can send data from multiple DTEs over one cable medium to a packet-switched node (DCE). The DCE is a multiplexer or switch that is physically connected to several other DCEs. On an X.25 network, the DCE is a physical switch or multiplexer that can send data over several logical channels created by the X.25 protocol design. (These channels are virtual circuits, as discussed in the next section.) The multiplexer receives the transmitted packets and stores them in a buffer until the intended transmission channel becomes available. Then the packets are forwarded to their destination, where the DTE reassembles the packets back into their original order.

Because X.25 supports multiple channels, several DTEs can transmit at the same time. The multiplexer sequentially switches from channel to channel, transmitting the data from each DTE.

Figure 4–5 represents an X.25 network.

Figure 4-5

X.25 network

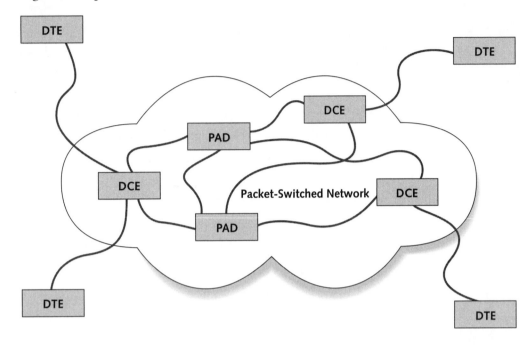

X.25 LAYERS

The CCITT specifications have defined three layers within X.25 for communications between DTEs and DCEs. The physical layer, or Layer 1, is described by CCITT's X.21 standard. This layer is associated with physical connections, data-bit representation, and timing and control signals. The physical interface is similar to the RS-232C standard for serial communications (now known as EIA-232C/D).

X.25's Layer 2 is equivalent to the OSI data-link layer. This layer provides the basic point-to-point connection between the DTE and the network. It is responsible for data transfer, error checking, and flow control.

Layer 3 is like the OSI network layer. This layer handles packet formatting and packet-switching. It can multiplex (switch) up to 4,095 simultaneous logical connections over one link-level physical connection.

The Layer 3 protocol level includes the X.25 packet format, which consists of a header and user data. The header is composed of a general format identifier that specifies the overall format of the packet header, a logical channel identifier containing the virtual circuit ID, and a packet type identifier to designate the kind of information in the packet.

Layer 2 is implemented by Link Access Procedure-Balanced (LAPB). LAPB allows the DTEs and DCEs to initiate communication. LAPB ensures that the frames arrive at the receiving node in the correct sequence, and that they are error free.

Figure 4-6

LAPB frame
format

Flag	Address	Control	Data	FCS	Flag
1 byte	1 byte	1 byte	variable	2 bytes	1 byte

The LAPB frame fields within Layer 2 (see Figure 4-6) consist of the following:

- The *flag field* shows the beginning of the LAPB frame.

- The *address field* indicates the destination of the frame.

- The *control field* shows whether the message is a command or response, and it indicates the frame sequence number.

- The *data* portion of the frame holds the body of the message.

- The *frame-check sequence* (FCS) field permits error checking using CRC.

- The *flag* field shows the end of the frame.

Figure 4-7 shows the Layer 1, 2, and 3 X.25 frame structure.

Figure 4-7

X.25 frame
format

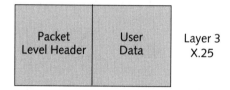

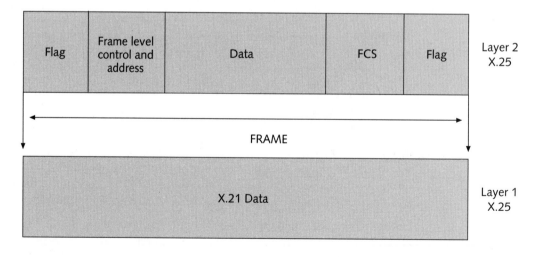

Once a virtual circuit is established, X.25 puts a sequence number on each packet. A maximum number of packets to be sent is established without a further request from the receiving DTE. Normally, the packet limitation is based on the allocated subscription time (for public networks).

X.25 USE

At 64 Kbps, X.25 is not as fast as newer technologies such as ATM, but it offers many advantages until technology in less-developed countries catches up. For example, X.25 continues to be a reliable way to connect legacy mainframe, minicomputers, and early LANs.

ISDN

Integrated Services Digital Network (ISDN) was introduced in the 1970s by the CCITT to provide voice, data, graphics, and video digital services. The first CCITT set of standards was made official in 1984 and later refined in 1988. The "I" series of standards from 1988 includes the following:

- *I.100.* This portion of the standards provides an introduction to ISDN, and a glossary of terms.

- *I.200.* The services provided to users include:

  1. Complete guaranteed end-to-end compatibility.

  2. Standardized terminals and procedures.

  3. Listing of ISDN subscribers in an international directory.

  4. Standard testing and maintenance procedures.

  5. Charging and account rules.

- *I.300.* This series focuses on network issues such as numbering and addressing.

- *I.400.* This portion deals with network interface topics such as equipment configurations, transmission rates, and protocol specifications.

- *I.500.* This defines the interface between ISDN and dissimilar networks.

- *I.600.* Subscriber installation, access services, and general architecture are defined here.

The benefits of ISDN are summarized in Table 4-4. Implementation of ISDN standards has been slow. Since ISDN is entirely digital, old analog and electromechanical switches have to be replaced. The major U.S. long-distance carriers, such as AT&T, MCI, and Sprint, are progressively implementing ISDN as they replace aging equipment. They also are working to support standardized equipment for message traffic across carriers. Progress also is being made in Europe, where there are many long-distance carriers supporting a wide range of communications equipment.

Table 4-4

ISDN advantages

ISDN Benefits
The ability to provide voice, data, and video services over one network
Communications channels offered in multiples of 64 Kbps, such as 384 Kbps and 1536 Kbps throughput
A layered protocol structure compatible with OSI
Network maintenance and management services offered via intelligent nodes
The ability to provide switched and nonswitched connection services
Provision for videoconferencing through high-bandwidth capabilities

I.200 SERVICES

The I.200 portion of the CCITT specifications for ISDN offers impressive networking capabilities. These are divided into bearer services, teleservices, and supplementary services. The bearer services include circuit mode and packet mode options. The circuit mode options are shown in Table 4-5. Packet-mode bearer services include virtual call and permanent virtual call circuits (modeled after X.25 virtual circuits). They also include connectionless service, which is currently under development.

Table 4-5

ISDN circuit mode options

Information Rate	Channel	Applications
64 Kbps	B	8 KHz General Purpose Communications
64 Kbps	B	8 KHz Digitized Speech
64 Kbps	B	3.1 KHz Audio
64 Kbps	B	8 KHz Alternate Transfer of Speech
384 Kbps		8 KHz Video and PBX Link Fast FAX CAD/CAM Imaging High-Speed Data LAN Internetworking
1,536 Kbps	H11	Same services as 384 Kpbs

The teleservices provide for 3.1 KHz speech communications. They also include teletex end-to-end text communications, telefax end-to-end FAX communications, and a mixed mode for combined text and FAX. Another teleservice is videotex, which provides for retrieval of digital mailbox information including text and graphics. Interactive text communications (telex) also are part of these services.

Supplementary services are primarily available for voice communications. These include number identification, multi-party calling, and call completion.

DIGITAL COMMUNICATIONS

Two common interfaces are supported in ISDN: basic rate interface and primary rate interface. The basic rate interface (BRI) has an aggregate data rate of 144 Kbps. Since many conventional LANS have data rates of 1–16 Mbps, ISDN BRI is not suitable for some network applications, such as file transfer, and graphics applications.

The primary rate interface (PRI) supports faster data rates, particularly on channel H11, which offers switched bandwidth in increments of 1536 Kbps. As higher-speed networks are developed, it is anticipated that broadband ISDN will become available. This would offer data rates of 155–622 Mbps.

ISDN is designed to be compatible with many existing digital networks, such as ATM, X.25, and T1 (T1 has a data rate of 1.54 Mbps). As illustrated in Table 4-5, ISDN is divided into 64-Kbps channels. These include channels B, D, H11, H12 (used in Europe), and H4X (proposed broadband). Digital signals are placed on the network in two ways. One method is time compression multiplexing (TCM). This method sends 16–24-bit blocks of data in alternating digital bursts. There is a quiet period between bursts to allow the line to settle before the next burst. Consequently, the first burst goes in one direction, followed by a pause. The pause is followed by a burst in the opposite direction. Each burst is 288 Kbps. Because of the direction switching, the total data rate is 144 Kbps. The data bursts are managed by a central timing control.

The second method is echo cancellation. This method transmits data in two directions at the same time. A device called a hybrid is used to connect the transmitter and the receiver to the subscription line. The two-way simultaneous transmissions often cause reflection (echo) of the transmitted signal. Echo of signals on the line may be three times greater than the power of the true signals, thus obscuring the data. ISDN uses an **echo canceler** to overcome the reflected signals. The echo canceler determines the amplitude of the echoed signals and subtracts the amplitude from the incoming signals. Since the amount of echo can vary, the echo canceler employs a feedback circuit that enables it to continuously measure the amplitude of the signal reflection.

RELATIONSHIP BETWEEN ISDN AND OSI

ISDN incorporates the physical, data-link, network, and transport layers of the OSI model. Similar to X.25, it uses LAPB and the data-link layer to ensure maximum detection of communication errors.

IMPLEMENTATION

Extensive use of ISDN is several years away, since carrier companies will experience high equipment replacement costs. ISDN also is experiencing strong competition from high-speed technologies such as ATM and frame relay. The future for ISDN data networking will depend on how quickly broadband ISDN is implemented. As high-speed technologies continue to evolve, ISDN will likely share the network market with ATM and frame relay, which is described below.

FRAME RELAY

CCITT standards for frame relay were introduced in 1988 to meet the demands of high-volume, high-bandwidth WANs. Additional standards were approved in 1990, 1992, and 1993 to meet the evolving demand for frame relay. Nearly 60% of Fortune 1000 companies have adopted frame relay or plan to do so.

The concept behind this technology is similar to X.25, in that frame relay uses multiplexing along with virtual circuit techniques. Unlike X.25 and ISDN, however, frame relay is designed to interface with modern networks that do their own error checking. It achieves "fast packet" high-speed data transmission by recognizing that newer network technologies have error checking on intermediate nodes, and so it does not incorporate extensive error checking. For example, frame relay is used with TCP/IP or IPX based networks, where these protocols handle the end-to-end error checking at the DTE.

Frame relay does look for bad frame check sequences. If it detects errors that were not discovered by intermediate nodes, it discards the bad packets. It also discards packets if it detects heavy network congestion.

PACKET FORMAT

The frame relay packet is illustrated in Figure 4-8. The first field is the flag, which signals the beginning of the frame. The frame relay header comes after the flag field. The header is composed of the following parts:

- Data link connection identifier (DLCI). This portion of the header stores the virtual circuit number. Each virtual circuit created in frame relay is given an ID number to distinguish it from other circuits.

- Command/response bit (CE). This bit indicates whether the packet holds a command or a response type of communication.

- Forward explicit congestion notification (FECN). When a node detects network congestion, it changes the FECN bit to notify the receiving node.

- Backward explicit congestion notification (BECN). This bit is changed to notify the sending node that there is network congestion.

- Discard eligibility indicator (DE). When this bit is changed, it signals the receiving node to discard packets due to network congestion.

- Address extension bit (EA). This bit shows that extended addressing is used. It means that additional virtual circuits have been created. EA has not yet been implemented for practical use.

Figure 4-8

Frame relay
packet format

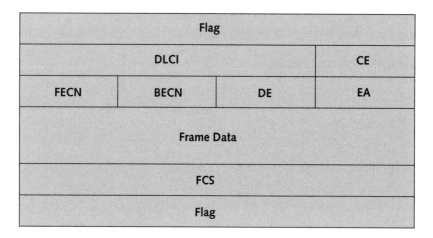

Following the frame header is the information field. It contains the data for the destination node. The size of this field is different for different vendors. Some vendors package 32,768 bits of data and others package 65,536 bits in this field.

The information field is followed by a frame-check sequence field that uses CRC error checking. The frame format is closed by a flag field to indicate the end of the frame.

VIRTUAL CIRCUITS

Frame relay uses multiple virtual circuits over a single cable medium. Each virtual circuit provides a data path between two communicating nodes. As is true for X.25 communications, the virtual circuits constitute a logical rather than physical connection. Two types of virtual circuits exist within frame relay: permanent and switched.

Permanent virtual circuit

A permanent virtual circuit (PVC) is a continuously available path between two nodes. The path is given a circuit ID that is used in the DLCI field of each transmitted frame. Once the circuit is defined, it remains open, so communication can occur at any time.

PVCs apply only the physical and data-link layers of the OSI model. Signal transmission is handled at the physical layer, and virtual circuits are part of the data-link layer. A single cable medium can support multiple virtual circuits to different network destinations.

Switched virtual circuit

A switched virtual circuit (SVC) transmission is based on the need to establish a transmission session. A **call control signal** is sent between the nodes to establish communication. Once the communication is finished, the call control signal issues a command for each node to disconnect.

An SVC connection is designed to allow the user network provider to determine the data throughput rate. It can be adjusted based on the needs of the application and the current network traffic conditions. Multiple SVCs can be supported on a single cable from point to point. SVC standards were issued in early 1994. SVC is a newer technology than PVC.

SVCs use the physical, data-link, and network portions of the OSI model. The physical and data-link layers perform the same functions as in PVCs. The network layer is used for call control signaling protocols.

TRANSMISSION MEDIUM

Frame relay is used with fiber optic, T1 (high speed telecommunications), and T3 mediums. Currently, it can deliver packets at speeds up to 1.544 Mbps (T1 speeds). Once it is adapted to broadband applications, it will be capable of speeds up to 44.7 Mbps.

CELL RELAY

Cell relay is a developing technology that takes frame relay a step further. Because frame relay breaks data into packets designed for store-and-forward transmission, it is not suitable for voice and video applications. Cell relay creates large fixed-length data entities called cells. When transmitted, a cell may be empty or full of data. The cell relay technology enables information to be sent without the packet-switching delays in frame relay.

SUMMARY

Protocols are the communication languages that make internetworking possible. In particular, TCP/IP has played a founding role in linking computers worldwide. TCP/IP has not only provided a common basis for the transmission of data, it also has provided critical application services. These services are TELNET, FTP, SMTP, and DNS.

IPX has played an important role by providing communication services for Novell LANs. Many large-scale networks began as small LANs with NetWare and IPX. Today, IPX continues to play a central role in data communications.

Like TCP/IP, X.25 has linked very different computer systems and LANs into wide-area networks (WANs). It has been predominant in European and other foreign networking systems. X.25 has played an important role by providing the packet-switching technology that has made newer protocol systems, such as frame relay, possible.

In the future, communication barriers on our planet will continue to melt away due to technologies like ISDN, frame relay, cell relay, and others. The multiple channel and virtual circuit capabilities of these networking systems are making high-speed communications a global reality.

KEY TERMS

Term/Acronym	Definition
Call Control Signal	This signal is used to initiate communication between two nodes using a switched virtual circuit on a frame relay network. The signal also is used to disconnect communication between the nodes.
Datagram	TCP/IP breaks data into these smaller units, which can be transmitted in streams on the network.
Data Communications Equipment (DCE)	A network device that performs packet switching.
Data Terminal Equipment (DTE)	Terminals, workstations, and host computers that operate on a packet-switching network are called DTEs.
Dotted Decimal Notation System	The most common IP address scheme, where address references are separated by periods.
Echo Canceler	This device is used to eliminate signal reflection in the cabling of a network. Echo cancelers are used on ISDN networks.
Hop	Each time a packet travels through a router, it has gone one hop. The number of hops is tracked by some protocols to determine if a packet should be discarded as lost or aged.
NetWare	A commonly used file server operating system that provides file services, print services, and access security to network workstations through the IPX protocol.

NetWare Core Protocol (NCP)	Novell file servers use this configuration of drivers to communicate with nodes and other file servers on a network.
Network File System (NFS)	This network file transfer protocol ships files as streams of records.
Network Shell	Each workstation on a Novell network is equipped with drivers that are called the network shell. These drivers enable the workstation to communicate with file servers and other workstations.
Packet Switching	A simultaneous parallel conversation of data along separate paths in the same switch.
Subnet	Many networks are really composed of several smaller networks that combine to make a larger network. The smaller networks are subnets.
User Datagram Protocol (UDP)	This TCP/IP protocol defines how to construct datagrams and transmit them on the network.
Xerox Network System (XNS)	XNS was developed to provide a means for nodes to communicate on Ethernet networks. The IPX protocol is modeled after XNS. XNS packet construction is similar to the IEEE 802.3 format.

REVIEW EXERCISES

1. Can the same network support TCP/IP and IPX communications? If so, how is this accomplished? If not, why not?

2. What applications are a part of the TCP/IP protocol, and what functions do they perform?

3. How is TCP/IP implementation similar to the OSI model? At what layers does the X.25 protocol employ the OSI model? How does frame relay correspond to the OSI model?

4. How does packet switching work? How do virtual circuits work? What protocols employ these techniques? Why does this technology hold promise for new directions in fast-packet communications?

5. What are the advantages of X.25 compared to frame relay? What are the disadvantages? How would you compare the advantages of ISDN to X.25 and frame relay?

6. Explain how TCP/IP communications work. Why has this protocol been important to the Internet?

7. How does IPX work on a network? How is this protocol used by NetWare?

8. Explain IP addressing. Research the IP addressing schemes used on your campus.

9. What is SPX? How is it used?

10. Is SMTP an X.400-compliant protocol?

11. Where is X.25 primarily used?

12. What protocol is used on the Internet?

13. Are subnetworks used at your campus? If so, what are some of the subnetwork addresses? (You will need to contact your campus network administrator to answer these questions).

14. What data transport methods are supported by NetWare?

15. If you have internet access, log in to Microsoft's web page at http://www.microsoft.com. See if you can find information about data transport methods supported by Microsoft NT.

16. What is the domain name used to designate your campus on the Internet?

17. How is error checking performed in a frame relay packet?

INTERNETWORKING DEVICES

On the surface, a network may simply appear to consist of long runs of wire interspersed with boxes containing blinking lights. But as you learn more about networks, you will see that they are similar to organic units. Each portion of the network has a specific function. Some network devices play a small role, such as amplifying data to lengthen transmission distances. Others have a larger role, such as intelligently directing data traffic to avoid congestion. As a whole, the wire and boxes combine to enable computer users to communicate over vast distances. A functioning network becomes a large, complex entity of people, data, and machines working interactively.

AFTER READING THIS CHAPTER YOU WILL BE ABLE TO:

- DESCRIBE THE EQUIPMENT USED TO BUILD MODERN NETWORKS, SUCH AS COMMUNICATION SERVERS, REPEATERS, BRIDGES, ROUTERS, AND HUBS
- EXPLAIN THE SPANNING TREE ALGORITHM
- PROVIDE A BACKGROUND IN BRIDGING AND ROUTING TECHNIQUES
- DESCRIBE WIRELESS NETWORKING OPTIONS

This chapter describes the network equipment that makes data communications possible. The simplest devices include communication servers, multiplexers, and repeaters. These devices have little internal intelligence but are very effective in small networks. As user productivity grows, so does the need for increased intelligence in network devices. There is a demand to interpret protocols, block designated network traffic, and find the fastest route for sending data. Devices with built-in intelligence include bridges, routers, and hubs.

COMMUNICATION SERVERS

Communication servers provide a way to connect terminals, PCs, modems, and printers into a network. A single communication server has multiple serial ports available for use, and a port that is connected to the network.

A typical use for a communication server is to connect terminals to a network so they can reach a host system such as an IBM mainframe computer. Communication servers are used under these circumstances to enable organizations to retain their investment in terminals. They offer a means to implement networking and to delay the cost of immediately replacing dumb terminals with workstations. Figure 5-1 illustrates IBM 3270 terminals connected to an IBM ES9000 by way of the network.

Figure 5-1

Terminal server connecting IBM 3270 terminals to the network for connection to a mainframe

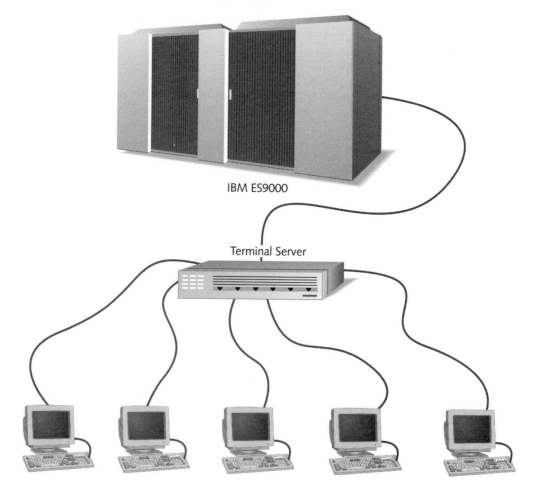

IBM ES9000

Terminal Server

The communication server also may connect several modems to a network. The modems can be accessed remotely by workstations or terminals. On a college campus, this would enable a student to access a network host from home. Using a PC and modem, he or she could dial into a modem bank at the college from his or her apartment. The modem would be connected to the communication server, which is connected to the network (Figure 5-2). The ability to connect modems to a network paves the way for **telecommuting** opportunities, where employees can work from home or a remote computing site.

Figure 5-2

Communication server for a modem network

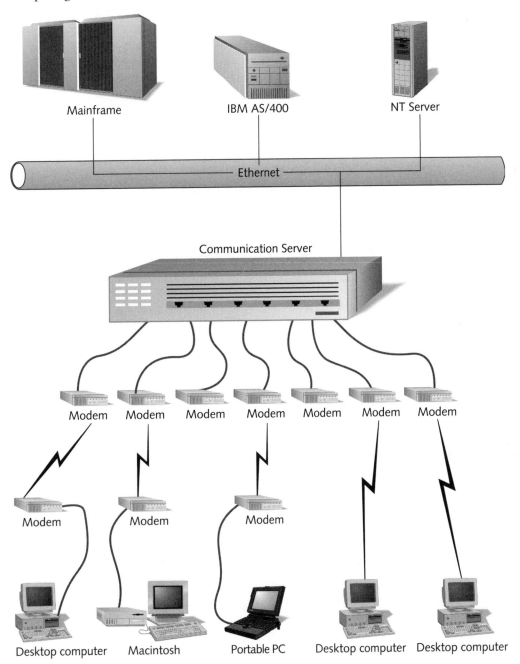

Mainframe   IBM AS/400   NT Server

Ethernet

Communication Server

Modem Modem Modem Modem Modem Modem Modem

Modem   Modem   Modem

Desktop computer   Macintosh   Portable PC   Desktop computer   Desktop computer

MULTIPLEXERS

Multiplexers are network devices that can receive multiple inputs and transmit them to a shared network medium. X.25, ISDN, and frame relay use multiplexers for packet-switched communications. In these technologies, the multiplexer (packet-switched node) receives data from several nodes. The multiplexer is connected to a single cable medium, which is divided into channels or virtual circuits. The multiplexer stores the received packets until it can open the intended channel.

The multiplexer simply switches from channel to channel, placing each packet on the channel specified in the packet's data link connection identifier (DLCI). Each packet is stored until the multiplexer opens its channel for transmission. Figure 5-3 shows a diagram of a multiplexer.

Multiplexing is accomplished by one of three methods: time division multiple access, frequency division multiple access, and statistical multiple access.

Time division multiple access (TDMA) divides the channels into distinct time slots. Each time slot is designated for a particular network node, as if it were a dedicated line. The multiplexer rotates from time slot to time slot for each channel. TDMA does not guarantee the most efficient use of the network medium, since transmission occurs on only one channel at a time. The timing of node transmission also is important, since a node may transmit at an interval that is out of synchronization with its time slot.

Frequency division multiple access (FDMA) divides the channels into frequencies instead of time slots. Each channel has its own broadcast frequency. The multiplexer switches from frequency to frequency as it sends data.

Statistical multiple access, or statistical multiplexing, is used by X.25, ISDN, and frame relay. This method is more efficient than TDMA or FDMA, because the physical medium bandwidth is dynamically allocated based on the application need. The multiplexer continuously monitors each channel to determine the communication requirements. For example, at one moment a channel may need to transmit a large graphics file, and then be quiet. Algorithms on the multiplexer determine the bandwidth needed to transmit the file. After the file is transmitted, it will reallocate bandwidth to another channel.

REPEATERS

Once a network is installed, more and more departments are likely to request connectivity to the network. Network growth can be significant in terms of new users and the distances between the users. Extending cable plant runs throughout a floor or building presents a challenge. Several users in a department may be spread over distances that require cabling to extend beyond the IEEE distance specifications.

The repeater is an inexpensive solution that enables a network to reach users in distant portions of a building. A repeater amplifies an incoming signal, retimes it, and reproduces it along multiple cable runs (see Figure 5-4 on page 88). Retiming helps to avoid packet collisions once the signal is placed on the cable.

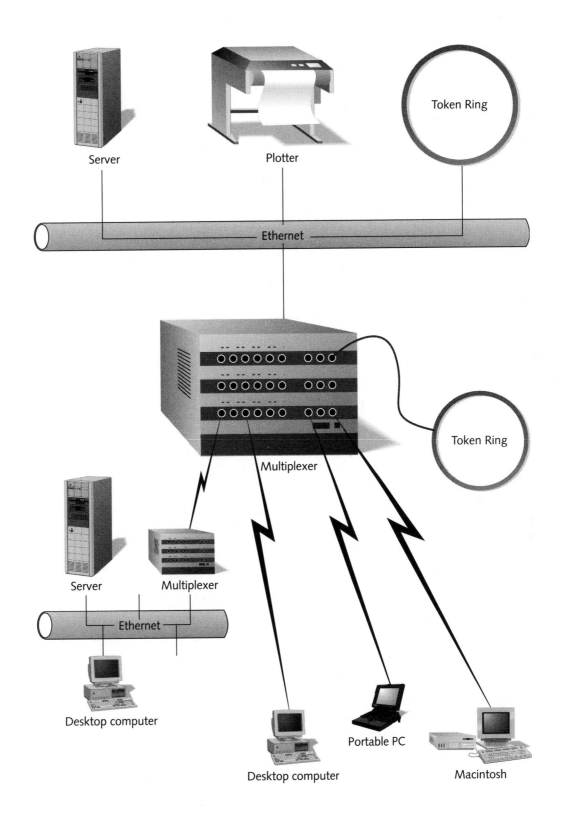

Figure 5-3

Multiplexers

Figure 5-4

A repeater
connecting
network nodes

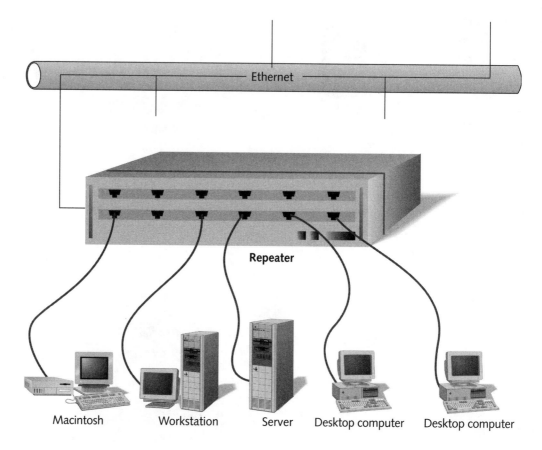

Each cable run is treated by the network as a normal cable segment. For example, a 10BASE5 Ethernet repeater can put a received signal on multiple cable runs 500 meters in length. Each cable run supports up to 99 connected nodes and a terminator at the end of the segment. A 10BASE2 repeater supports 185 meter runs, with 29 nodes on each run. According to IEEE specifications, and depending on the network topology and media, a single packet can travel through up to four repeaters.

Cabletron's MR2000C is one example of a multi-port repeater. It takes one inbound thick or thin IEEE 802.3 Ethernet segment, amplifies the signal, and places it on two to eight full-length segments. The MR2000C also has an AUI port for connection to a coaxial or fiber optic cable backbone.

When the MR2000C receives data packets, it retimes them before placement onto the extended segments. If the repeater detects a problem on an individual segment, such as excessive collisions, it will halt transmission of data to that segment. This method of closing down a segment is called **partitioning**. For example, a segment may be partitioned if an Ethernet interface is malfunctioning and sending excessive packet traffic. One segment on a multi-port repeater can be partitioned without affecting the others. The segment also can be reset at the repeater for resumed transmission as soon as the network problem is fixed.

BRIDGES

A bridge is a network device that connects one LAN segment to another. Bridges are used in the following circumstances:

- They are used to extend a LAN when the maximum connection limit has been reached, such as the 30-node limit on an Ethernet segment.

- They are used to extend a LAN beyond the length limit, such as 500 meters for Ethernet.

- They are used to segment LANs to reduce data traffic bottlenecks.

- They are used for security, to prevent unauthorized access to a LAN.

The first bridges were developed by DEC in the early 1980s. DEC's work on bridges was incorporated in the IEEE 802.1 standard. Today, bridges are very popular on Ethernet/IEEE 802.3 networks. Because their implementation is unseen by users, the term transparent bridge is commonly used. Bridges are described as operating in "promiscuous" mode which means they look at each packet's address before sending it on. Figure 5-5 shows a bridge connecting two IPX-based Ethernet LANs and a TCP/IP Ethernet LAN.

Bridges operate at the media access control (MAC) sublayer of the OSI data-link layer. A bridge intercepts all network traffic and examines each packet as it is received. It reads the destination address on each packet and determines if the packet should be forwarded to the next network. If the packet is intended for a local node, the bridge will **filter** the packet to that node on the originating LAN. A standard Ethernet bridge can filter about 30,000 packets per second and forward about 15,000 packets per second.

Bridges provide full network access because they are protocol-independent. They only look at the MAC address. A single bridge can forward TCP/IP, IPX, and X.25 packets without regard to the frame structure. Bridges do not attempt to convert packets from one network protocol format to another.

Figure 5-5

Bridged
network

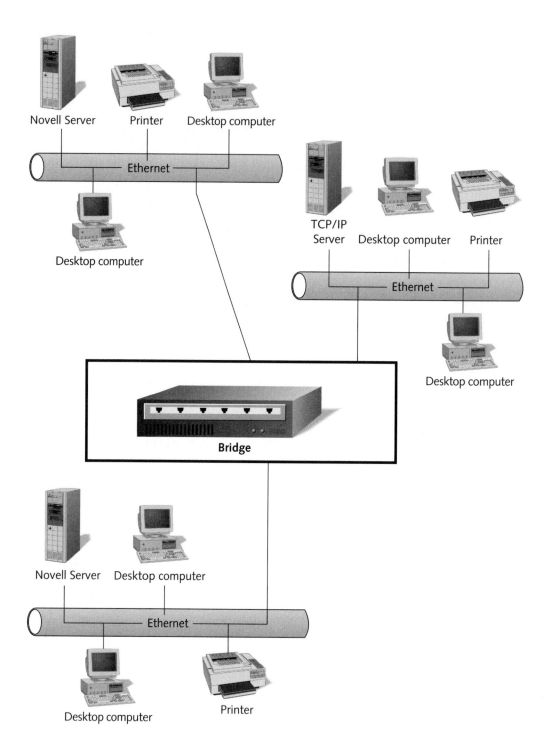

There are two types of bridges: local and remote. A local bridge is used to directly connect two LANs in close proximity, such as two Ethernet LANs. It also is used to segment network traffic for the purpose of reducing bottlenecks. For example, a network might have a file server that creates high-volume network traffic. A bridge can be installed so packets from that file server only reach workstations in a designated area.

In another case, clustered minicomputers, graphics workstations, diskless workstations, and PCs accessing file servers may share the same network. Performance on this high-traffic network will suffer unless the network can be divided into separate strategic networks based on device and application use. Bridges can be placed on this network to isolate high-traffic areas into smaller network segments.

Remote bridges are used to join distant networks. To reduce costs, the bridges can be joined by a serial line. This is one way to join networks in different cities or states and combine them into a single large network. As discussed later in this chapter, remote bridging also is performed by routers.

BRIDGE FUNCTIONS

A bridge performs three important functions: learning, filtering, and forwarding. When it is "powered on," a bridge *learns* the network topology and addresses of devices on all attached networks. The bridge learns what is on the network by examining the source and destination addresses in the packets it receives. By this means, each bridge builds a bridging table so it knows the address of every network node. Most bridges can store a large range of addresses in their bridging tables. A Bay Networks Ethernet bridge, for example, can store up to 8,192 entries in its bridging table. DEC FDDI bridges can store 14,000 entries.

The bridge uses its table as the basis for *forwarding* traffic. When a packet is received, the bridge reads the destination address and looks up the address in the bridging table. If an association is found, the bridge forwards the packet to a known destination. If no association exists, the frame can be **flooded** to all ports on the bridge, except the port from which the frame was sent.

A bridge also may contain instructions entered by the network manager to not flood packets from specified source addresses. Or it may have instructions to discard certain packets instead of forwarding them. These instructions enable the bridge to *filter* network traffic.

CASCADE AND MULTI-PORT BRIDGES

Some bridges only can link two network segments. These bridges are used to **cascade** network segments. For example, bridge A connects LAN 1 and 2. Bridge B connects LAN 2 to LAN 3. A packet from LAN 1 will have to go through both bridges A and B to reach LAN 3.

There also are **multi-port bridges** that can tie several segments into one network. Some vendors offer multi-port bridges with up to 52 ports or interfaces. Using the previous example, if bridge A were a multi-port bridge, it would have three ports to enable it to connect LANs 1, 2, and 3. A packet from any one of these LANs would travel through only one bridge to reach its destination; the bridge's table would contain addresses of all the nodes on each LAN.

REDUNDANCY

Bridges are installed in parallel on many networks to provide for **redundancy**. If one bridge fails, the other will continue to operate so there is minimal network interruption.

The disadvantage of using bridges in parallel is that it creates a situation where packets are duplicated by each bridge. This can be fatal on an Ethernet network, because a looping condition may result, in which two identical packets are picked up by both bridges and forwarded to the next LAN. The receiving LAN may forward the packets back to the originating LAN. The loop will continue until one of the bridges stops forwarding. Figure 5-6 illustrates looping.

Figure 5-6

Parallel bridge looping

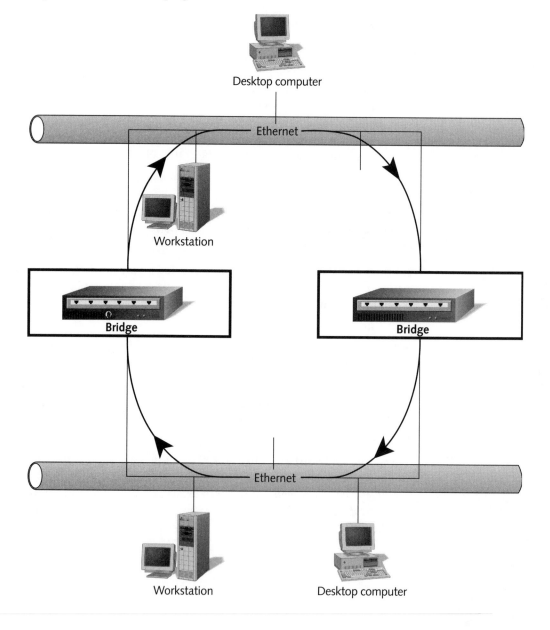

SPANNING TREE ALGORITHM

Networks that employ more than one bridge (including redundant networks) use the **spanning tree algorithm** to bridge packets. This algorithm is defined according to the IEEE 802.1d standard. The spanning tree algorithm is designed to accomplish two goals. One goal is to ensure that a packet cannot be caught in an endless loop on the network. When many network segments are connected by bridges, it is possible for packets to travel in a loop and never reach their destination. At minimum, this eventually causes some network congestion. On a large scale, the looping packets can result in so much traffic that they cause a **broadcast storm**.

A second goal of the spanning tree algorithm is to forward packets along the most efficient route. Efficiency in this case means the distance the packet must travel and utilization of cable resources. The spanning tree algorithm deals with looping packets by creating a one-way path around the network. All bridges on the network communicate with each other to establish the direction in which packets are bridged. Part of this communication process involves selecting a root bridge. Each bridge is given an ID and a priority. The root bridge has the highest priority. The spanning tree algorithm protocol enables bridges to "talk" to one another using reserved multicast packets called bridge protocol data units (BPDUs), which allow bridges to learn about each other. The BPDU frame format is shown in Figure 5-7.

Figure 5-7

BPDU packet format

Proto ID	Vers	Mess Type	Flags	Root ID	Root Path Cost	Brdg ID	Port ID	Mess Age	Max Age	Hello Time	Forw Delay
2	1	1	1	8	4	8	2	2	2	2	2

The fields represented in Figure 5-7 are the following:

- *Proto ID:* This is the protocol identifier, which is 0 for BPDU frames.

- *Vers:* This field contains the version number and is always 0.

- *Mess Type:* The message type is also 0 for BPDU frames.

- *Flags:* The TC bit in the flag signals a topology change. The TCA bit is set to acknowledge receipt of a configuration message with the TC bit set. The other six bits are unused.

- *Root ID:* This identifies the root bridge with a two-byte priority followed by a six-byte bridge ID.

- *Root Path Cost:* This contains the "cost" of the path from the bridge sending the configuration message to the root bridge. (Cost is explained below.)

- *Brdg ID:* This field contains the priority and ID of the bridge sending the message.

- *Port ID:* This contains the ID of the port or interface from which the configuration message was sent. This field allows the bridge to detect looped configurations.

- *Mess Age:* The message age field shows the amount of time since the root bridge sent the message.

- *Max Age:* The maximum age field indicates when the current message should be deleted.

- *Hello Time:* This shows the time period between root bridge confirmation messages.

- *Forw Delay:* The forward delay contains the length of time that bridges should wait before transitioning to a new state after a topology change. (Topology Change Messages consist of only four bytes. They include the protocol ID field, which contains the value 0, a version field, which contains the value 0, and a message type field which contains the value 128.)

The first stage in the creation of a bridged network is to determine which bridge has the highest priority. The bridge with the lowest MAC address is assigned the highest priority and becomes the root bridge. The other bridges are given a priority number based on their MAC address. Bridges with lower MAC addresses have higher-priority assignments.

Once a root bridge is designated, it sends out root BPDUs to find loops. The other bridges place selected ports in a blocked (one-way) state to prevent looping. Ports are blocked based on a determination of **cost**. Each port is assigned a cost value, which is either a default number or a number assigned by the network administrator. The cost of a path to the root bridge is based on line speed and distance. A T1 line running at 1.544 Mbps will have a higher cost than a 10-Mbps Ethernet line. Also, a bridge that is farther than others from the root bridge will block ports due to higher cost of transmission (a longer path to the root bridge).

Once the spanning tree network is established, the root bridge transmits **Hello BPDUs** once every few seconds. If the other network bridges do not receive a Hello BPDU within a given time (the default is 20 seconds), it is assumed that the root bridge is off-line or malfunctioning. The bridge that detects this first issues a topology change configuration BPDU to establish another root bridge.

The spanning tree algorithm allows only one path to any network in a bridged network. By coupling this with cost determination, network congestion is minimized and network efficiency is maximized.

ETHERNET BRIDGING

On an Ethernet network, cost calculations are of equal value. Since this is the case, the total number of bridges in a linear path between two nodes is limited to eight. Exceeding eight bridges can result in packet timing problems for CSMA/CD algorithms. While this is not an official standard of the spanning tree algorithm, it is followed by conscientious network managers.

TOKEN RING BRIDGING

Token ring bridges use **source routing** to forward packets on the network. Originally proposed by IBM, source-route bridging has been incorporated into the 802.5 token ring LAN specification. Source-route bridges perform routing at the OSI network layer.

Source-route bridging (Figure 5-8) places the complete source-to-destination route into all inter-LAN frames sent by the source. The bridges store and forward frames as indicated by the route specified within the frame.

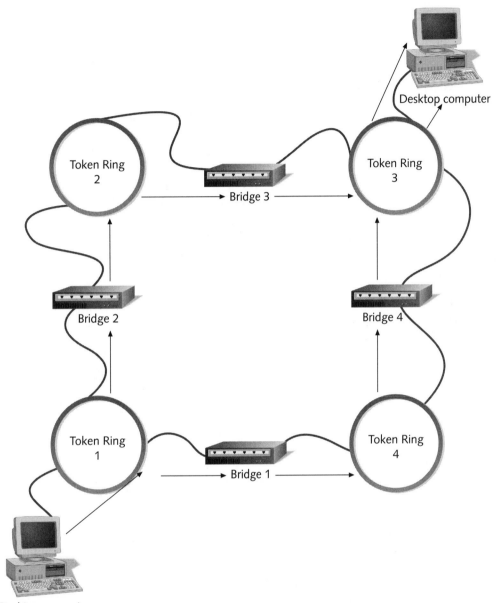

Figure 5-8

Source-route bridging

When a node anticipates sending a packet on a bridged network, it issues an explorer packet. Each bridge that receives this packet copies it onto all outbound ports. Route information is appended to the explorer packets as they travel throughout the internetwork. When the sending node's explorer packets are received by the destination node, the destination node replies to the sending node using the accumulated route information. Then the sending node must select a path to the destination node. The path is determined by three factors: the route taken by the first packet received back, the minimum number of hops to the destination, and the path that will enable the largest packet size (4 Mbps network segments have 4,000-byte packets and 16 Mbps networks have 17,800-byte packets). After the path is determined, the path information is placed in the RIF (routing information field) of the 802.5 packet. The presence of routing in the 802.5 packet is indicated by setting the RII (routing information indicator) in the packet.

If redundant bridges are used, each bridge is assigned a different number so the two paths are seen as distinct. Token ring networks are limited to a maximum of seven bridges.

ROUTERS

A router performs functions similar to a bridge, such as learning, filtering, and forwarding. Unlike bridges, however, routers have built-in intelligence to study network traffic and to quickly adapt to changes detected in the network. Routers connect LANs at the network layer of the OSI model, which enables them to interpret more information than bridges from packet traffic. Routers can connect networks that have dissimilar data-link layers. For example, an Ethernet network using the TCP/IP protocol can be connected to a packet-switched frame relay network that also uses IP.

Unlike bridges, which are transparent to the end-node, routers are known to the end-node. Nodes regularly communicate with a router to confirm their address and presence. Routers are designed to send packets along paths with the lowest volume of traffic and with the lowest cost. They also can isolate portions of a network to contain areas of heavy traffic from reaching the broader network system. This characteristic enables them to prevent network slowdowns and broadcast storms.

As a network grows in complexity, the need to ship packets along the shortest, most efficient path grows proportionally. Bridges often are replaced by routers to ensure that growing network traffic is efficiently handled and network congestion avoided. Also, when large networks must be joined, routers are more efficient than bridges in linking these networks.

ROUTING TECHNIQUES

Routing is performed in one of two ways. Static routing is accomplished by the network manager setting up the routing tables so there are fixed paths between any two routers. The network manager also intervenes to update routing tables when a network device fails. A static router can determine that a network link is down, but it cannot automatically re-route traffic without intervention from the network manager. Because it is labor intensive, static routing is not commonly used by most network managers.

Dynamic routing occurs independently of the network manager. Dynamic routers monitor the network for changes, update their own routing tables, and reconfigure network paths as needed. When a network link fails, a dynamic router will automatically detect the failure and establish the most efficient new paths. The new paths are configured based on the lowest cost as determined by network load, line type, and bandwidth.

Some routers support only one protocol, such as TCP/IP or IPX. Multiple protocol routers offer protocol conversion between dissimilar networks.

ROUTING TABLES

Routers maintain information about node addresses and the network status in databases. The routing table database contains the addresses of other routers and of each end-node. Dynamic routers automatically update the routing table by regularly exchanging address information with other routers and with network nodes.

Routers also regularly exchange information about network traffic, the network topology, and the status of network links. This information is kept in a network status database in each router.

When a packet arrives, the router examines the destination address. It decides how to forward the packet based on network status information and a calculation of the number of hops required for the packet to reach its destination.

SINGLE- AND MULTI- PROTOCOL ROUTERS

Routers exchange information by means of a routing protocol. The routing protocol enables routers to exchange network status and network address data.

Routers that use a single protocol (such as TCP/IP), maintain only one address database. A multi-protocol router has an address database for each protocol it recognizes (such as a database for TCP/IP nodes and a database for IPX nodes). Multi-protocol routing is accomplished by three methods: ships-in-the-night, encapsulation, and integrated routing.

Ships-in-the-Night (SIN)

This method involves using separate routing protocols for each protocol supported by the router. For example, a router that supports TCP/IP, IPX, and OSI would use three distinct routing protocols. The routing protocols would be OSPF, RIP, and IS-IS (specific routing protocols are explained in the next section).

The SIN method can degrade router performance because of the need to maintain the rules for each routing protocol. The more protocols that are supported, the more overhead is created in the router. Another cost of the SIN approach is the greater need for router management. Multiple routing protocols mean the creation of multiple virtual circuits to manage. Tuning a SIN-based router can be very difficult as the number of virtual circuits increases.

Encapsulation

Encapsulation is a technique that simplifies transmitting packets between routers. Using this method, multi-protocol routers encapsulate all data into a proprietary protocol or into the IP protocol. The danger in using a proprietary protocol is that you are locked into purchasing all routers from the same vendor, because only routers made by that vendor can de-encapsulate the packet at the receiving end. Adopting a router that encapsulates packets in a generic IP fashion provides more flexibility than proprietary schemes. This allows routers to be purchased from a wide range of vendors.

Integrated Routing

Integrated routing serves multiple protocols with one protocol routing scheme. Many vendors are adopting a single integrated routing protocol so that one network can have routers from different vendors. Integrated routing makes network management easier and provides good network performance.

ROUTING PROTOCOLS

Vendors use different routing protocols to transport data between routers. The most common protocols are the routing information protocol and the open shortest path first protocol.

Routing Information Protocol (RIP)

This protocol is based on determining the fewest hops between two network nodes. As networks become more complicated, RIP is beginning to fade as a choice of vendors. RIP requires high bandwidth and network resources, because each RIP router sends a copy of its routing table to every other router as often as twice a minute. RIP also is limited in other ways. For example, it cannot select the best path for transmitting data when two or more lines are available at different speeds. Also, RIP cannot determine the best path based on line delay, bandwidth, or network traffic.

Open Shortest Path First (OSPF)

This protocol does not have the limitations of RIP. Each OSPF router transmits a description of its local links, instead of its entire routing table. There is minimal network congestion because these routing packets are relatively small.

OSPF provides eight classes of service so the network manager can control how data are transmitted along given paths. Data transmission can be based on line speeds, bandwidth, and network traffic. For example, packets that are not time-sensitive can be directed onto low-cost paths, whereas more urgent packets can be sent on high-speed paths.

LOCAL AND REMOTE ROUTERS

Routers that join networks within the same building or that link adjacent networks on a campus are called local routers. For example, a local router might join two Ethernet networks on the same floor of a building (see Figure 5-9). Another example is a router that joins two building networks on a college campus, such as the engineering building network with the mathematics building network.

Figure 5-9

Local routing

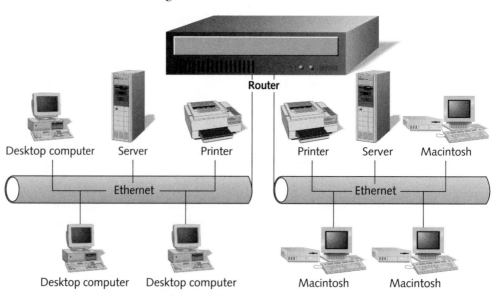

A typical Ethernet router can route 5,000 or more packets per second. The same router may handle 15 different network protocols, such as IP, IPX/SPX, and AppleTalk.

Local routers continuously monitor their constituent networks so that routing tables can be updated to reflect network changes. They monitor changes in line speeds, network load, network addressing, and network topologies.

In the process of joining networks, local routers are used to segment network traffic and to enforce security. A local router can be used to limit certain types of packets from leaving a specific network segment. It can be used to control which network nodes are able to reach a segment containing sensitive business information. When you employ a router for security, it becomes a **firewall** on your network, protecting the network from hackers and unwanted traffic.

A remote router enables networks to be connected over long distances, such as New York to Los Angeles. A single router in Los Angeles might connect a business in that city to remote business routers in Denver, St. Louis, and New York. Another example would be a remote router at a major university campus connecting with corresponding routers at satellite campuses throughout the state. Figure 5-10 illustrates how networks located in different cities are connected into one network through remote routers.

Figure 5-10

Remote routing

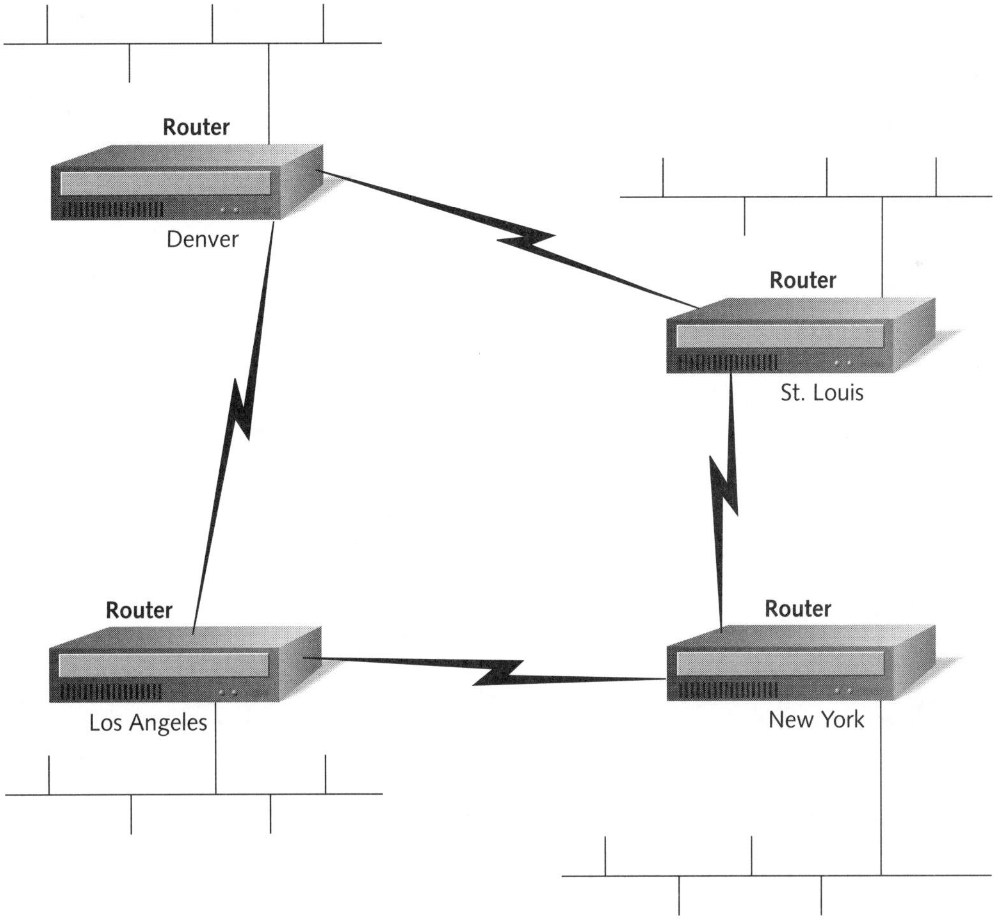

Remote routers connect ATM, frame relay, high-speed serial, and X.25 networks. Similar to a local router, a remote router can forward packets at a rate of 5,000 frames per second or more. Remote routers support multiple protocols, thus allowing communication with many kinds of distant networks.

Remote routers can be set up to filter incoming and outgoing packets. They enable the network manager to control the network load and to determine which network nodes will have access to a given network. For example, a network manager may allow only the accounting department, company executives, and auditors to access the company accounting network.

Many remote routers can be rebooted through the use of remote management software. This enables the network manager, from a remote location, to reset the router after a power failure or network interruption. Software upgrades for remote routers can also be performed through remote download features.

MULTIMEDIA ROUTER

A complex network may need the capability to route several protocols across short and long distances. A *multimedia router* is designed to handle several protocols, such as FDDI, token ring, and Ethernet. Figure 5-11 illustrates how a multimedia router can link networks.

Figure 5-11

Multimedia routing

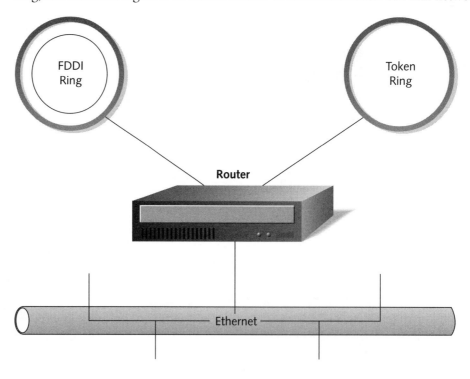

The multimedia router normally performs routing and bridging functions. For example, one multimedia router may support bridging using FDDI as a link between Ethernet and token ring networks. The multimedia router also may support token ring bridging, such as source routing.

In large networks, the multimedia router is used to enable high-speed connectivity. One application is to implement an FDDI 100 Mbps backbone connected to various Ethernet and token ring networks. Packets from a 4- or 16-Mbps token ring network are quickly delivered to a 10-Mbps Ethernet network by routing them through the FDDI backbone.

APPLETALK ROUTING

There are many Apple Macintosh networks installed on college campuses and in business environments. They may be used within education colleges, engineering schools, in art departments, or for specialized business applications. These networks employ the AppleTalk protocol for communication between nodes.

As institutions grow, there is a need to connect isolated AppleTalk networks with enterprise-wide networks. Multimedia routers have been developed to provide connectivity between AppleTalk, Ethernet, FDDI, and token ring networks. Bay Networks, for example, incorporates AppleTalk routing in its LattisTalk router/repeater software. A LattisTalk router enables AppleTalk twisted-pair devices to link up with Ethernet networks and to share data with computers on TCP/IP networks. In this way, a Macintosh can communicate with a networked IBM ES9000 mainframe on a TCP/IP Ethernet network.

Macintosh communications with a host have been improved through the development of MacAPP. MacAPP consists of programming tools to help exchange information between Macintosh computers and hosts, such as mainframes and minicomputers.

HUBS

Network hubs come in many "flavors." The simplest hubs increase network connectivity by enabling a logical Ethernet bus network to be physically connected as a star. More complex hubs are used to replace bridges and routers to reduce network congestion. Advanced hubs provide very high-speed connectivity for FDDI, frame relay, and ATM networks.

In general, hubs provide one or more of the following services:

- Permit large numbers of computers to be connected on single or multiple LAN
- Reduce network congestion
- Provide multi-protocol services, such as Ethernet to FDDI connectivity
- Consolidate the network backbone
- Enable high-speed communications

10BASET HUB

The simplest hub is the 10BASET hub used on an Ethernet LAN. It also is one of the most popular ways to connect work groups on small and large LANs. This hub uses a physical star topology to connect PCs to the central hub. Additional hubs are added by connecting one hub to the next through a backbone, such as with thick or thin Ethernet as the backbone cable plant. Figure 5-12 illustrates a 10BASET hub connected to PC workstations.

Figure 5-12

10BASET hub

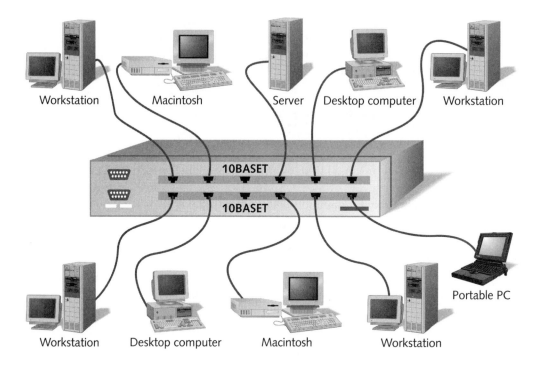

Management of the LAN is handled by software at the hub instead of through individual devices connected to the LAN. A physical star topology is easier to maintain than a physical bus, because only one device is connected to one port, or devices are daisy-chained (connected one to another) to a limited extent. If a NIC on a single port malfunctions, you simply disable that port until the card can be replaced. Workstations on the other ports continue operation without interruption.

Racal InterLan offers low-end 10BASET hubs with 8 to 16 ports. On larger networks, their InterLAN*Link* hubs can be stacked together for up to 96 ports with only one logical repeater hop. When hubs are stacked in this way, management of all hubs is controlled from a single hub in the group.

The InterLAN*Link* hubs use management software called FaultAlert to monitor the network. A network problem, such as a malfunctioning segment, is detected on a monitoring station with the FaultAlert software.

Hewlett-Packard manufactures a 10BASET hub that provides 16 ports. Their hub also supports routing for IP and IPX packets.

SWITCHING HUBS

Switching hubs permit you to significantly increase the throughput capability of an existing 4-Mbps, 10-Mbps, or 16-Mbps network by taking full advantage of existing bandwidth capabilities.

On a standard Ethernet or token ring network, only one packet can be transmitted at a time. As more nodes are added, transmission delays and packet collisions become frequent. And even though the cable plant has greater bandwidth available, only a fraction of it is put to use.

Switching hubs allow an existing network to be separated into multiple smaller segments, each independent of the other and each able to support packet transmissions at regular network speeds. No additional network equipment is needed. This makes switched Ethernet a low-cost way to increase network throughput as demands on a LAN increase, particularly with the implementation of client/server applications and database servers.

Switching hubs can be installed on LANs in a wide-area network where specific LANs are experiencing increased network traffic. The switching hub can divide network bandwidth into two or more segments. This means that network throughput is at least doubled and sometimes increased even more, depending on the capabilities of the switch.

The Bay Networks BayStack Ethernet Workgroup switch uses dedicated RISC processors to support six ports. With this switch, 10 Mbps of bandwidth are available on each of the six segments. The Ethernet Workgroup switch also comes with a fast Ethernet switched port to support 100BASET products.

Cabletron has an MMAC-8FNB switch that can manage up to 168 10BASET connections. This switch also has bridging capability. The switch configuration includes dual power supplies for redundancy.

Although switching hubs provide a good initial solution to increased network traffic, eventually they may no longer be appropriate for growing network needs. Applications may emerge that require large amounts of bandwidth and very high network speeds. Such applications may include the transmission of electronic forms or access to digitized pictures stored in a database. The advantages and disadvantages of switching hubs are summarized in Table 5-1.

Table 5-1

Advantages and disadvantages of switching hubs

Advantages	Disadvantages
Reduce network congestion	Do not solve problems where much larger bandwidth is needed
Use existing network installation	Not appropriate where a high-speed solution is needed
Cheaper to implement than FDDI or ATM	Not a good solution for time-sensitive transmissions
Quick installation	

SWITCHING FABRIC

The technique used by a hub to provide switching is called the **switching fabric**. Two switching fabrics are used by hubs: cut-through and store-and-forward.

Cut-Through

Cut-through switching is accomplished by forwarding portions of packets before the entire packet is received. The packet is forwarded as soon as the destination address is read. This method affords relatively high transmission speeds. Fast transmission also is accomplished by foregoing error checking.

Store-and-Forward Switching

In this switching method (also known as buffered switching), the packet is not forwarded until it is completely received. Once a packet is received by the switch, it is examined for errors before being sent to the destination node. Hubs using store-and-forward switching also employ routing to establish the fastest path to the destination via the switch. These hubs are designed to circumvent broadcast storms and replicated packets.

At first, most hubs employed cut-through switching to take advantage of the high-speed transmission feature. The introduction of CPU capabilities in store-and-forward switching hubs has yielded impressive gains in speed over cut-through switching. Some CPU-based store-and-forward switching hubs can transmit packets up to 25% faster than cut-through switching hubs.

EIFO HUBS

As a network grows to hundreds of users, the need for high-speed communications grows as well. Client/server applications require high-performance and high-bandwidth networks. A common means to achieve high performance is to place the servers on 100-Mbps FDDI rings over UTP or fiber optic cabling plants. In many installations, this requires linking existing Ethernet segmented networks to one or more FDDI rings.

Ethernet-In-FDDI-Out (EIFO) client/server switching hubs provide the capability to connect coaxial or 10BASET Ethernet networks to FDDI rings. A typical EIFO hub is able to connect 10 or more network connections. These hubs switch at the MAC layer to ensure low-delay and high-speed performance. One EIFO hub can handle 1,000 network nodes.

EIFO hubs provide an easy upgrade path to a high-speed network. An EIFO hub can be installed with no changes to adapters, software drivers, or cabling.

EIFO hubs also enable the network manager to reduce network congestion on routes to high-demand client/server application servers. This is accomplished in two ways. First, the congestion is reduced by placing servers on the high-speed FDDI ring. Second, EIFO hubs allow you to segment your network. For example, EIFO hubs may be "stacked" by connecting several hubs to an FDDI backbone or by interconnecting hubs directly. Bandwidth at the hubs is 100 Mbps, which reduces packet collisions and congestion. Figure 5-13 illustrates an EIFO hub network.

Figure 5-13

EIFO hub
network

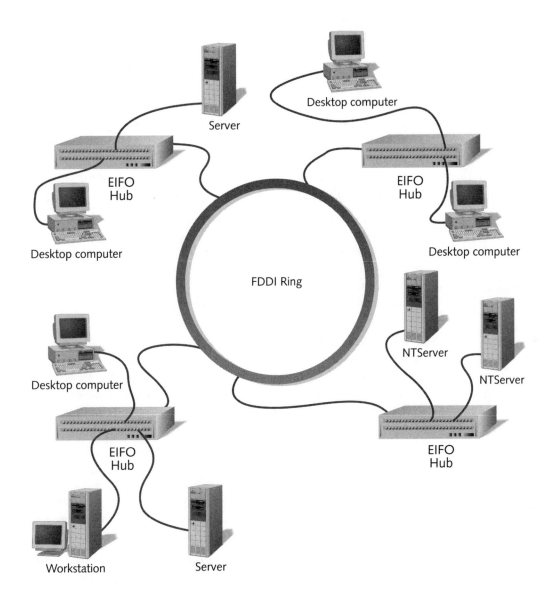

100BASET HUBS

Fast Ethernet has gained broader acceptance within networking circles since it was proposed in the early 1990s. Multimedia, video, and GUI client/server applications have fostered the need for high-bandwidth, high-speed technologies. 100 Mbps Ethernet is one answer to this demand.

In early 1994, AT&T developed a chip set called Regatta to support 100 Mbps. Several manufacturers, including Kalpana, DEC, and Hewlett-Packard, have implemented the chip set in their 100BASEVG networking switch technology. Other vendors, such as Bay Networks, 3Com, and Grand Junction Networks, also have developed fast Ethernet products, but their equipment uses the 100BASE-X standard.

Bay Networks offers a 100BASET hub that can house 12 or 24 100BASE-TX ports (UTP ports). These hubs also can be outfitted with a 100BASE-FX port to connect to a fiber optic cable backbone. And when the hubs are stacked, they support up to 132 100BASE-TX ports.

INTELLIGENT HUBS

Many enterprise-wide networks have grown to include Ethernet, fast Ethernet, token ring, and FDDI segments. This growth is often accompanied by the presence of a variety of repeaters, bridges, routers, and switches. Network support becomes very complex as the number of independent network boxes grows in number and as these boxes are spread over large geographic areas.

One solution to unifying network equipment needs is to implement a central intelligent hub or concentrator. Concentrators work particularly well for physical star topology networks that require a variety of network equipment.

At the heart of the concentrator is a backplane circuit board. Some concentrators come with redundant backplanes and redundant power supplies, in case one of these components malfunctions during live network operations. The concentrator backplane has multiple slots (multiple buses) for "plug-in" type network circuit boards. Each plug-in circuit board may handle a different network function. For example, one circuit board may perform bridge functions, one may act as a token ring hub, one may support a 10-Mbps Ethernet segment, and one may provide a 100-Mbps FDDI interface.

The concentrator represents a strategy to unify network equipment and to manage the network at single points of origin. This enables the network manager to gather and distill performance data close to the source. At the same time, the network is more easily scaled upward as expansion needs arise. For example, if a new Ethernet segment is required in a building wing, this growth is accommodated by adding a circuit board to the concentrator.

Since the concentrator performs as an intelligent hub, data about the network are gathered at the concentrator. It collects, analyzes, and reduces the raw data into meaningful information. The data are forwarded to a central network management station. Since network equipment is unified within the hub, the network manager does not have to sift through raw information from individual network components spread throughout an area. The concentrator collects data from each of its components and provides an instant snapshot.

When the network grows, new intelligent hubs are installed in key places to provide network services. Each hub gathers and reduces network performance data to transmit to the central management station. Even though the network is growing, management can be centralized. One advantage of this approach is that the network management can occur remotely by an off-site manager or team. Another advantage is that management software upgrades are easily installed on each intelligent hub and on the central management station. Advances in network management capabilities are implemented more easily than if individual repeaters, bridges, routers, and switches have to be upgraded in multiple network locations.

Several manufacturers offer intelligent hubs. Cabletron's MMAC series is one example of the technology. The MicroMMAC, MMAC, and MMAC-Plus hubs support token ring, Ethernet, FDDI, and SNA. The MMAC-Plus hub handles over 200 users and provides switching capabilities. All three hubs employ Intel I960 microprocessors for scaleable CPU operations as software demands grow.

Bay Networks has a 3000 Premises Concentrator that handles Ethernet, token ring, and FDDI. The Ethernet component also uses a retiming module to provide an IEEE 802.3 repeater ability. The 3000 has 12 slots that connect to a backplane and power supply, with redundant power supply capability. Modules also can be added to provide network segmentation.

Bay Networks and Cabletron both follow the IEEE, ISO, CCITT, and ANSI standards. This is important because their equipment does not rely on proprietary standards. Networks built with equipment that adheres to the standards are easier to support and expand than networks containing nonstandard equipment.

ATM SWITCH

An ATM switch provides high-speed, fast-packet switching at 155 Mbps. ATM switches enable voice, video, or data to be transmitted over a network using existing UTP or fiber optic cabling. Fast-packet transmissions can be brought to the desktop.

The ATM switch provides high-speed communications with dedicated bandwidth by means of fast MAC-layer transport. Virtually any type of data can be transmitted directly from one node to another through the MAC layer. Through ATM, LANs are connected in star physical topology without redundancy (see Figure 5-14).

Figure 5-14

ATM switch with UTP 5/fiber

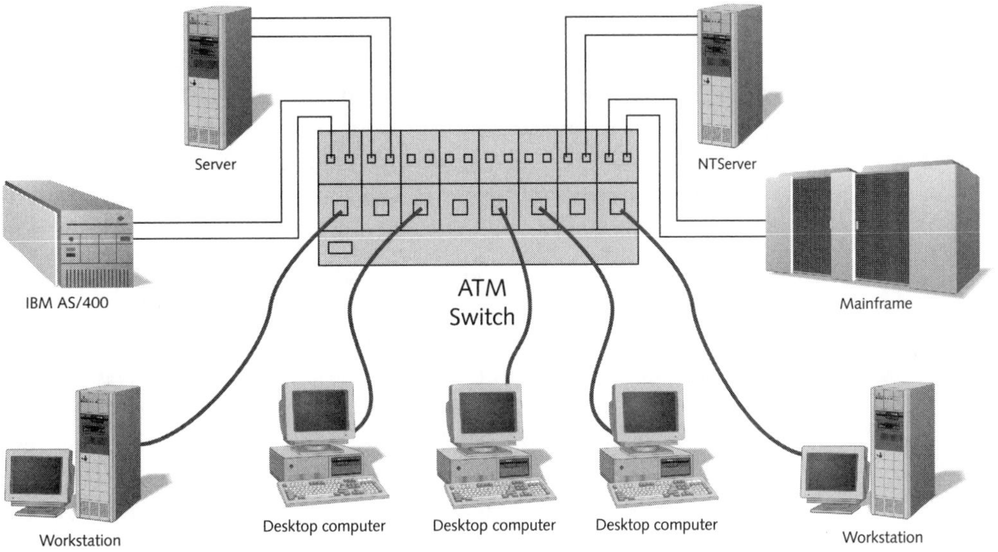

An ATM switch has 10, 16, or more ports. Many ATM switches are built to handle unshielded twisted-pair using modular RJ-45 SONET/SDH (Synchronous Optical Network/Synchronous Digital Hierarchy) interfaces. (See Chapter 11 for a description of SONET.) The supported UTP is Category 5.

Fiber optic ATM switches handle fast-packet transmissions on 62.5/125 micrometer (μm) and 50/125 μm multi-mode cabling. They also provide intermediate-distance communications through 8.5/125 micron single-mode fiber optic cable. Some switches have slower speed 44.7 Mbps for T3 WANs on 75-ohm coaxial cabling.

Bay Networks has individual ATM switches for UTP and fiber optics. They also have an ATM switching capability for T3 WAN transmissions. Output buffers on a Bay Networks ATM switch can hold up to 1,024 cells to capture and transmit multiple-burst type data streams. Network traffic within the Bay Networks switches is coordinated by their Connection Management System software.

A drawback to ATM communications is cost, although costs are going down rapidly. Some manufacturers, such as IBM, offer 25-Mbps switches at much lower cost than 155-Mbps switches. However, the 25-Mbps ATM data transmission technology is not standard.

WIRELESS NETWORKING EQUIPMENT

Many organizations are discovering the need to connect users in remote or hard-to-reach locations. An urban university may want to link networks in two adjoining buildings where there are no underground cabling tunnels. A small business may need to link separate buildings, but may not have the budget to dig trenches and lay fiber optic cable. Wireless networking equipment provides an answer to these types of situations.

The two prevalent wireless alternatives are remote bridges and hubs.

REMOTE BRIDGE

Several vendors offer remote wireless Ethernet and token ring bridges. Remote bridges are implemented using two bridge units. One bridge is attached to an existing LAN and has a wireless side that connects to an antenna. The other bridge is connected to a different LAN in a nearby building or within the same building. It also is equipped with an antenna to transmit and receive packets. Omnidirectional antennas are used for transmissions within a building; directional antennas are used for communications between LANs in separate buildings.

Packets are transmitted as radio waves (packet radio) at ultra-high frequencies. The high-frequency ranges offer greater bandwidth transmissions at higher speeds than would be possible at lower frequencies. Because of the relatively high wave bandwidths, these are known as **spread spectrum** radio frequencies. Wireless bridges operate on spread spectrum radio frequencies in the 902–928 MHz range. Radio transmissions in this frequency range are called **line-of-sight transmissions** because waves only travel short distances. Wave lengths at lower frequencies, such as 20 MHz, are able to skip long distances in the atmosphere. They can travel several hundred or several thousand miles, but they do not have the high bandwidth characteristics needed for fast-packet radio transmissions.

Besides high bandwidth, the 902–928 MHz range offers several other advantages. One advantage is that transmissions at these frequencies are very difficult to intercept. The military has long used these high frequencies to enhance security on its radio transmissions. Additionally, radio frequency interference (RFI) is much lower on spread spectrum frequencies than it is on conventional radio frequencies. Spread spectrum communications also are not subject to interference from weather conditions. Another advantage is that the Federal Communications Commission (FCC) does not require licensing for radio transmissions in the 902–928 MHz range. (Countries other than the U.S. may require licensing and these laws should be checked before installing remote bridges.) See Table 5-2 for a summary of spread spectrum radio frequency advantages.

Table 5-2

Spread spectrum
wireless
communications

Advantages of Ultrahigh Frequency Communications
Relatively high bandwith
Fast packet transmission
Security from interception
Negligible RF interference
Not subject to adverse weather
No FCC licensing requirement

Persoft, Inc. manufactures Ethernet (802.3 compliance) and token ring (802.5 compliance) remote bridges. Both types of bridges are capable of 2-Mbps packet transmissions. These bridges are able to connect LANs up to three miles apart. A Data Encryption Standard (DES) security chip can be installed in the bridges to encrypt packet transmissions for special security requirements. The bridges are SNMP compatible and operate via the MAC layer. The Persoft bridges enable filtering by protocol or by address. They use the Spanning Tree algorithm and connect to thick, thin, and twisted-pair cable media.

Cabletron offers remote bridges for communications within a building or to connect LANs between buildings. These units support SNMP management (see Chapter 8 for an explanation of SNMP) and provide extra security through a pre-established ID code used by the hub and the wireless remote. The Cabletron bridges follow IEEE 802.3 specifications. Other companies that produce wireless bridges are Aironet, Cylink, and Solectek.

REMOTE HUB

The purpose of a remote hub is to eliminate wiring needs for short distances within a building, such as in an office area. Wireless hubs operate in a physical star fashion. They use spread spectrum communications and normally support SNMP management.

A single hub may provide up to 50 or 60 wireless connections over a range of several thousand square feet. The wireless communications are achieved by equipping the hub with transceivers. Each node also has a transceiver and communicates with a specific transceiver in the hub. The hub and node transceivers are equipped with antennas for radio communications. (See Figure 5-15.)

Figure 5-15

Wireless
networks

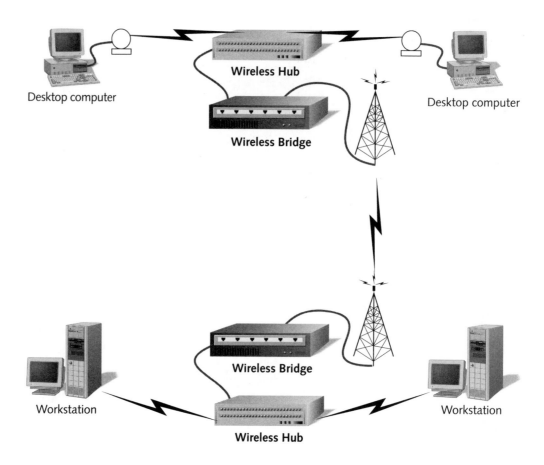

Cabletron's FreePort is an example of a wireless hub. This product provides signal coverage of 200,000 sq. ft. The FreePort hub supports up to 62 nodes equipped with wireless transceivers. The hub will communicate with a node 263 feet away.

Due to the slower speeds, wireless communications are not as widely used as cable-based systems. However, these systems have advantages in situations where it is expensive to run cable.

SUMMARY

The networking equipment described in this chapter makes users more productive as they demand more from themselves and their network. Each device described enables the network administrator to increase data throughput as user demand grows. Further, as users move to electronic forms, client/server computing, more complex GUI applications, and sound and video, they need a robust network to accommodate this software.

The communication server is a first step in providing connectivity for basic devices such as terminals and modems.

Multiplexers enable network expansion on a single cable for input from several nodes. This technology is particularly important for packet-switched applications. Repeaters are an inexpensive way to extend the cable plant as a network moves out to reach more offices or classrooms.

Bridges offer the ability to connect separate LAN segments into one larger network. They also provide the option to make a network more fail-safe through redundancy. Routers add networking intelligence to optimize packet traffic on the cable plant.

Intelligent hubs vary from basic to complex modular units. They serve to increase network connectivity, improve ease of network monitoring, and permit high-speed communications.

Wireless networking is growing today as more people want the ability to connect to their network remotely. This type of networking is cost-effective in situations where physical cabling expenses are very high.

KEY TERMS

Term/Acronym	Definition
Broadcast Storm	This situation occurs when a network segment is saturated with more packets than can be effectively handled.
Cascade	A bridging technique where each bridge is connected to two networks.
Cost	This value is used to determine the most efficient pathways on a network. It is calculated based on line speed and distance to the root bridge.
Filtering	The ability of a bridge to determine that a packet should be directed to its originating LAN and not forwarded to a connecting or different LAN.
Firewall	These devices (and software) protect networks and file servers from unauthorized access. They also help reduce unwanted network traffic.
Flooding	When a bridge cannot determine the destination of a packet, it may forward the packet to all known networks.
Hello BPDU	Packets transmitted by a root bridge at a specified interval. The packets acknowledge to other bridges that the root bridge is working.
Line-Of-Sight Transmissions	Relatively short-distance radio signal transmissions that travel from point to point along the Earth's surface.
Multi-Port Bridges	These bridges can link several individual segments into one network.
Partitioning	Some networking equipment, such as a repeater or hub, is able to detect if there is a communications problem on a given cable segment. It disconnects or partitions that segment until the problem is resolved.
Redundancy	Alternate network routes or alternate equipment are built into some networks to ensure that packets reach their destination in the event of equipment failure. For example, when one bridge fails, packets can be redirected to a different bridge on their way to the destination node.

Source Routing	A technique used by token ring bridges to forward packets to a network.
Spanning Tree Algorithm	This algorithm is used to ensure packets are not transmitted in an endless loop. Also, it enables packets to be sent along the most cost-effective network path.
Spread Spectrum	A wide-bandwidth electronic signal transmission frequency.
Switching Fabric	The switching method used by a hub.
Telecommuting	Some employers offer a program to allow employees to work from home or from a remote computing site. The employee uses telephone lines or wireless communications to access the host computers at a central work site.

REVIEW EXERCISES

1. Under what circumstances would you install a multi-port repeater?
2. Describe how a bridge might be used to reduce network traffic problems.
3. What network conditions might cause a network segment to become partitioned?
4. What is a multiplexer?
5. What are the three methods used for multiplexing? Which method works best for high-speed data transmissions?
6. What is the spanning tree algorithm? How does it work?
7. Describe a network scenario in which you would replace an existing bridge with a router. When would you employ a multimedia router?
8. Show the layout of a small college campus with an administration building, the central computer center, two classroom buildings, a dorm, and an engineering building. There is a network that connects all buildings, as well as a LAN within each building. The LAN in the engineering building is home to 20 high-traffic scientific workstations. How would you set up your network to ensure optimum flow of data?
9. ATM allows a data transmission rate of _____.
10. Approximately how many packets can an Ethernet bridge filter in a second?
11. How is a concentrator used on a network?
12. What are the advantages of spread spectrum communications?
13. What are OSPF and RIP?
14. Draw a small network showing how you would connect terminals to access a mainframe.
15. How is bridging done on an Apple-based network?
16. What is stored in a routing table?
17. Explain how cut-through switching fabric works.

CHAPTER SIX

BEGINNING NETWORK DESIGN

Up to this point we have discussed networking theory and the pieces that make up networks. Now we will see how each of these pieces is joined to make a functioning network.

Just as there are many types of network equipment, there are many ways to design a network. Some network designs offer more opportunity for growth than others. Some offer more opportunity to take advantage of new high-speed technologies. The foundation you create with your first design will affect your ability to expand in the future.

This chapter presents introductory Ethernet network design methods, beginning with basic coaxial installation. We build on each design to illustrate how to expand a network from an office area to multiple floors in a building. The advantages and limitations of each design are discussed to help make you a more effective network designer.

AFTER READING THIS CHAPTER YOU WILL BE ABLE TO:

- DESIGN A SIMPLE ETHERNET NETWORK WITH ONE CABLE SEGMENT

- ADD COMPUTER PERIPHERALS TO A NETWORK SEGMENT

- ADD NETWORK SEGMENTS

- DESIGN A NETWORK FOR A SINGLE ROOM, SUCH AS A COMPUTER LAB OR OFFICE

- DESIGN A NETWORK FOR A FLOOR IN A BUILDING

- DESIGN A NETWORK FOR SEVERAL FLOORS IN A BUILDING

- EXPLAIN HOW THE PHYSICAL LAYOUT OF A BUILDING INFLUENCES NETWORK DESIGN

BASIC ETHERNET MODELS

A very simple Ethernet network design for a small office may consist of a single **segment** of wire that runs from a file server to several workstations. Up to 30 nodes can be attached to the segment, counting workstations and the file server. This simple network is shown in Figure 6-1.

Figure 6-1

Simple Ethernet network

Server

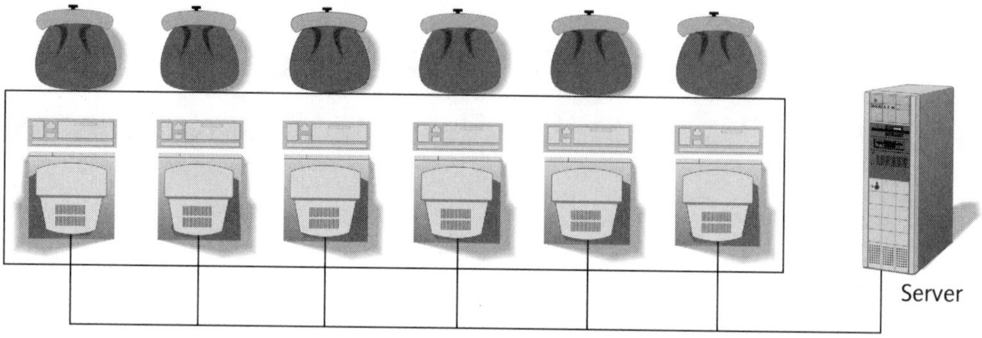

In this network, the server is near the workstations. The cable that joins the server and workstations is thin coaxial, 10BASE2, 50-ohm cable (RG-58A/U). **BNC T connectors** are used to link the cable with each node. There are two terminators on this network. One is on the BNC connector at the left-most workstation, and one is on the server's BNC connector.

Since this network uses coaxial cable, the cable should be run so there are no kinks or tight bends that might damage it.

ADDITION OF A PRINT SERVER

The network shown in Figure 6-1 has no printers. Because of the simplicity of the network, a printer is not difficult to add. For this example, assume that you have a laser printer with an internal print server card that has a coaxial interface. Before you add the printer, check the length of the cable that is already installed. Next measure the cable length required to reach the printer. The combined length should not exceed 185 meters (refer to Chapter 3). Figure 6-2 illustrates how the network might look with the addition of a printer. To add the printer to this network, the terminator has to be detached from the left-most workstation and placed on the BNC connector attached to the print server card in the printer.

Figure 6-2

Printer added
to the network

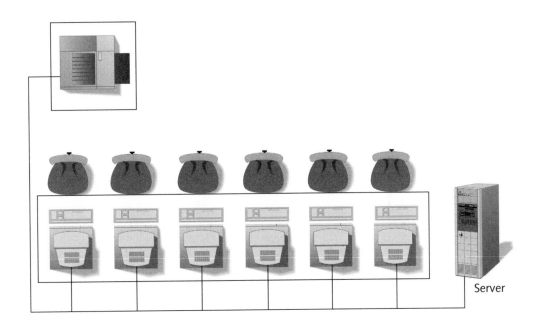

Server

AN ADDITION TO THE NETWORK

Assume that the network in Figure 6-2 is a Novell network in a statistics lab at a college. Adjacent to the statistics lab there is a business lab that has computers that need to be connected to the Novell file server. One way to do this is to extend the existing cable segment into the lab. The problem is that the segment will be over 185 meters long if you extend the cable to the farthest node in the business lab.

One solution is to add another NIC to the Novell server. This enables you to create a separate segment for the new business lab. Figure 6-3 illustrates how the network looks after the segment has been added.

A different solution is to install a multi-port repeater. For example, a multi-port repeater with eight Ethernet slots and two AUI slots will enable the network to grow in the future. With this option, you can have up to eight segments and add a fiber optic backbone for communications with other networks. Figure 6-4 shows the two labs joined by the repeater.

Figure 6-3

Adding a
segment by
adding a server
NIC

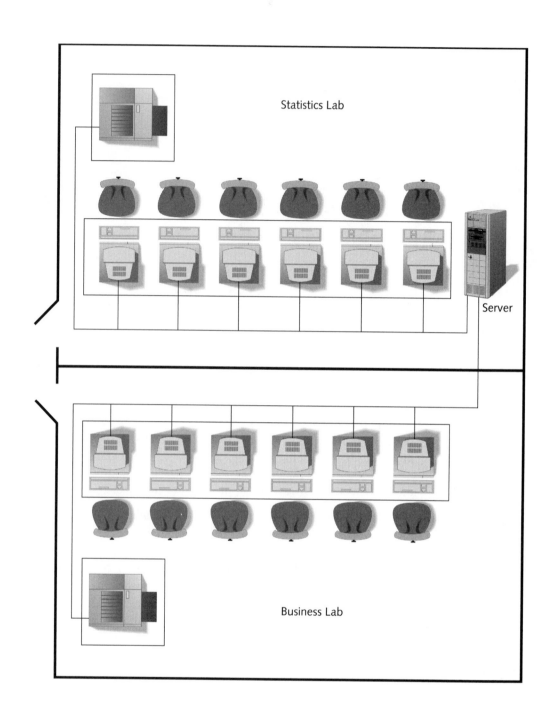

Statistics Lab

Server

Business Lab

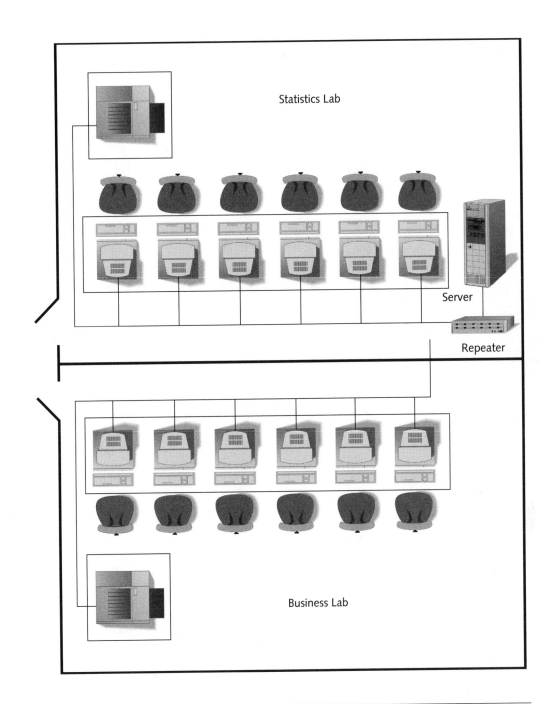

Figure 6-4

Adding a segment by adding a repeater

JOINING MULTIPLE LABS

If you are networking a classroom building with many computer labs, the multi-port repeater gives you an option to network several labs to one file server. Building on this example, you can connect several labs from one well-placed repeater. Figure 6-5 shows how this is accomplished.

Figure 6-5

Building
multiple
segments from
a single
repeater

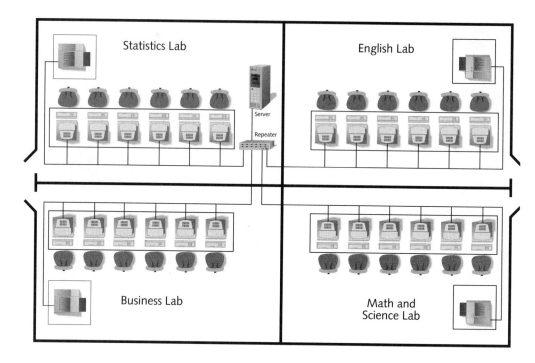

In Figure 6-5 there are five segments from the repeater. Each Ethernet segment must be terminated at both ends to meet IEEE specifications. Also, no segment can be over 185 meters in length. Including workstations and printers, there are nine nodes on each segment. Six nodes are workstations, one is the printer, and two are the terminators. The segment with the server has three nodes—the server and the two terminators. The repeater is also counted as a node.

By putting the server on its own segment, you can isolate the server from problems created by another network node. On the other hand, if you had placed the server on the statistics lab segment along with the six workstations and printer, the entire network could have lost access to the server if a problem had occurred on that segment. When a server is isolated on a segment, however, the number of problems that can make the server unavailable to the rest of the network are kept at a minimum.

As you plan to expand the access to the server, keep in mind the server's capabilities. Do you have enough server CPU to run the anticipated software? Do you have enough licenses for the software? Do you have enough licenses for the server operating system?

Table 6-1 reviews the basic design issues to consider when expanding a network.

Table 6-1

Expanding an
Ethernet segment
length

Basic Design Issues
Design for future expandability.
Properly terminate all segments.
Follow the IEEE specs for distance.
Isolate the server to minimize problems from other nodes.
Determine if the server has enough CPU horsepower.
Determine if there are enough software licenses.
Determine if there are enough database licenses.
Determine if there are enough server operating system licenses.

EXPANDING AN ETHERNET SEGMENT LENGTH

Let's continue with the computer lab example to address how to reach labs that are too far away for one 185-meter segment. If you have an existing coaxial network with a repeater, you can extend the reach of a segment by adding another repeater. Figure 6-6 shows how you can add a repeater to extend the reach of your network.

Figure 6-6

Adding a repeater to extend a segment

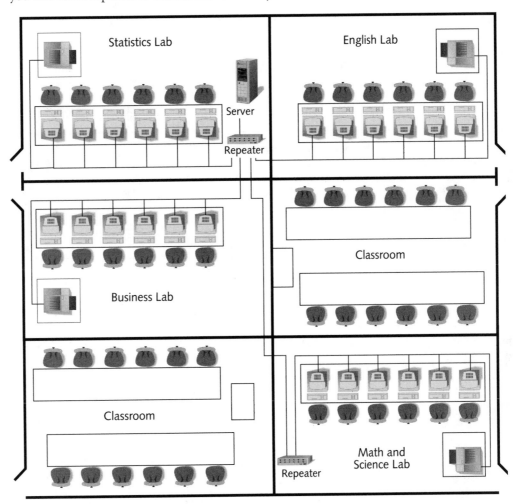

In Figure 6-6, one segment length is used to go to the second repeater in the math and science computer lab. The segment connecting the first and second repeater has no other equipment connected, minimizing problems that might take the segment down. This new segment can be up to 185 meters in length. In this example, the second repeater also is a multi-port repeater. Additional 185 meter segments can be added to the second repeater to reach labs or offices beyond the math and science lab. For example, Figure 6-7 shows how to connect two offices to this repeater.

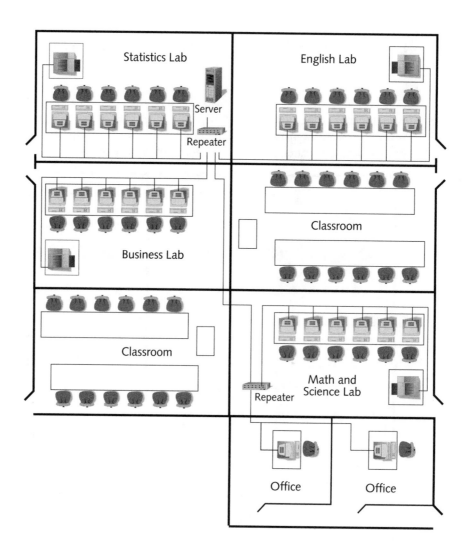

COAXIAL NETWORK LIMITATIONS

These networks are functional and relatively simple to build. Many early networks were built like these models, using coaxial cable and BNC connectors. As mentioned earlier, coaxial cable is subject to damage if it is twisted or bent. BNC connectors also can be damaged when workstations are moved. When working with existing coaxial equipment, use segments as much as possible, as shown in Figures 6-3 through 6-7. This will make network problems easier to trace or isolate.

For coaxial networks, use only high–quality cable and connectors. Periodically check each area of your network to be certain the connectors are still in good condition and that the cable is properly attached to the connectors. Replace connectors where shielding is exposed or where the wire insulation is damaged. Also inspect terminators to ensure they are working.

Protect coaxial cable as much as possible. Route the cable away from high traffic areas and away from sources of heat, such as radiators.

AN IMPROVED MODEL FOR SINGLE-ROOM NETWORKS

An alternative to the design model shown in Figures 6-1 and 6-2 is to use a concentrator to connect the workstations and printer. The concentrator enables you to build an Ethernet network with a logical bus topology but a physical star configuration. Figure 6-8 shows this design method.

Figure 6-8

A single-room network model using a concentrator

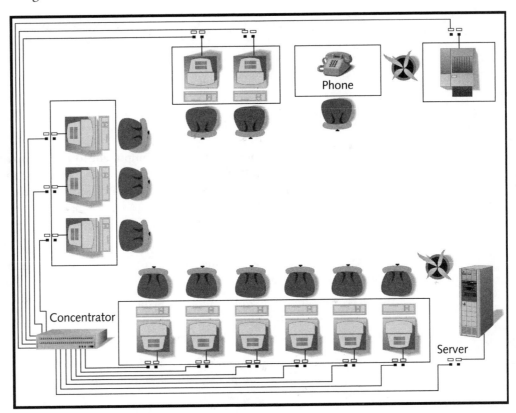

In Figure 6-8, the concentrator (in the lower left part of the diagram) is used to connect each node to the network. The connection pattern is in the physical form of a star, with each node on its own cable segment, so the network is easier to maintain. Because of the star configuration, a defective node can be traced and repaired quickly.

The cable plant for the room in Figure 6-8 is 10BASET or twisted-pair wire. Twisted-pair has several advantages over coaxial, including the following:

- Greater reliability
- Easier to work with
- Compatible with future technologies
- Lower cable costs
- Less expensive connectors

Twisted-pair is more reliable than coaxial cable because it is not as likely to be damaged if stepped on or bent. For the same reason, it is easier to work with as it is pulled through walls, in ceilings, and around corners.

Twisted-pair also is more compatible with future technologies than is coaxial cable. Equipment made for twisted-pair, such as concentrators, offers more opportunities to expand a network, and to take advantage of high-speed communications options in the future. Later in this chapter we will show you how easily the network in Figure 6-5 can be expanded with a concentrator.

If you plan to continue adding to your network, you will find twisted-pair cable and connectors to be less expensive than coaxial and BNC connectors (although price reductions are making fiber optic cable competitive with twisted-pair). Also, twisted-pair connectors are easier to attach to the cable.

ROOM PREPARATION

When you install a network in a room, it is important to install a sound cable plant. The cable should be installed out of view, if possible. Cable should be run through walls or ceilings. If this cannot be done, wire molding or cable track should be considered to protect the cable plant. As the cable is installed, check to ensure that each cable run avoids sources of electrical interference, such as light fixtures and power outlets.

Measure the cable distances while the cable is being installed to ensure that cable runs meet IEEE specifications. Once the cable is in, test the cable lengths and characteristics with a **cable scanner** (described in Chapter 10).

Before you install the cable, plan ahead for printers, plotters, fax machines, and other equipment. Run extra cable and install extra wall jacks, so additional nodes can be added and so people can move desks around the room in the future.

Consider in advance the best location for network equipment. The location of a concentrator or repeater should be planned to allow optimum distances for cabling and for the placement of the network nodes.

If the room has "public access," the network equipment should be located in a secure place, such as a closet. If the secure enclosure is kept locked, make a key available to the people who know how to maintain the network, for those times when a file server, repeater, or concentrator has to be re-booted or checked for problems.

SINGLE-FLOOR NETWORK MODEL

If you are the network manager in an office area on a single floor, you may be asked to provide network access to each office. Before you begin, do a thorough investigation of the physical layout of the floor. This will help you plan the cable runs so that the network conforms to IEEE specifications. Advance planning also will help you to keep cable and other equipment costs to a minimum. Another reason to carefully inspect the area is to determine the best location for file servers and other network equipment.

Check the local construction codes to determine if there are any special requirements. This will help you to purchase the right type of cable to meet the codes. For example, fireproof plenum cable may be required in one region, whereas another region may specify that cable be run through conduit.

The model presented in Figure 6-8 can be extended to network a single-floor office area. Figure 6-9 illustrates how a network might be designed for this set up. This design uses twisted-pair cable and a concentrator to connect each node. Assume that the file server is configured for Macintosh and Intel-based PC communications. By using a concentrator, this network design will allow both.

Figure 6-9

Single-floor model with concentrator

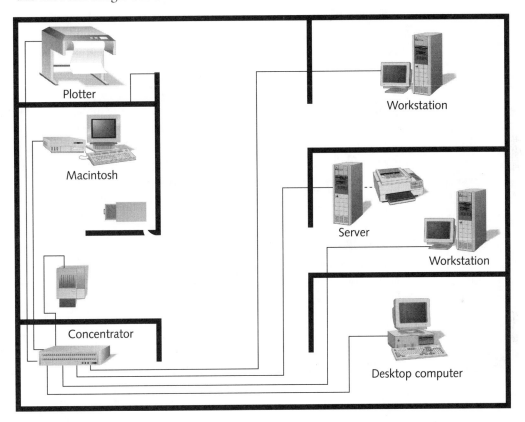

Two network printers and a file server printer are available to the office. The network printers are a plotter and a laser printer. Both have internal print server cards to allow connection to the network.

SINGLE-FLOOR DESIGN CONSIDERATIONS

The network equipment and wiring "punch-downs" should be well protected from public access. This is for the safety of the users as well as for the security of the cabling plant. The most common solution is to build a **wiring closet** for the network equipment. A wiring closet is a small enclosed room that is used to store network equipment and to centralize network wiring. Figure 6-9 includes a wiring closet for the concentrator.

The wiring closet location is an important part of the physical design of your cable plant. It should be located for centralized placement of cable runs and network equipment. If your organization is building or remodeling the office area, ensure that the wiring closet is in the best possible location. Make certain the closet is less than 90 meters (allow for a 10 meter patch cable for future expansion) from the most distant network equipment or network node.

If you are adapting an existing office, plan to make a thorough investigation of the building construction and floor configuration. You might make a floor plan to scale, showing the location of each office. This will help you determine point-to-point distances and available locations for the wiring closet.

If new construction is planned, emphasize the need to put in twisted-pair cable. Begin planning with the contractor and building designers as soon as possible. Your early input will have a strong impact on the success of the network.

As you would do for a single-room installation, have extra cable and wall jacks installed so people can move equipment and office furniture in the future. Test the length of all cable runs to ensure that they are within IEEE specifications. Also inspect and test the cable after it is installed to make certain it is network grade. Finally, check the cable runs for proximity to sources of electrical interference. Table 6-2 is a list of single-floor design recommendations.

Table 6-2

Single-Floor Design
Use 10BASET instead of coaxial if possible.
Design using concentrators to better isolate problems.
House the cable for safety and reliability.
Install the cable away from sources of electrical interference.
Keep network equipment in a safe place.
Install extra cable outlets for flexibility.

MULTIPLE-FLOOR NETWORK MODEL

Once a network has been installed in an organization, other departments will show an interest in having network connectivity. Some companies plan for a new building-wide network, as part of their competitive strategy. Thus, as a network manager, you likely will have an opportunity to set up a network that involves several floors of a building.

The plan shown in Figure 6-9 provides one building block for designing a reliable multiple-floor network. Figure 6-10 shows an example of a network that connects four floors, using the prototype established in Figure 6-9. This design uses a concentrator on every floor except the bottom floor. The bottom floor has two file servers and a plotter connected to a hub. Each concentrator also is connected to the hub.

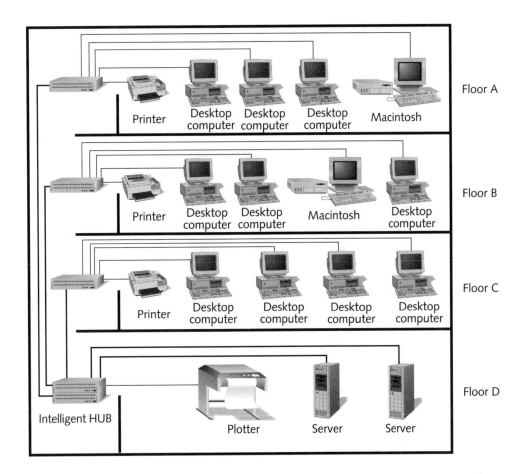

Figure 6-10

Multiple-floor
network model

In this model, every concentrator is on a separate segment. This architecture enables you to isolate problems to a particular floor, which helps to speed problem resolution. The servers and plotter also have their own connection to the hub.

This design offers a significant advantage, in that equipment failure at one level does not prevent the other equipment from continuing to operate. For example, if a desktop computer on the top floor fails, the other nodes on that floor continue working (as well as the nodes on the rest of the network). If a concentrator fails on one floor, the other floors are still operational. If one server fails, the other server continues to provide service. And if a board fails in the hub, such as the one connected to the concentrator on the top floor, the remainder of the network continues to operate.

Another advantage of the design is that you can purchase an intelligent hub that allows network monitoring. This will allow you to track the status of the network from a single monitoring station in your office, so you can be aware of network problems the moment they occur. (Chapter 9 describes network management software.)

The disadvantage to the network design in Figure 6-10 is that the hub is a single point of failure. If the hub fails, the network cannot operate. A solution to this problem is to purchase a hub with fault tolerance, which might include a redundant backplane and a redundant power supply. Also, you will be able to provide faster problem solving if you have spare network boards for the hub.

MULTIPLE-FLOOR EQUIPMENT DESIGN ISSUES

The network design shown in Figure 6-10 uses fast Ethernet or **fat pipe** technology from the central wiring closet at the bottom level to up-links going to each concentrator and server. This design reduces bottlenecks from high network traffic on the backbone between floors.

The fat pipe technology uses copper or fiber optic cable for the network backbone. Fiber optic cable is a good choice for vertical riser cable, because it ensures you will be ready to adapt to higher-speed technologies as they develop.

Many vendors are offering 100BASET fat pipe NICs for workstations. At the same time, the cost of fiber optic cable is dropping, making high-speed communications to the desktop more affordable. High-speed connectivity is important if applications that require high bandwidth, such as CAD software, will be used.

MULTIPLE-FLOOR PHYSICAL DESIGN CONSIDERATIONS

The physical layout of multiple floors affects your options for setting up a network. Layout affects wiring closets, network peripherals, and AC power.

Wiring Closets

As is true for a single-floor plan, the wiring closet locations are critical, because they affect the kind of network equipment you can use and the ability to reach all proposed network nodes. If you are designing a network for a new building, ask to have input into the wiring closet locations. The best choice is to stack them vertically overhead on each floor (as shown in Figure 6-10). This will reduce wiring costs and increase the total reach of your network. If you are working in an existing building, prepare a diagram of each floor and use it to help determine the best wiring closet locations.

As mentioned in the single-floor design, security for wiring closets is very important. On a large network, such as the one in Figure 6-10, security needs mount as the number of nodes increases. Access to wiring closets should be kept to a minimum, to prevent the connection of unauthorized "snooping" equipment and to prevent unauthorized changes to the physical configuration of the network.

Wiring closets should not be used for multiple purposes, such as for storage, to limit problems caused by someone accidentally turning off equipment or damaging the equipment due to spills.

The wiring closet should be kept cool and dry, to prevent humidity from damaging network equipment. Also the wiring closet should be kept clean; if equipment becomes excessively dirty it will overheat and be subject to extra wear or damage.

Patch panels (the cable wiring panels) should be built by professionals following the EIA/TIA 568 specifications. Patch cords should follow all distance limitations.

Network equipment location

As you plan the network cable plant, take into account the organization's current and future needs for file servers, printers, high-speed printers (such as for large mailings), fax machines, CD-ROM changers, and other network equipment. Enter the locations of network equipment on the floor diagram to help place wiring closets. You will need to plan the placement of printers, plotters, and faxes so they can be used effectively in each office area. The placement of file servers is important for the maintenance and security of each server. For example, you may want to locate file servers in an office or "machine room" where access is limited and where you can install a UPS to provide fail-safe power.

The location of hosts and file servers also is important so you can segment the network to limit bottlenecks. (Segmenting network traffic is covered in Chapter 7.)

AC power

All AC power to each floor in the building should come from the same AC power source. A true ground should be available at the wall sockets used for network and computer equipment to prevent electric shock hazards as well as equipment failures.

PHYSICAL AND EQUIPMENT DESIGN

As the last two sections show, the physical design of a building and the equipment design both affect the kind of network you are able to install. In many situations, you will encounter problems that require you to adapt as best as possible. For example, in new construction, building plans may be changed and the anticipated wiring closet locations may be altered. Or the cable may be pulled with lengths beyond IEEE specifications. In an older building, you may have to extend a coaxial network that was poorly designed from the start, or the wiring closet locations may create design problems.

The best approach is to carefully plan before you start and to follow as closely as possible the design concepts we have discussed.

Table 6-3 summarizes design issues for multiple-floor network design.

Table 6-3

Multiple-Floor Design
Use a modular design.
Provide redundancy in critical network equipment.
Use fat pipe technology for future growth.
Design the building plan for vertically stacked wiring closets.
Secure wiring closets.
Secure file servers.
Plan for the location of peripherals.
Check the ground at power outlets.
Check the AC power source on each floor.

SUMMARY

This chapter has presented a variety of design models for Ethernet networks. The first model is a simple coaxial network for a small network situation. We built on that model to show how it can be expanded to include additional network segments, and how one or more repeaters can be used to extend a network.

10BASET networks can be less expensive than coaxial networks and are easier to maintain. Examples of 10BASET networks are shown for single-office, single-floor, and multiple-floor designs.

For all designs, it is important to build your network in a modular fashion to minimize the impact of a single problem on the rest of the network. The physical layout of a building has a strong influence on your ability to create a well-designed modular network.

When you design a network, create options to expand. Most importantly, include in your network design a growth path to take advantage of high-speed networking advancements.

Understanding the basics of network design presented in this chapter will prepare you to build networks that are ready to deliver the high-speed communications of the future.

KEY TERMS

Term/Acronym	Definition
BNC T Connector	This coaxial connector is in the shape of a T. The top ends are connected to the cable (or one may be connected to a terminator). The bottom of the T goes to the network node.
Cable Scanner	This testing instrument is used to measure cable length on a network.
Fat Pipe	High-speed fiber optic or copper cable (fast Ethernet or 100 Mbps) used to link network equipment on a backbone.
Segment	A network can be divided into smaller units, called segments. A segment on an Ethernet network is terminated at each end and supports up to 30 nodes (reserving one node for a repeater or hub connection).
Wiring Closet	This small room or closet provides a place for network equipment and central network wiring, such as punch-downs and patch panels.

REVIEW EXERCISES

1. Why is the location of a wiring closet important?
2. Why should the wiring closet be kept secure?
3. Show how you would add a second server to the configuration shown in Figure 6-3.
4. Redesign the network in Figure 6-5 to use twisted-pair cable and one or more concentrators.

5. Design an example network to connect two offices to one file server. Include two printers for each office area and one fax.

6. What are the advantages of using twisted-pair instead of coaxial cable?

7. Design a two-floor network using four servers, 40 PC workstations, and five network printers.

8. Find an existing coaxial Ethernet network at your school or in an office. Show how you would redesign this network to isolate critical network components. How would you prepare the network for high-speed communications?

9. Why is a good ground important on a network?

10. Describe two situations that might cause electrical interference to a cable run.

11. What is fat pipe? Why is it important to use this technology in your network design?

12. Find a computer lab that is networked on your campus. Can you identify the possible points of failure along the campus network that might affect services to this lab?

13. Find a lab on campus that is not networked. Describe how you would provide network services to this lab.

14. Identify areas on your campus where high-speed communications might be needed in the future (or where they are presently being used). Describe why high-speed communications might be needed.

15. What would you inspect after new cable is installed for a network?

ADVANCED NETWORK DESIGN

Designing networks involves taking on new challenges to meet the computing requirements of an organization. A growing business originally may have installed a token ring network and want to convert to Ethernet. A company may need to provide network access to employees working from home. A university may want to establish network communications between its remote campuses. Or a corporation may need to set up a high-bandwidth multimedia training lab.

This chapter addresses each of these design issues. The chapter begins with an explanation of token ring design and shows how to join separate token ring networks. It also shows how a token ring network can be converted to Ethernet. More complex designs using bridges and routers are presented to show how network traffic can be directed and controlled.

The best designs emphasize modular networks. This chapter uses the flexibility of intelligent hubs to show how networks can be designed modularly for efficiency and expansion.

AFTER READING THIS
CHAPTER YOU WILL BE ABLE TO:

- DESIGN TOKEN RING NETWORKS
- DESIGN BRIDGED NETWORKS
- CREATE A NETWORK USING ROUTERS
- EXPLAIN HOW INTELLIGENT HUBS CAN BE USED TO BUILD A NETWORK
- EXPLAIN STRUCTURED NETWORKING TECHNIQUES
- CONNECT AN IBM MAINFRAME TO A NETWORK
- SET UP REMOTE ACCESS COMMUNICATIONS TO A NETWORK

TOKEN RING NETWORKS

A token ring network involves a logical ring topology in a physical star design. The network is built around multistation access units (MAU). Each node on the network is connected to an MAU, with a maximum of eight nodes per each MAU. Figure 7-1 illustrates the design of a simple token ring network.

Figure 7-1

Token ring network on a single floor connected by a MAU

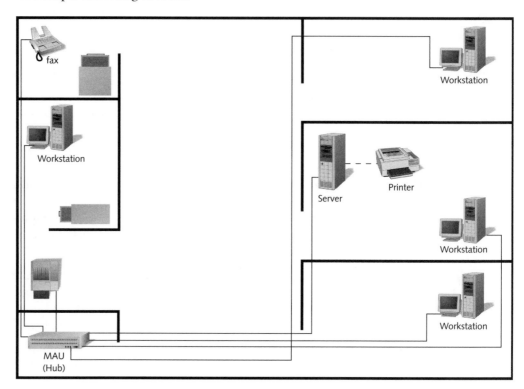

The cable plant is twisted-pair wire. If type 1 (see chapter 3) is used, the maximum segment length can be 300 meters (if only one MAU is present). For other cable types, the maximum segment length is 100 meters.

Notice that the network in Figure 7-1 is very similar in design to that shown in Figure 6-9. In some instances, a token ring network can be converted to Ethernet by replacing the NICs, connectors, and the MAU with a concentrator. This is useful to remember, if you need to convert an existing network to move to high-speed technologies or to have compatible monitoring of all networks.

Up to 12 MAU units can be used on a single ring. The MAUs are connected with a patch cable, which can be up to 100 meters in length. Figure 7-2 shows two MAUs connected to form one token ring network.

Figure 7-2

Token ring
network with
two MAUs

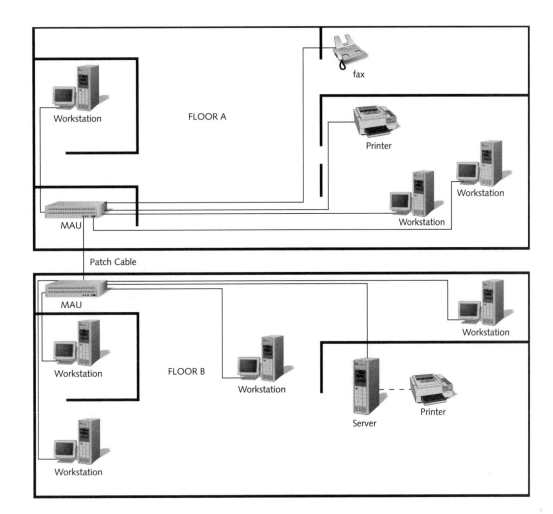

The total number of nodes that can be supported on one ring using cable types 1, 2 or 9 (shielded twisted-pair) is 260. If cable type 3 (unshielded existing telephone wire) is used, the total nodes supported per ring is 72.

The advantage of token ring networks is that they are reliable. The token-passing communications method provides more assured transmission than collision-prone Ethernet. If network reliability is a high priority in your design, a token ring solution should be considered.

Another advantage of token ring networks is that a malfunctioning node often can be located faster than on Ethernet (although, as we will see in Chapter 10, monitoring software for Ethernet is very effective for locating network problems).

A disadvantage of token ring is that it can be more expensive than Ethernet. For example, MAUs are expensive compared to equivalent Ethernet equipment, and it takes several MAUs to construct a large network. Another disadvantage of token ring is that there are more high-speed communications options available or under development for Ethernet networks.

Table 7-1 summarizes the connectivity rules for token ring.

Token Ring Connectivity Rules
Up to eight stations per MAU
Use twisted-pair cable types 1, 2, 3, or 9
Maximum segment length for type 1 cable with only one MAU is 300 meters
Maximum segment length for type 2, 3, or 9 cable is 100 meters
Maximum of 12 MAUs per ring
Supports up to 260 nodes on type 1, 2, or 9 cable
Supports up to 72 nodes on type 3 cable

BRIDGED NETWORKS

In some cases you will need to isolate network access for security and performance. For example, the accounting department in a publications company may need to control who has access to the file server used for accounting applications. However, they still need to be able to communicate with the rest of the company by electronic mail. In this situation, a bridge might be used to filter packets by address between the accounting office area and the rest of the network. Figure 7-3 illustrates the use of a bridge in this capacity.

Figure 7-3

Bridged token
ring network

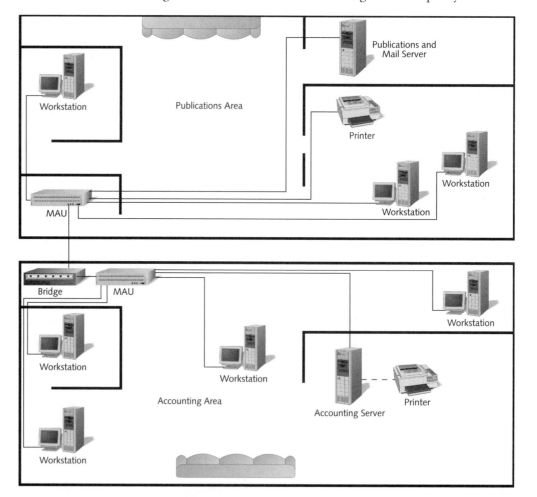

In Figure 7-3, the bridge is placed so traffic from the publications area is controlled. High traffic periods on the publications side will not impact the accounting side, since the bridge keeps the publications packets isolated to the publications network. Also, access to the accounting server is limited to the accounting side. Electronic mail can still be shared, since these packets are allowed to go through the bridge.

BRIDGING ETHERNET NETWORKS

Ethernet networks can be bridged for the same reasons as token ring networks. Bridging enables you to isolate network traffic between separate LANs or between LAN segments. Designing a network to isolate traffic between LANs is called **segmenting** the network. For example, assume you have three buildings on your network, each with its own LAN. One is the Business and Administration Building, and the other two are research labs. Both research labs use workstations with CAD and other high-traffic applications. A bridge can be used to isolate the high-traffic research areas, but will still permit electronic mail and other communications to flow between the buildings. Figure 7-4 illustrates how you would bridge the three LANs.

Figure 7-4

Bridged Ethernet networks

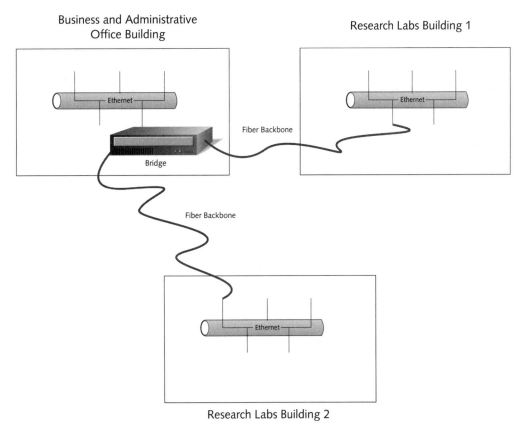

BRIDGING NETWORKS TO EXTEND DISTANCES

Another application performed by bridges is to link networks to extend the reach of network services. For example, assume there is a coax Ethernet LAN in the art department building of a large university campus, with one segment that has reached the distance and node maximums. The art department is interested in linking their network with the performing arts department on the same floor. The performing arts department also has a coax Ethernet network. The two networks can be extended into one by using a bridge. Figure 7-5 shows how the bridge can be used to join the networks.

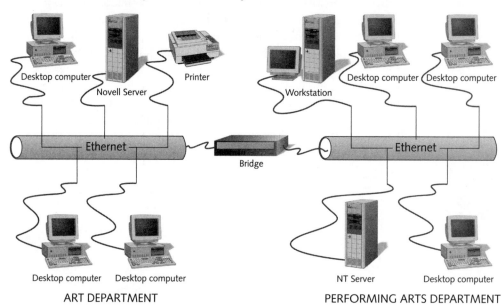

Figure 7-5

Bridging two networks to extend them into one

ROUTER APPLICATIONS

On larger networks, packets can be sent along the most efficient path by installing routers. Like bridges, routers can filter packets to isolate network traffic. They go beyond this, however, and direct packets along the most efficient route, to provide an increased level of network performance.

To compare use of a bridge to that of a router, assume you are linking Ethernet segments between five buildings. Figure 7-6 shows a bridge joining the segments.

Notice that electronic mail sent from the server in the top left network is transmitted by the bridge to all points on the network. The bridge does not have the information needed to send the mail packets to the exact destination, so it forwards them to each of the five LANs. As the arrows show, this creates unnecessary network traffic.

You can reduce the amount of traffic by installing a router in place of the bridge. The router can determine the destination of each packet and send the packet along the shortest route. (The router can "see" into the appropriate network layer to route the message, whereas a bridge cannot.) Figure 7-7 shows how mail is transported on the same network using a router instead of a bridge.

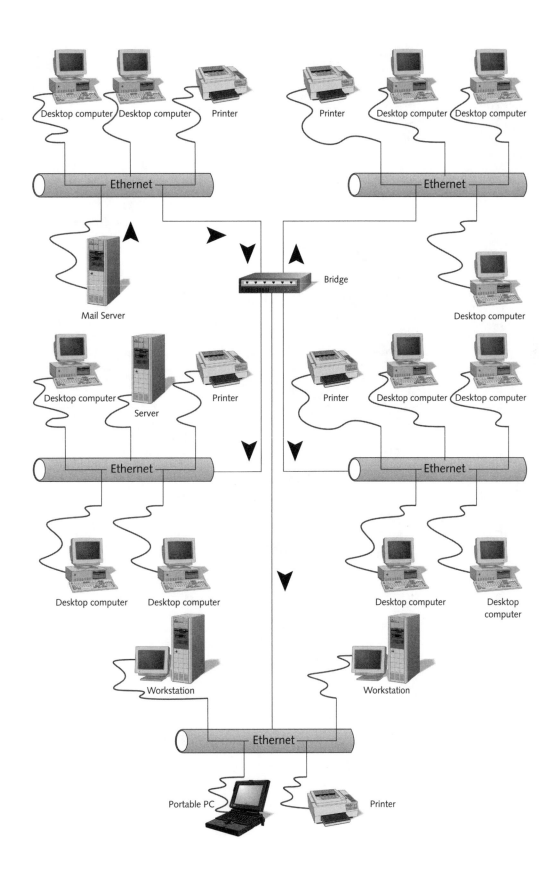

Figure 7-6

E-mail sent on a bridged network

Figure 7-7

E-mail sent on
a network
joined by a
router

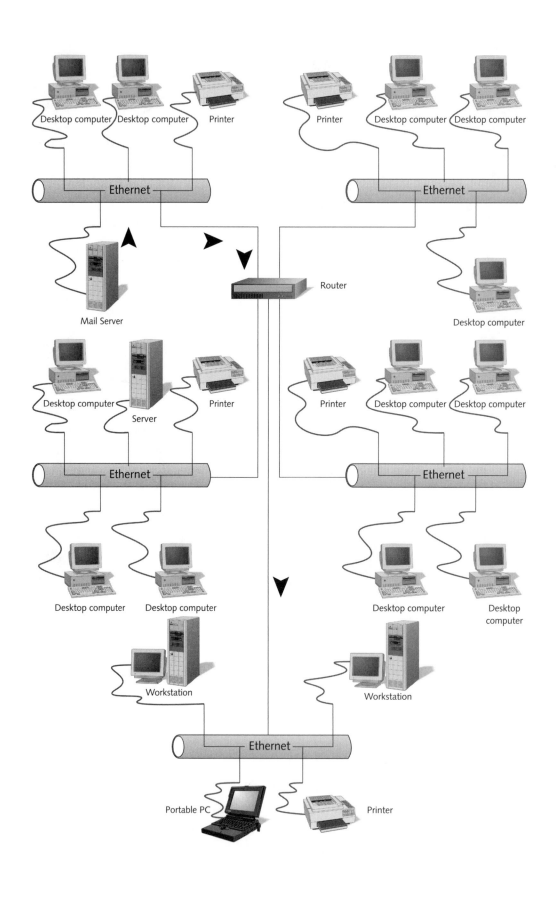

As the arrows in Figure 7-7 indicate, the e-mail is sent only to the network at the bottom of the illustration. No extra packets are sent to the other networks, because the router tables contain information about the best path to reach the appropriate destination.

LONG DISTANCE COMMUNICATIONS THROUGH ROUTERS

Routers are used to link remote networks as well as networks within a business or college campus. Let's use a multi-campus university as an example. This university system has four campuses, each over 50 miles apart. One way to link these campuses into an enterprise-wide network is to go through a router at each campus location. Figure 7-8 illustrates how the campuses could be joined.

Figure 7-8

Linking remote campuses through routers

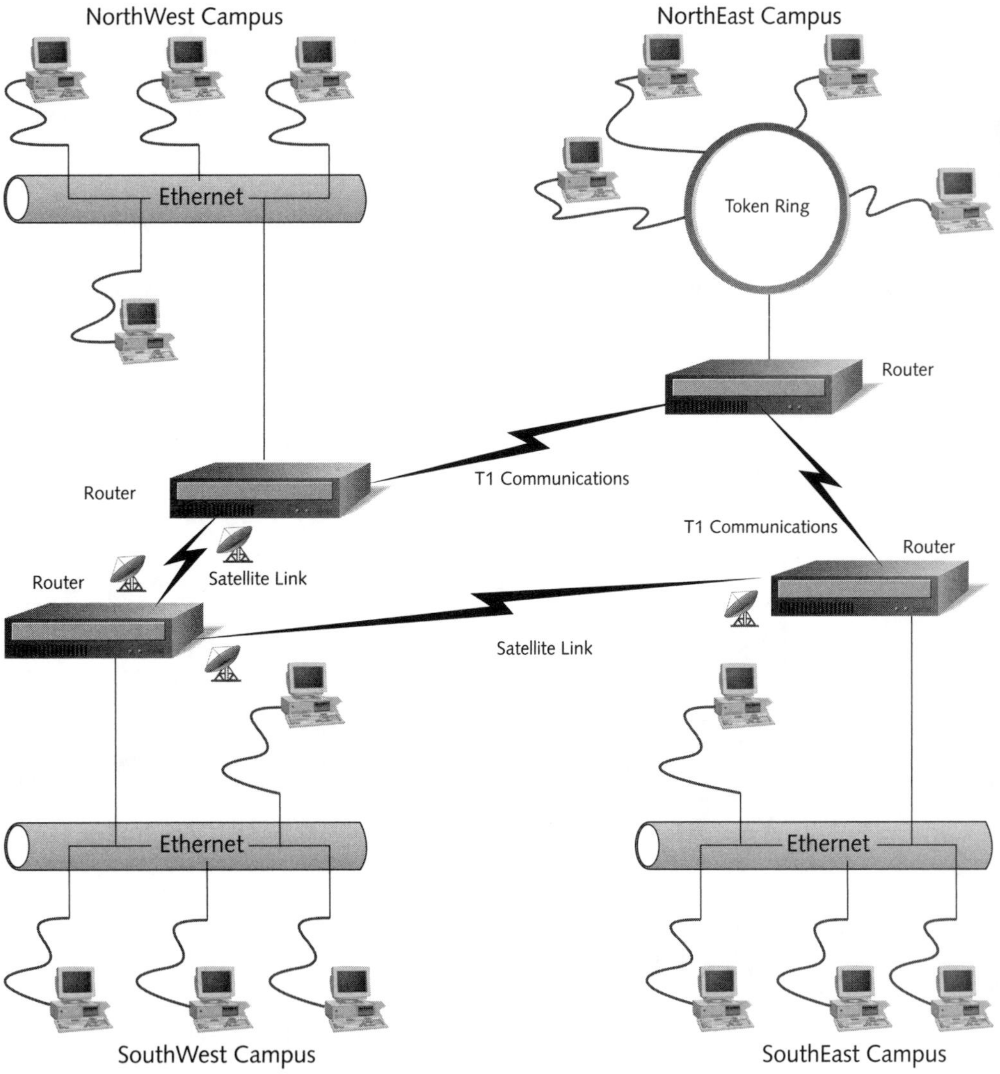

In this example, a router on one campus links to routers on two other campuses. NorthWest Campus is linked to SouthWest Campus by satellite communications. The same is true for the link between SouthWest Campus and SouthEast Campus. NorthEast Campus is linked to NorthWest Campus and SouthEast Campus by dedicated T1 telecommunications lines.

Each campus has a unique network identification, so the routers can quickly identify packets destined for each campus. The digital information is transferred from the routers to the communications links by using **Channel Service Unit (CSU) and Data Service Unit (DSU)** devices connected between each router and the communications link. The CSU provides an interface to connect to the communications link. The DSU converts data so they can be sent over the link and it converts received data to be forwarded onto the network. The CSU/DSU works on a principle similar to a high-speed modem that converts and compresses or uncompresses data transmitted over telephone lines.

ROUTERS AND BRIDGES COMPARED

The decision to use a router versus a bridge depends on your resources and what you need to accomplish. Both enable you to segment networks for security and to reduce unnecessary traffic, and both connect multiple LANs.

Bridges are relatively easy to configure and are less expensive than routers. They also filter packets faster than routers. If you have a network that uses protocols such as NetBEUI, NetBIOS, or SNA, a router is not a good investment, because none of these protocols can be routed.

Routers offer the ability to automatically "learn" the network and reduce network traffic in places where bridges may contribute to traffic problems, such as in Figures 7-6 and 7-7. A disadvantage to using routers is that they are more expensive, harder to configure, and can require more maintenance. Table 7-2 summarizes the advantages and disadvantages of bridges and routers.

Table 7-2

Implementing bridges versus routers

Bridges	Routers
Can join networks	Can join networks
Can segment networks	A good solution for linking remote networks
Relatively easy to configure	Can route packets to reduce network bottlenecks
Relatively inexpensive	Are relatively expensive
Filter packets faster than routers	Are more difficult to set up
Cannot route packets	Cannot route some common protocols

INTELLIGENT HUBS

Intelligent hubs combine the best features of repeaters, bridges, switches, and routers by combining all three into one unit. In Chapter 6, we introduced the use of an intelligent hub to connect concentrators on three floors in a single building (see Figure 6-10).

Intelligent hubs centralize network equipment functions into one modular unit. The unit may contain several modules such as repeater modules, bridge modules, and router modules. Depending on the hub, additional modules may be available for FDDI and token ring media. Each module is a board that plugs into a **backplane** in the hub. Hubs that support FDDI and token ring modules have separate backplanes for these media.

There are two types of intelligent hubs. One type comes is a small unit with a limited number of plug-in modules. This is called a stackable hub. As you add to the network, you can add more hubs. The hubs are joined via a common backbone. These hubs are designed for use on medium-sized networks.

Another type of hub is a large all-in-one unit that can house several modules and backplanes. These hubs are used in large networks such as a university campus or an enterprise-wide business network.

Intelligent hubs come with software to monitor and control the network, such as to automatically partition a malfunctioning segment. Some have firewall software to help control access to network servers and to encrypt data.

One important capability of an intelligent hub is the option to segment networks within the hub. This confines maintenance to one location in a network. For example, look at the network design shown in Figure 6-10. As discussed in Chapter 6, an advantage of this design is that it segments the file servers so they are unaffected if problems occur in other parts of the network. The design also includes the capability to segment the networks on each floor. Now take the concept of segmenting one step further. For example, assume there are two buildings, each with a design similar to the one shown in Figure 6-10. Since each building has a hub, connecting the buildings together is easily accomplished. You simply connect the hubs with a fiber optic backbone between buildings. Figure 7-9 shows this network design.

STRUCTURED NETWORKING

Figure 7-9 illustrates how the cable plant and network equipment can be designed to make a network modular. This type of design has roots in the designs used for telephone (voice) cable plants, in which twisted-pair telephone wire is often run in a horizontal fashion on each building floor, connecting to a centralized punch-down in a wiring closet.

In the late 1980s, network equipment manufacturers began to develop concentrators that could take advantage of existing twisted-pair cable plants installed for voice. These concentrators enabled data communications to take place over the type 3 twisted-pair cable previously only used for voice communications.

The development of these concentrators suggested the same techniques could be used for new installations, using twisted-pair cable to connect each network node to a concentrator or intelligent hub. As mentioned previously, the advantage is the ability to more easily trace a problem to a single node and then to isolate the node from the rest of the network. This approach, which is called structured wiring, is illustrated in Figure 6-10 and Figure 7-10.

Figure 7-9

Linking two buildings via intelligent hubs

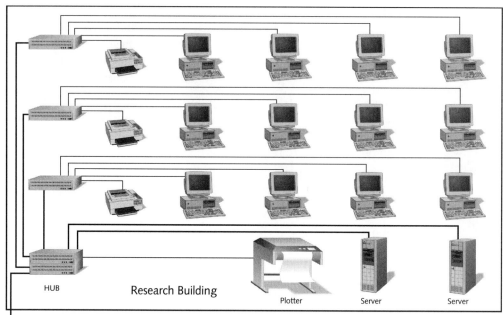

HUB

Research Building

Plotter Server Server

← Fiber Optic Backbone

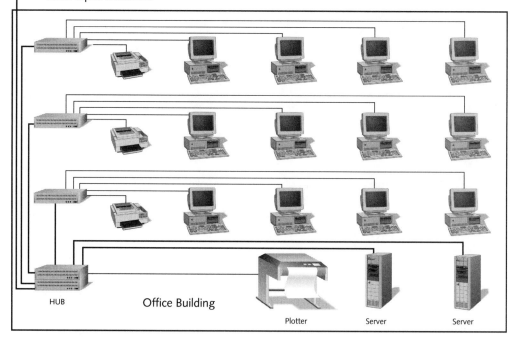

HUB

Office Building

Plotter Server Server

Figure 7-10

Horizontal (single floor physical star topology) structured wiring

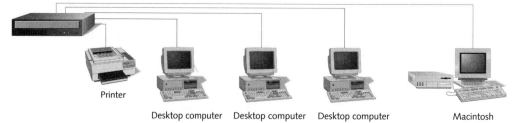

Printer Desktop computer Desktop computer Desktop computer Macintosh

The important components of structured wiring include:

- Use of inexpensive flexible cabling, such as twisted-pair
- Wiring nodes into a physical star
- Horizontal cabling plants within building floors
- Use of hubs (concentrators) for centralized wiring
- Intelligence built into the hubs to detect problems at the nodes

Structured wiring was soon followed by the concept of structured networking. Structured networking architectures enable the network manager to use the advantages of the modular star concept throughout a network. This is made possible by modular intelligent hubs. By centralizing cable media, gateway, repeater, bridge, and routing modules, modular hubs provide the option of building vertical (multiple floor) as well as horizontal cable plants (see Figures 6-10 and 7-11).

Figure 7-11

Vertical
structured
networking with
intelligent hubs
connected by fat
pipes

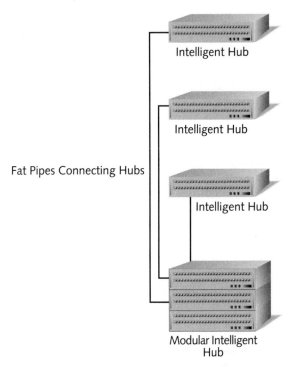

Intelligent Hub

Intelligent Hub

Fat Pipes Connecting Hubs

Intelligent Hub

Modular Intelligent
Hub

The key features of a structured network include the following:

- Centralized network management
- Vertical and horizontal network design
- Ability to reconfigure the network physically and logically
- Ability to segment the network according to business patterns
- Ability to add redundancy
- Ability to quickly introduce high-speed network equipment advances

CENTRALIZED NETWORK MANAGEMENT

Centralized network management means that central points are established for critical network functions. For example, network monitoring can be performed at a management station connected to the modular intelligent hub. Information-gathering nodes are dispersed throughout the network to provide the management station with continuous information about all parts of the network. (See Chapters 9 and 10 for more discussion of network management and remote network monitoring.)

With centralized network management, much of the network maintenance can be done from a central area, reducing the need to travel to multiple geographic locations on a network. This is especially important on large networks.

Centralized network management also simplifies activities such as maintenance of file servers and hosts. Servers and hosts can be centralized in areas where they are easy to maintain, such as in computer rooms. Backups and software upgrades can be done from one location instead of many. The computers can share one UPS and conditioned power source, saving the cost of multiplying these resources to several locations.

VERTICAL AND HORIZONTAL NETWORK DESIGN

As we discussed, vertical and horizontal design offers several advantages. It makes it possible to physically isolate each network node for greater network reliability. It also makes it possible to upgrade a specific section of the network for special purposes, such as installing an FDDI ring for high-speed communications with servers. It makes it possible to quickly address high-traffic network problems. Network segmentation can be performed horizontally, such as dividing one floor into two or more segments. Segmentation also can be done vertically by segmenting floors to reduce the impact of network traffic. Also, traffic can be reduced by installing one or more fat pipes on the vertical uplinks in a building and between buildings.

RECONFIGURING THE NETWORK PHYSICALLY AND LOGICALLY

Structured networking enables you to make network changes as needed. The modular design means you can physically upgrade the network in several places. For example, a concentrator can be replaced by a modular hub or by stackable hubs. A high-speed 100BASET link can be added to a specific node.

The ability to physically reconfigure a network means you can segment the physical portions of a network to save on the number of bridge and routing modules that must be purchased.

The intelligent hub software also enables you to reconfigure segments logically. From the central management station, you can add a new logical segment, remove a segment, or add a new node to an existing logical segment.

SEGMENTING THE NETWORK ACCORDING TO BUSINESS PATTERNS

The ability to segment the network logically means that you can organize network segments by work patterns. For example, in a chemical research plant you might organize nodes into a research chemist **workgroup**, a sales workgroup, a purchasing workgroup, an administrative workgroup, and a plant operations workgroup. Later you may wish to segment the chemists into an experimental research workgroup and an engineering workgroup. This capability is especially important as client/server software is implemented. (Chapter 11 discusses the impact of client/server technologies on networking.)

REDUNDANCY

Structured networking provides more opportunities to add redundancy to your network. You can add redundant parts to the intelligent hubs, such as power supplies and backplanes. You can create redundant paths so critical data can always get to their destination. You can perform a **hot swap** in a modular hub to replace a defective module without taking down the hub.

HIGH-SPEED NETWORK IMPLEMENTATION

The modular design of a structured network enables you to implement high-speed networking advances as they come to the marketplace. Many components for high-speed networking are currently in the introductory stages, including 100BASET NICs, ATM switching devices, and SONET networks (see Chapter 11).

One example is to install ATM switching for current high-speed needs. For example, your organization might wish to install a lab for multimedia training. Multimedia training systems usually contain voice and video files that require a lot of bandwidth. On a structured network, you can add an ATM switch to provide the needed bandwidth as shown in Figure 7-12.

As you add the ATM switch to the network, you can include in your design plans the option to eventually connect to a high-bandwidth SONET network when one becomes available in your area. Figure 7-13 shows use of an ATM switch to connect to SONET.

IMPLEMENTING STRUCTURED NETWORKING GRADUALLY

Your budget and the existing cable plant may place limitations on your ability to have a completely structured network. You may have to implement this a step at a time, replacing equipment as funds become available. You can gradually replace multi-port repeaters with concentrators. Selected bridges and routers can be replaced with modular intelligent hubs. For example, the routers in the multi-campus example could be replaced with intelligent hubs, as shown in Figure 7-14.

Figure 7-12

Connecting an
ATM switch

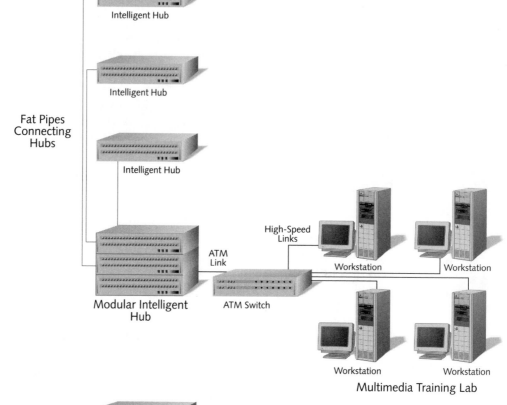

Figure 7-13

Adding ATM
communications
with a SONET
network

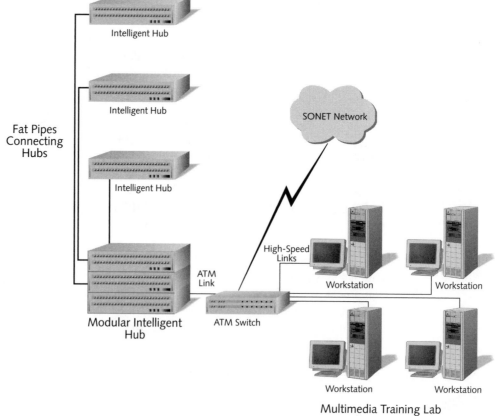

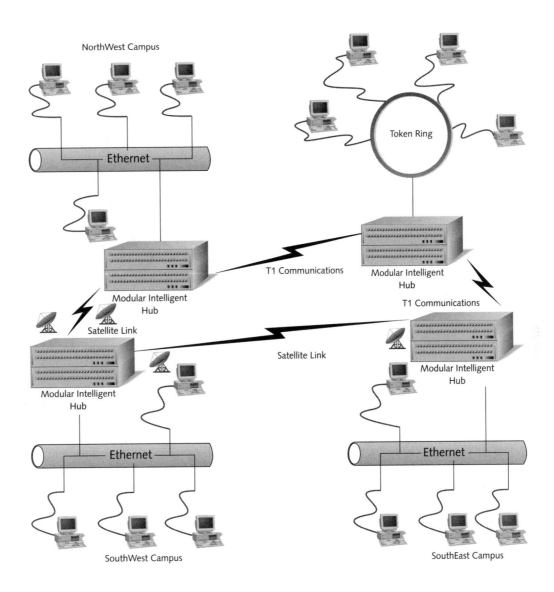

Figure 7-14

Linking remote
campuses
through
intelligent hubs

A feature of the design shown in Figure 7-14 is that network management can take place at any of the hubs. If a connection problem develops on one of the campuses, information about the problem can be viewed wherever a management station is located. This is useful for dispatching people to work on the problem and for keeping users informed about the problem and the estimated repair time.

OTHER CONNECTIVITY ISSUES

As you develop a network, you will have connectivity issues for very specific types of situations. Four common connectivity issues include connecting an IBM mainframe to the network, X.25 communications, remote access to the network, and wireless connectivity. Each of these is discussed in the sections that follow.

CONNECTING AN IBM MAINFRAME

There are two frequently used methods to connect an IBM mainframe to your network. One is to connect through a front-end processor, such as IBM's 3745 communications controller. The 3745 can be equipped with one or more Ethernet NICs for use on a TCP/IP network. The 3745 uses IBM's Network Communications Program (NCP) to provide the software communications management. Figure 7-15 shows how the 3745 is used on a network.

Figure 7-15

IBM host connected via front end and TCP/IP

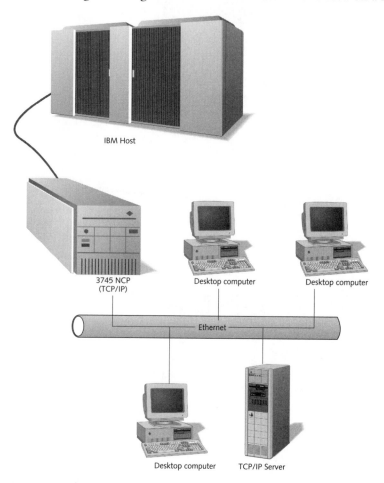

Another way to connect the IBM to a network is through a **systems network architecture** (SNA) gateway. SNA is a protocol used by IBM to communicate with terminals and other IBM mainframe computers. The SNA gateway is placed between the network and the IBM, as shown in Figure 7-16.

In both connection methods, you will need to provide software to access the IBM from PC workstations, since connectivity is designed for IBM terminals. Several **terminal emulator** programs are available, such as Novell's LAN Workplace and the 3270 Winsockets IBM emulator.

Figure 7-16

IBM host
connected via
SNA gateway

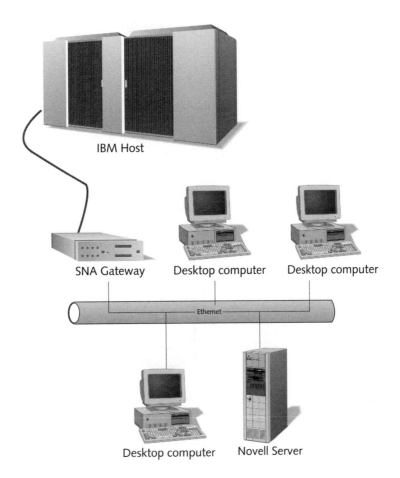

IBM Host

SNA Gateway   Desktop computer   Desktop computer

Ethernet

Desktop computer   Novell Server

X.25 COMMUNICATIONS

Some multinational corporations build international data communications using X.25 packet-switching networks. Many of these corporations build networks for overseas communications by using a remote X.25 router to link with a public X.25 packet-switching network. One way to set up X.25 communications is through a TCP/IP network, with a router (or router module in an intelligent hub) sending the IP packet to an IP-compatible X.25 network. Figure 7-17 illustrates this using an intelligent hub router module.

REMOTE NETWORK ACCESS

Business travelers, telecommuters, students, and others often need to access network software and files from remote locations. Corporations, universities, and government organizations are providing remote access from network servers dedicated for this purpose.

Novell and Microsoft provide remote network access services through their NetWare Access Server (NAS) and Remote Access Server (RAS) options. Novell's NAS is a PC-based computer configured with NAS software to operate as an access server. The NAS can be connected to a bank of modems for dial-up service to the network. A remote user can dial up the server through a DOS, Windows with DOS, or Macintosh computer. A NAS will handle up to 16 users at the same time. To the user, the NAS acts as a remote PC, with a specified amount of disk space allocated to the user. It allows the user to connect to one or more Novell servers on the network.

Figure 7-17

Connecting to
an X.25
packet-switching
network from a
router module

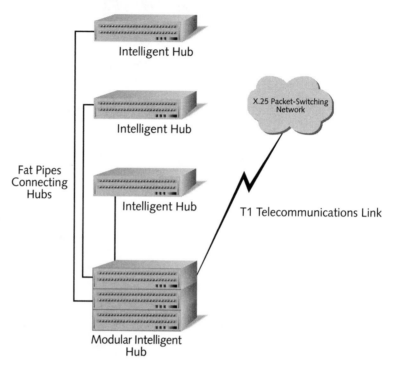

Microsoft's RAS is more versatile than NAS because it supports remote communications with Microsoft NT or Novell NetWare servers. Remote communications are made possible by using point-to-point protocol (PPP) or serial line internet protocol (SLIP). PPP is a protocol developed for transmitting data remotely. SLIP is a remote communications protocol originally developed for UNIX environments. SLIP and PPP support communications for TCP/IP, IPX, and NetBEUI over telephone lines. They also support data transfer through X.25 packet-switched networks and ISDN telecommunications networks.

An NT server can be configured to operate the RAS server software. Users reach the RAS-enabled server through a bank of modems that support the PPP and SLIP protocols. The modems can be connected to the network through a communications server. Figure 7-18 illustrates how RAS is used on a network providing access through a modem bank.

A user who wishes to dial in needs a computer with a modem and Microsoft Windows. The client computer is configured in Windows to use PPP, SLIP, and the protocols needed for the network being accessed. For example, if the client PC is accessing a network with NT and NetWare servers, it needs to be configured for NetBEUI and for IPX.

Before a client can access the RAS server, that client must have a domain account name registered to the NT domain (list of authorized users). Also, the network manager must use the RAS administration utility to grant the RAS server access to the client domain name.

Figure 7-18

RAS access on a Microsoft NT network

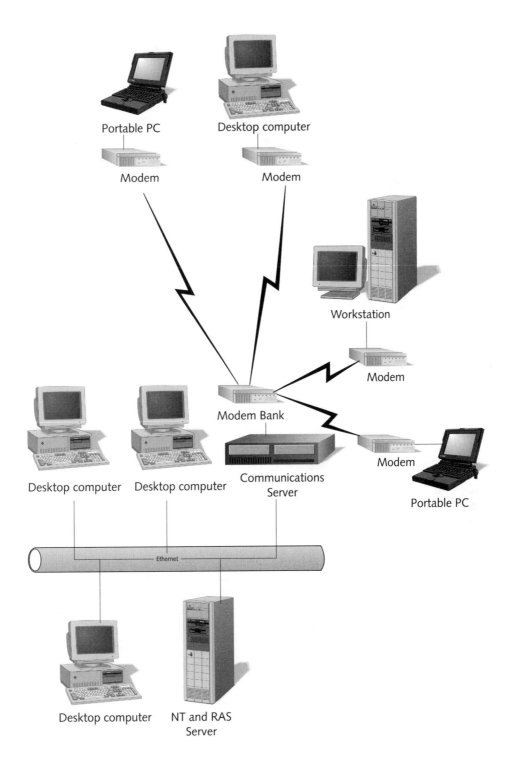

WIRELESS CONNECTIVITY

Wireless network communications sometimes provide less expensive solutions than running network cable. For example, you may have a situation where it is very expensive to run cable between buildings, but you still need to connect the networks inside various buildings to one another. In this example, wireless networking is an alternative to consider.

Two wireless bridges can provide the link between networks so long as the buildings are within line-of-sight communications (as specified by the manufacturer). Figure 7-19 shows two wireless bridges connecting Ethernet networks in a city college. One network is in the administration and classroom building, and the other is in a second classroom building. The remote bridge antennas are placed on the roofs of each building.

Wireless network communications have two important disadvantages: They transmit data at relatively low speeds (often 2 Mbps), and no specifications have been defined for wireless communications, which increases the risk of becoming dependent on one vendor.

Figure 7-19

Connecting networks using wireless bridges

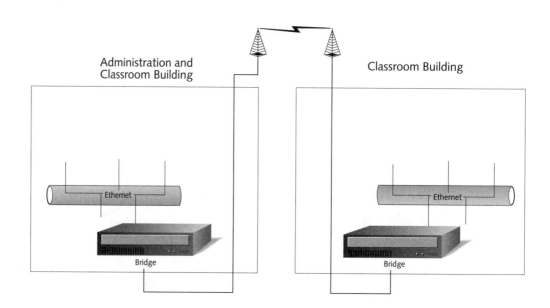

SUMMARY

Token ring networks provide a reliable networking environment, but they are limited in terms of bandwidth and flexibility. Like Ethernet networks, token ring networks can be expanded by using bridges.

Bridges and routers provide design options to isolate traffic where network performance is a concern due to increasing traffic. Intelligent hubs have all the capabilities of bridges and routers, and they provide an expansion path to high-speed networking. They also provide the opportunity to centralize network management.

Structured networking is a design concept that is vital to building flexible and dependable networks. A structured network provides a foundation to let you adjust network traffic flow, to manage your network, and to create a network that reflects the workgroup patterns of your organization.

KEY TERMS

Term/Acronym	Definition
Backplane	Modular equipment has a main circuit board or backplane with plug-in connectors for the modular boards. The main circuit board provides connections between the modular boards, power to the modular boards, and grounding.
Channel Service Unit (CSU)	This device provides an interface between a router communications port and a communications line, such as T1.
Data Service Unit (DSU)	This unit is used along with a CSU for communications over a T1 line. The DSU converts data to be sent over the line, and it converts data received from the line into a readable digital format.
Hot Swap	Some network equipment allows you to replace defective boards without powering down the equipment. These hot swaps are a form of fault tolerance.
Segmenting	In this process, the network manager isolates a portion of the network to reduce bottlenecks and to reduce the impact of a network malfunction on other portions of the network.
Systems Network Architecture (SNA)	This communications protocol is used by IBM for communications between IBM mainframe computers and terminals.
Terminal Emulator	Some mainframes and minicomputers are designed to communicate with terminals instead of PC workstations. A terminal emulator software program is run on a workstation to make it act like a terminal.
Workgroup	To a network-aware operating system such as Microsoft Windows, Microsoft NT, or Novell NetWare, a workgroup is a logical grouping of computer users for the purpose of sharing files, executables, and other computer functions.

REVIEW EXERCISES

1. What devices are used to connect a router to a communications link?
2. A _____ acts as a hub on a token ring network.
3. Show how you would connect networks in three office buildings in downtown New York City.
4. What are the advantages and disadvantages of token ring networking?
5. What are the features of structured networking? What advantages are there to building structured networks?
6. Go to a lab at your school and observe the cable plant. Are there any changes you would make to achieve structured wiring?
7. Under what circumstances is it ineffective to place a router on a network?

8. What is network segmenting? What network problems might segmenting solve?

9. What protocols are used for remote access to a network?

10. What are the functions of RAS and NAS?

11. Find a building on campus that is not networked (or one in the business area of your town). Design a network for this building using structured networking concepts.

12. One way to connect an IBM mainframe to a network is through

_____ .

13. How would you change the network in Figure 7-4 to provide better service between buildings?

14. What are the advantages to using type 3 cable on a token ring network in a building? What are the disadvantages?

15. Why is the backplane important to a modular hub?

16. What are the advantages of centralized network management?

CHAPTER EIGHT

NETWORK MANAGEMENT: THE ESSENTIALS

Several years ago a large college installed a campus-wide network for administrative and academic computing. They built a coax-based 10-Mbps Ethernet network and, at first, used it for two academic labs. In the early stages, the performance was exceptional. Later they extended the network to reach the administrative offices for use with word processing and spreadsheet software. Soon another lab was added for computer aided design (CAD) software, and yet another to teach desktop publishing for journalism classes.

There was little planning with each addition. With every growth step came serious network "slow-downs." The college paid little attention to network management, and the network began to have a negative reputation. Finally, performance became unacceptable when a new system was added to enable students to view their progress toward degree requirements.

Many organizations neglect network management until serious problems occur and faith in the network reaches a low point.

**AFTER READING THIS
CHAPTER YOU WILL BE ABLE TO:**

- EXPLAIN NETWORK MANAGEMENT ESSENTIALS
- EXPLAIN SNMP FOR NETWORK MANAGEMENT SOFTWARE
- DESCRIBE NETWORK SECURITY NEEDS FOR DATA PROTECTION AND NETWORK RELIABILITY
- DESCRIBE PRINT SERVICES
- EXPLAIN DISK SHARING SERVICES

Solid network management is as important as the initial design. Network management is a process that needs to start when the network is installed. As the network grows, so should the network management techniques and tools. This chapter provides an introduction to network management. It outlines important management concepts and issues such as use of SNMP, the need for security, network printing, and disk sharing.

SNMP

The Simple Network Management Protocol (SNMP) is a widely used protocol that enables network managers to continuously monitor network activity. SNMP was developed as an alternative to the OSI proposal for network management, Common Management Interface Protocol (CMIP). CMIP has been slow to emerge and has relatively high system overhead. Many vendors have chosen SNMP instead because of its simplicity.

SNMP has several important advantages over CMIP. First, it is supported by all major vendors of network management tools (see Table 8-1). Several hundred networking devices currently support SNMP. These include file servers, network interface cards, routers, repeaters, bridges, and hubs. In contrast, CMIP is used by IBM in some token ring applications, but is not used on many networks.

Table 8-1

Some SNMP-based network management products

Manufacturer	Product
Bay Networks	OPTIVITY
Cabletron	SPECTRUM
Digital Equipment Corp. (DEC)	POLYCENTER
Hewlett-Packard	OpenView
IBM	SystemView

Another advantage of SNMP is that it operates independently on the network, which means that it does not depend on a two-way connection at the protocol level with other network entities. This quality enables SNMP to analyze network activity, such as incomplete packets and broadcast activity, without depending on possibly faulty information from another node. CMIP, on the other hand, connects to network nodes at the protocol level, which means its analysis of problems depends on the accuracy of a node that may be malfunctioning.

SNMP also has an advantage in that management functions are carried out at a network management station. This is in contrast to CMIP, where management is distributed to the individual network nodes that are also being managed.

Another advantage of SNMP is that it has lower memory overhead than CMIP. CMIP needs up to 1.5 MB at the node for operation, whereas SNMP only needs a maximum of 64 KB.

HOW SNMP WORKS

SNMP functions through two entities, the **network management station (NMS)** and **network agents**. The NMS monitors networked devices that are equipped to communicate via SNMP. The managed devices run agent software that is in contact with the network management station. Most devices connected to modern networks are agents. These include routers, repeaters, hubs, bridges, PCs (via the network interface card), print servers, communications servers, and UPSs.

A network manager can use the console at the NMS to send commands to network devices and obtain statistics on performance. The NMS can build a map of the entire network. If a new device is added, the NMS can "discover" it immediately. Software on the NMS has the ability to detect if an agent is down or malfunctioning. The agent may be highlighted in red or an alarm may sound, or both. All NMS software is now written in graphical user interface (GUI) format so it is easier to display.

Many NMS software packages have graphical representations of meters to show network utilization, flow of packets, and other network performance information. Application programming interfaces allow customized programming features.

Each agent maintains a database of information, such as the number of packets sent, the number of packets received, packet errors, the number of connections, and so on. An agent's database is called the Management Information Base (MIB).

The NMS uses a range of commands to obtain or alter MIB data. The retrieved data enables the network manager to determine if a device is down or if a network problem exists. The NMS may even allow the network manager to reboot a device remotely.

The messages transmitted between the NMS and the agent are packaged into the **User Datagram Protocol (UDP)**. The packaged unit consists of a message version ID, a community name, and a protocol data unit (PDU). The community name is a password shared by the NMS and the agent. The PDU is a command sent from the NMS to the agent (see Figure 8-1). The commands are in the form of a Get or a Set instruction. For example, a GetRequest or GetNextRequest command enables the NMS to interrogate MIB table variables. A GetRequest might be issued to obtain information on how many packets have been rejected at a bridge. In another example, the SetRequest command permits the NMS to change variables. This command might be used to reset a time-until-reboot variable on a bridge to zero, enabling the NMS to immediately reboot the bridge.

MANAGEMENT INFORMATION BASE (MIB)

The MIB stores data on network objects such as bridges, routers, hubs, and repeaters. The core set of variables contained in a MIB are listed in Table 8-2.

The MIB table was originally defined according to the Management Information Base-I (MIB-I) standard. This standard tracks information about a device, incorporating a range of variables as shown in Table 8-2. MIB standards are defined by the Internet Engineering Task Force (IETF).

MIB-I permits vendors to add proprietary MIB extensions. The extensions enable vendors to manage unique functions of a particular device. Several hundred vendors have implemented additional variables. Vendors submit an application to the Internet Assigned Numbers Authority to create extensions.

Figure 8-1

Network management station monitoring a bridge and a hub

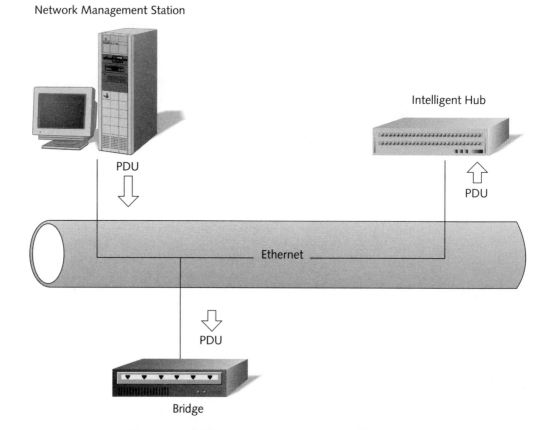

Network Management Station

Intelligent Hub

PDU

PDU

Ethernet

PDU

Bridge

Table 8-2

MIB core variable groups

Group	Description
Address Translation Group	Converts network addresses to physical or subnet addresses
Interfaces Group	Tracks the number of network interfaces or the number of subnets
Internet Protocol (IP) Group	Tracks the number of input datagrams received and the number rejected
System Group	Provides information about the device containing the agent software
Internet Control Message Protocol (ICMP) Group	Tracks the number of source messages sent and received
Electronic Gateway Protocol (EPG) Group	Provides information about an agent's network neighbors
User Datagram Protocol (UDP) Group	Provides information about the current UDP listening agent/device (the agent contacted by the NMS)
Transmission Control Protocol (TCP) Group	Contains information about TCP connections, such as IP address and timeout characteristics
SNMP Group	Tracks information about PDU commands and communications with the MIB

A second standard, MIB-II, has been developed to improve on MIB-I. This standard includes improved security, support for token ring, support for high-speed interfaces, and support for telecommunications interfaces.

The MIB standards are still evolving to include two important plans for the future. One is to make MIB compatible with popular relational databases. Microsoft, Informix, Sybase, and Oracle have strongly supported this enhancement. All of these companies market successful relational databases.

The manufacturers of remote portable PCs also are pushing for the standardization of MIB extensions, which will be called Mobile MIB. Compaq, Zenith Data Systems, IBM, and Motorola have all expressed interest in development of Mobile MIB for management of wireless notebook PCs.

SNMPv2

SNMP had some shortcomings that have been addressed in version 2, which is called SNMPv2. Security is a particularly important issue, since SNMP has lacked strict security measures. For example, with SNMP the community name is sent by the NMS without encryption and can be intercepted. Someone might be able to capture this password and get access to the Set command. He or she would then be able to remotely configure a router or hub, compromising the security on a network.

SNMPv2 provides better security in several ways. First, data are altered in transit so they are more difficult to interpret. Messages also are sent in unpredictable order or delayed so that they are harder to intercept. Another improvement is that the community name is encrypted.

Besides security, other improvements have been built into SNMPv2. For example, there is improved error handling and multiprotocol support. The transport protocols, IPX and AppleTalk, also are supported. The speed of data transmissions is improved by enabling retrieval of more information at one time.

NETWORK SECURITY

Providing and maintaining security is critical to the daily management of a network. As a network grows, so does users' dependence on the network to perform vital business, academic, and research functions. An interruption of network service or loss of data can generate costly losses.

Network security management involves minimizing downtime and data loss resulting from natural hazards and human intervention. To reduce threats to the network or to data, the network manager is responsible for addressing the following areas:

- Passwords and password maintenance
- Access privilege management
- Encryption
- Power protection

- System and data backups
- System fault tolerance and redundancy
- Firewalls
- Virus monitoring
- Disaster recovery

NETWORK PASSWORDING

Passwords are a front line of defense to secure network nodes. All types of network nodes should have password protection (see Table 8-3).

Table 8-3

Password protection

Network Node	Type of Password Protection
File Server	Supervisor accounts, workgroup administrator accounts, user accounts, guest accounts
Host Computer	Supervisor accounts, user accounts, guest accounts
Database Server	System administrator, database administrator, database groups, user accounts
Application Server	Supervisor accounts, workgroup administrator accounts, user accounts
Network Equipment	System administrator
User Workstation	User access

File servers

All accounts on UNIX, Microsoft NT, Novell, Banyan Vines, and other file server systems should require passwords. File servers have several different types of accounts that can be created. These include a supervisor account, workgroup administrator accounts, user accounts, and guest accounts. The supervisor account should be limited to a small group of people who are responsible for managing the file server. This type of account has access to all directories and functions of the file server, and supervisor account holders must be careful to keep their passwords secure. Many places require supervisor passwords to contain eight or more characters and to be constructed so they are difficult to guess. Supervisor passwords also should be changed on a regular basis, such as once a month, for added security.

Workgroup administrators have limited management capabilities over a group of users, as specified by the file server supervisor. They may have authority to create new accounts for the workgroup, assign directory access rights, and set up utilities for the workgroup. As is true for a supervisor, a workgroup administrator should have a password that is difficult to guess and that is changed on a regular schedule.

Each file server user has a personal account. He or she has update-and-read access to his or her home directories and other directories shared by a workgroup. These accounts also should require passwords, to be set by each individual user. Account holders should be advised to not share their passwords. Many organizations suggest avoiding a password that is the name of a family member or that is an easily guessed common name, such as the name of a school.

Guest accounts are sometimes created to enable "anonymous" users to log onto a file server. Their purpose in accessing the server may be to view public documents or files. Guest accounts normally allow files to be read or copied, but they usually do not have access to write files to the server. Guest accounts are often called anonymous FTP sites. They may be open to a group of people on the network or to the entire Internet community.

Host computers

Host computers, such as mainframes, minicomputers, and shared workstations, should have password access accounts, like a file server. These systems have supervisor accounts, user accounts, and guest or anonymous FTP accounts. As with a file server, the passwords on any host computer account with supervisor privileges should be changed frequently.

Database server

A database server is a key component of any network running client/server applications. Database servers are home to data stored in relational databases for business, administrative, and scientific uses. Oracle, Sybase, Microsoft SQL Server, Gupta, and Informix are some commonly used database systems. Each vendor's database comes with several levels of security. The **system administrator (SA)** is an account with global access to all databases and system administration features. This account should be well protected, with hard-to-guess passwords that are changed often.

Within each database system, there may be one or more dedicated databases. For example, a Sybase server might have four databases: one for human resource information, one for accounting data, one for sales tracking data, and one for purchasing data. Each database will have a **database administrator (DBA)** account. Like the SA, the DBA must protect his or her account via password and by regularly changing that password.

Database servers also have user accounts defined to the server. The user accounts should require passwords. Further, each account should be granted access only to data appropriate for that user. In our previous example, the accounting database might be accessed by an accounting manager and accounting technicians for each department in a company. The accounting manager will have full access to the accounting database. The accounting technicians will have access only to their particular department's data.

Some database servers enable an SA or DBA to designate security groups. Each user account is associated with a specific group, and that group is granted limited access to data. Access may be granted by table, database view, database row, or database column. Because database information is often critical to an organization, database security is a very important network function.

Application server

A network that supports database servers will have accompanying application servers. An application server houses the program applications needed to access or update data on a database server. These applications can include accounting general ledger programs that use an accounting relational database, or payroll programs that use data from a human resources database. The application server has supervisor, workgroup administrator, and user accounts that require passwords. A user account for payroll applications should require a password to ensure that only an authorized person can run payroll calculations and print payroll checks.

On some networks, the application server may run FTP programs. Schools and companies may choose to limit FTP access by placing passwords on these accounts.

Network equipment

Bridges, routers, switches, and hubs use administrator accounts to manage program and table functions. It is critical that these administrative accounts have passwords and that the passwords are changed often. Any network intruder can gain access and perform extensive damage if these accounts are not protected to the fullest measure.

User workstation

Workstation operating systems such as Windows for Workgroups, Windows95, NT Workstation, and UNIX permit the user to set up password protection on the workstations. All workstations connected to a network should require a password for access to the workstation.

ACCESS PRIVILEGE MANAGEMENT

Most network servers and host operating systems come with security capabilities (see Table 8-4). If a system does not have built-in security, it may be necessary to purchase a security system from the original vendor or a third party. For example, the IBM mainframe operating system, MVS, does not have a native security package. Many IBM customers opt to purchase the IBM security add-on, RACF.

Operating system security and security packages enable the system administrator to establish multiple levels of access privilege. One level of security enables the system manager to create security access for a single user or for groups of users. For example, the computer system security officer may have access to all data areas on a computer. To speed security management, the security officer may wish to create groups of users for security purposes. The payroll group might consist of members who can only access payroll information. The financial security group could contain people who can access the accounting files and data.

A second level of security determines access capabilities, such as read only, write, write/update, program execute, file creation/deletion, and directory ("library" for IBM hosts) creation privileges. The security officer can assign one or any combination of these privileges to a single user or to a specific group.

Another level of security determines who is able to access specific directories or libraries. This security can be specified to the subdirectory level, or on an IBM host it may be to the partitioned data set level (PDS).

Most security systems enable the security officer to control security down to the level of a specific file or data set. For example, the payroll office may be able to read, write, and update employee payroll files. The human resources office group may be able to read the payroll files, but not to perform updates.

Modern relational databases come with security capabilities. Oracle, Sybase, Microsoft SQL Server, Informix, and DB2 are some examples of database systems that have built-in security. These systems enable the security officer to establish security based on database, table, view, stored procedure, trigger, row, and column.

Table 8-4

Common Security Combinations
Single user and group
Read, write, write/update, program execute, file creation/deletion, and directory/subdirectory creation
Directory and subdirectory
File access
Database access via database, table, view, stored procedure, trigger, row, and column

ENCRYPTION

It is relatively easy for an enterprising hacker to build a network interface and software to capture packets on the network. With this capability, someone could "listen" for user IDs and passwords. He or she also might extract confidential data, such as a credit card or bank account number.

Data encryption techniques have become increasing important to protect critical information from interception on networks. A common method for encrypting data is to require "keys." The **encryption key** is a digital code or password that must be known to both the sending node and the receiving node. Some security schemes use keys with up to 512 digits.

One method that employs keys is the public-key encryption technique. In this technique, the key is divided into two parts. One part is published in a directory that is available to all network nodes. The second part is kept private by the sending and receiving nodes. Both portions of the key must be known by the receiving node before data packets can be decrypted.

The National Institute of Standards and Technology (NIST) and IBM have created a public-key encryption method called **Data Encryption Standard (DES)**. DES uses keys containing either 56 digits or 112 digits. Half of the key is used to encrypt information, and the rest of the key is used for decrypting the received data.

Some vendors have designed private-key encryption methods that give unique keys to the sending and receiving nodes. No portion of a key is published in a common directory. Keys are generated by a specialized encryption computer that verifies each node's authorization to transmit data. The specialized computer contains a database of information on each node such as IP address, user ID, user name, time, date, and so on. The key codes for the sender and the receiver must be known before information can be decrypted.

The public-key and private-key techniques both incorporate an additional encryption step for each packet that is sent. This step includes a message authentication code (MAC), an encrypted checksum attached to the stream of data. The checksum enables the recipient to determine if data were sent without error. And it provides a second level of data security, because both the sending and the receiving nodes must be able to compute the MAC.

POWER PROTECTION

Reliable power is critical for network equipment. There are two components to power protection: clean power and uninterrupted power.

Clean power involves filtering power to prevent fluctuations. Power surges and spikes are power increases, which can damage key network equipment such as file servers, host computers, hubs, and routers. Likewise, power sags, which involve voltage drops, can also damage equipment.

When the power goes out in a region, computer services can be interrupted, which brings the risk of data loss. Power outages also cause heavy wear on disk drives and some electronic components.

Power filters and surge protectors are a good investment for all key network equipment. A **power filter** protects equipment from sags and surges. It conditions power so a constant level is delivered to all connected equipment. A **surge protector** blocks power spikes but does not prevent low power situations from affecting equipment. In most situations, a power filter or conditioner is a better investment than a surge protector. Inexpensive surge protectors are not equipped to handle strong power spikes or spikes that last for several minutes.

An **uninterruptible power supply (UPS)** is an important investment for a network. A UPS is a box of rechargeable batteries that supplies power to equipment during a power outage. Some UPS products combine power filtering and uninterrupted power in one box. These are sometimes called hybrid UPSs.

There are two categories of UPS: off-line and on-line. The off-line UPS offers the least protection and is not well suited for critical file server and host computers. This type of UPS diverts a small amount of power to charge its batteries, and sends the main power directly to the attached equipment. There is a very brief switchover period to battery power when a power outage occurs. During the switchover period, power is lost to the equipment. The switchover may result in the equipment rebooting and in associated data loss.

The most protection is offered from an on-line UPS. This type of UPS draws power to continuously charge its batteries. The power to attached computer equipment is taken directly from the batteries. When a power failure occurs, there is never an interruption to the attached equipment. Power is still supplied directly from the batteries. The only change is that there is no outside power to continue charging the batteries. Because most power outages are brief, the batteries will start charging again quickly, as soon as the outside power resumes. For longer power outages, the reserve power in the batteries provides enough time to save data and properly shut down critical equipment.

SYSTEM AND DATA BACKUPS

Regular backups of all systems and data are as important as updating or reporting on data. On any computer or network equipment, there will be times when an equipment failure causes lost data. A backup system is the most cost-effective way to restore data and resume service. The alternative, manually rebuilding the data, is very expensive when calculated in terms of personnel and production time, as well as in loss of confidence in the network and services provided to users.

Types of backup include:

- *File backups.* Files in all directories should be backed up regularly. LAN servers will have word processing, spreadsheet, applications, and other files that need to be restored in the event of a system failure. Host workstations and mainframes have user files and data that should be backed up.

- *Database backups.* Many servers and hosts contain relational or network databases that must be backed up nightly. These may include Oracle, Sybase, Microsoft SQL Server, Informix, and other databases. Database backups can be taken of the entire database or just of individual tables.

- *System files.* Host and server computers have directories containing files that comprise the operating system or that contain parameters for the operating system. The system files enable the computer to boot and to execute commands. They also contain utilities for maintenance. A backup is made whenever changes are made to the files, as well as before and after making system upgrades, fixing bugs, and changing parameters.

- *System files on bridges, routers, hubs, and switches.* All network equipment with operating system files, tables, and parameter settings should be backed up. Backups are made after the equipment is first configured for service. They also are made before and after software upgrades, installation of bug fixes, and parameter changes.

BACKUP METHODS

Two backup methods can be used at the network level: full backups and incremental backups.

Full backup

This involves making a copy of all files and directories on a specific computer. There are two common ways to perform a full backup.

One method is called an **image backup**, which is a complete replication (a snapshot) of the data as they exist on a given volume. This is similar to a mirror image of the data and is done in binary format. One advantage of the image backup is that it can be performed quickly and restores are quick. Another advantage is that data compression is commonly done for image backups, which means fewer tapes are required. A disadvantage of an image backup is that individual files or directories cannot be restored. All information contained in the volume image—all files, directories, and security information—must be restored, which takes time if only one of the files is needed from the backup.

A second way to perform a full backup is called **file-by-file backup**. This method copies all files and retains the directory and subdirectory structures. For example, if the directory, CORPDATA, contains 25 files, all of these files will be stored on the backup under this directory. The advantage of the file-by-file method is that one or any combination of files can be restored. Also, entire directories, including subdirectories, can be restored. Plus, a file can be restored to a directory other than its original directory. For instance, if the file JAN.XLS is stored in the backup under the CORPDATA directory, it can be restored to a different directory, such as PRESDATA.

A disadvantage of the file-by-file backup is that it takes longer to complete than the image backup. A full restore also takes longer from a file-by-file backup than from an image backup. File-by-file backups frequently require more tapes than image backups.

Incremental backups

This type of backup also is known as a partial backup, because only part of the system is backed up at a given time. For example, out of eight volumes on a Microsoft NT server, the network administrator might back up only two per night. A different two volumes would be backed up each night until all the files have been backed up and the process rotation starts again from the beginning.

Another way to rotate incremental backups is by directory contents. For instance, the database and accounting directories might be backed up each Monday, Wednesday, and Friday night. The payroll, word processing, and spreadsheet files would be backed up on Tuesdays and Thursdays. System files would be backed up each Saturday.

BACKUP COMBINATIONS

Most network managers choose a combination of incremental and full backup methods. A common technique is to perform a full backup once a week on a slow production day, such as Sunday. Incremental backups are performed the other six days. This method ensures that the organization always can go back to one point in the week where all files can be restored. The "incrementals" can be restored one at a time after the full restore, if there is a need to go back to a given day in the week.

TAPE ROTATION

Many backup systems use a tape rotation to ensure that there is a way to restore data in the event of a tape failure. The Tower of Hanoi method is one of the most popular tape rotation methods. For example, on the evening of the full backup, two tapes might be used. There might to be four sets of backup tapes rotated over a span of eight weeks. Table 8-5 illustrates the rotation for the eight weeks. Tape set 1 is used four times, set 2 is used 2 times, and sets 3 and 4 each are used once during the eight week rotation period. If a problem is found with either set 1 or set 2 due to higher use, sets 3 and 4 are likely to be intact.

Table 8-5

Tower of Hanoi tape rotation

Week 1	Week 2	Week 3	Week 4	Week 5	Week 6	Week 7	Week 8
Set 1	Set 2	Set 1	Set 3	Set 1	Set 2	Set 1	Set 4

BACKING UP SECURITY RIGHTS

Novell NetWare, Microsoft NT, and other network operating systems store security and access rights information. This information governs file and directory access rights, the composition of security groups, and other access privileges. Some of the information is stored within directories and some is kept in system security files, such as the bindery in NetWare.

A backup system must be able to back up and restore access rights and security information. In the event of a hardware system or disk failure, this information is very difficult to recreate without a full back up/restore capability.

Popular backup systems, such as those offered by Palindrome and Cheyenne Software, provide options to back up security data, system files, data files, and all other server files. They also have options for full backups, incrementals, and tape rotation.

BACKING UP WORKSTATIONS

Network connectivity makes it possible to back up individual workstations in addition to file servers. Given the right software, any PC with a tape drive can be designated to back up other network workstations. The software used to back up file servers can be adapted to back up designated workstations at regular intervals. UNIX and Microsoft NT systems also come with the capability to back up neighboring workstations via the network.

COMPONENT FAILURES

Hardware components can and do fail. This includes components in any of the following devices:

- PC workstations
- File servers
- Print servers
- Repeaters
- Bridges

- Routers
- Hubs
- Switches
- Connectors
- Terminators

The hardware components most likely to fail are those with moving parts, such as disk drives and tape drives. Disk drives are particularly vulnerable to failure. This is partly because the read heads on disk drives are located as close as possible to the disk platters without physically touching them. Each time the disk drive is powered down, the read head is moved away from the platter as the drive is "spun down." The mechanical movement of spinning down a drive results in extra wear on the read head mechanism. Power failures, power sags, and power surges are particularly hard on disk drives, because they cause extra read head movement as the disk spins down and up.

Disk drives that are over 80% full also are subject to increased mechanical wear. Extensive fragmentation of files on a disk is another cause of extra wear. Full and fragmented drives cause the read head to move across the disk more extensively than in situations where disks are maintained regularly. Regular maintenance of disks involves moving files to less full disks and **defragmenting** disks. Defragmenting a disk is a process used to reorganize files to reduce the number of empty spaces between files. (The empty spaces are caused by deleting and creating new files.) Many operating systems come with software to defragment disks.

When a disk drive failure occurs, it is most likely to be a read head that has physically touched the disk platter. In all cases this causes damage to the platter, sometimes resulting in the release of metal fragments within the sealed module of the disk unit.

Because they have moving parts, tape drives also are subject to failure. Their failure rate is lower than that of disk drives, because the tape drive read heads and moving parts do not require such exacting tolerances or a 100% clean environment.

Other critical network components also can fail: for example, disk controllers. This type of failure can be difficult to diagnose, because the failure may be intermittent. A disk controller that is failing intermittently may cause a disk drive to fail completely, giving a false indication that the problem is in the drive and not the controller. For example, a university implementing a new client/server administrative system replaced several damaged disk drives before finding that the real problem was in a SCSI controller.

A power supply or backplane also can fail. Sometimes you can detect a faulty power supply by monitoring the power supply output. A bad power supply also may burn out completely. A faulty backplane is more difficult to detect, because damage may occur to the plugged-in boards before the problem can be diagnosed correctly.

The CPU is another critical component that can fail, although this type of failure is infrequent. CPU failure may be indicated by a system that will not boot, CPU clock timing errors, or a general protection fault (GPF).

SYSTEM FAULT TOLERANCE

The best defense against hardware failure is to implement **system fault tolerance** measures. System fault tolerance involves building in redundant hardware components. For example, because disk drives are most susceptible to failure, it is good practice to build in disk redundancy on critical file servers and network equipment. Disk redundancy is accomplished in two ways: by installing backup disks and by installing RAID drives.

Backup disks

Most file server operating systems permit the network manager to install two sets of disks. For each primary disk drive, a secondary backup drive automatically takes over if the primary drive fails. This capability is called disk shadowing (such as on UNIX, VMS, and MVS systems) or disk mirroring (such as on Novell and Microsoft NT systems). As information is updated on the primary drive, the same update is automatically copied to the secondary drive by the operating system. Disk mirroring is illustrated in Figure 8-2.

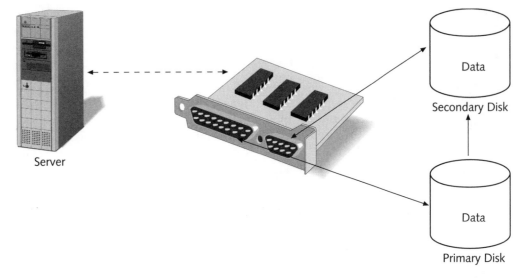

Figure 8-2

Disk mirroring

Server

Secondary Disk

Data

Primary Disk

Data

The backup drives can be on the same controller as the primary drives, or on a separate controller. Placing them on a separate controller creates an added level of redundancy or fault tolerance. If one controller fails, the remaining controller can take over. The use of a backup controller is called disk duplexing. Figure 8-3 shows a file server with a regular disk controller setup, and Figure 8-4 illustrates disk duplexing.

Figure 8-3

Regular disk configuration with one controller

Server

Data

Data

Figure 8-4

Disk duplexing with two controllers

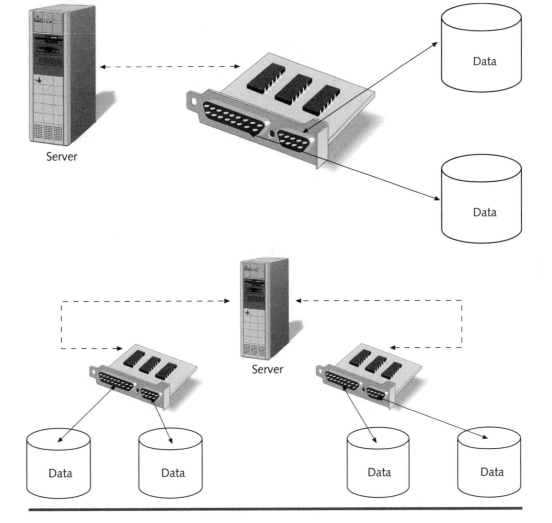

Server

Data   Data

Data   Data

RAID drives

RAID stands for Redundant Array of Inexpensive Disks. As the name suggests, multiple low-cost disks are employed to make the disk subsystem fault tolerant. There are six levels of RAID, as outlined in Table 8-6.

Although fault tolerance is particularly important for disks and disk controllers, equipment with redundant backplanes and power supplies also can be purchased. Various manufacturers of file servers, routers, hubs, and switches offer models with this redundancy built in. Cabletron, Cisco, and Bay Networks are examples of vendors who market fault-tolerant networking equipment.

Some equipment with built-in redundancy is designed to continue working when an equipment failure occurs. The defective power supply or backplane can be replaced without interruption of service to network users.

Fault tolerance can be purchased for CPUs on some types of file servers. Multi-processor computers are offered by manufacturers including IBM, Sequent, Hewlett-Packard, ALR, DEC, and others. The ability of the system to continue working after a CPU failure is dependent on the hardware architecture and the operating system.

Table 8-6

RAID levels of system fault tolerance

Level	Description
RAID Level 0	This is disk striping, a process by which data are spread over one or more volumes. Level 0 does not offer true fault tolerance, because if one disk volume fails, there is no automatic way to recover the lost data. The advantage of this approach is that the life of the disks is extended, since each disk houses less data. However, this advantage is quickly reduced as volumes fill up with more data over time.
RAID Level 1	Level 1 is the same as disk mirroring. All data files are replicated on two separate disks.
RAID Level 2	This level of fault tolerance combines disk striping with a method to store error correction data on the arrayed disks. If one disk fails, the remaining disks contain error correcting information that enables them to replicate the data on the failed disk.
RAID Level 3	This uses data striping as in levels 0 and 2. Level 3 employs data correction, but the information for data correction is stored on one disk. If that disk fails, its data cannot be rebuilt on the remaining disks.
RAID Level 4	In this level of fault tolerance, the disk subsystem strips data across the drives and stores data error correction information across the drives. It adds the capability of performing checksum integrity checks, with the checksum data stored on one of the drives in the array.
RAID Level 5	This level provides the best fault tolerance with data files, error correcting data, and checksums distributed across all drives in the array. Level 5 permits the network manager to "swap out" a failed drive without spinning down other drives. With this capability there is no interruption in service when a disk fails.

EQUIPMENT SPARES

Stocking extra equipment spares is another method to ensure "uptime" for your network components. Your spare equipment list may include disk drives, tape drives, disk controllers, bridges, routers, hub boards, and switch boards. It also should include network interface cards, cables, connectors, and terminators.

Part of your role as a network manager is to identify the critical file server and network operations, and plan to handle failures in these areas. For example, you might be responsible for two production servers and one test server. In this situation, you would want redundancy and spare parts for the production servers, but would be less concerned about the same service for the test server.

BUILDING FIREWALLS

Firewalls protect a network from intruders and reduce unwanted traffic. As network manager, for example, you might have a charge to protect the accounting system and payroll file server from being accessed by individuals outside the accounting department. You could restrict access by installing a firewall between the accounting office network segment and the rest of the network.

Routers are frequently used as firewalls, because they examine every packet before sending it on. The path through a router can be limited based on the local network address, subnet address, building address, and other IP addressing information.

If your network spans a large campus, or if it is connected to the Internet, router security may not be enough. For example, you might not be able to fine tune your router for adequate control over TCP-type protocols, such as FTP. An effective solution would be to install a device designed specifically to operate as a firewall. A dedicated firewall adds security options such as network address translation, logging, FTP management, SMTP proxy, HTTP proxy, network encryption, and virtual network encryption. These options are described in the following paragraphs.

- Network address translation: This is used to hide internal networks from view of the Internet. Knowledge of how to reach a particular node on your network is kept secret from Internet intruders. But communication to the Internet is unrestricted (or can be restricted if necessary) from your internal network nodes.

- Logging: The logging capability produces reports of intrusions so you can trace their origin. Some firewalls provide instant notification of intrusions.

- FTP management: A firewall can monitor all FTP sessions and the port number designated for a session. It can foil an intruder who is attempting to exploit FTP access by going through a port where he or she is not authorized. Firewalls also have FTP proxy. This feature enables the firewall to check an FTP session for Gets and Puts (send or receive a file). For example, it can be used to allow employees, but no one else, to transmit a file to a server from the Internet.

- SMTP proxy: A disadvantage of electronic mail is that header data often reveal information about the sender's network. When the message is sent, an intruder may intercept it and obtain sensitive network information. The SMTP proxy option enables you to remove this header data before the message leaves the firewall.

- HTTP proxy: Some firewalls have an HTTP proxy to protect World Wide Web (WWW or Web) applications. Through the HTTP proxy, only given users may access a specified Web page. If you work for a company that provides executive information reporting on the Web, HTTP proxy ensures that only the managers you designate can view the reports.

- Network encryption: Firewalls offer DES, proprietary, and other forms of data encryption for network-wide communications. Firewalls also may offer virtual or private network encryption. Virtual network encryption enables you to designate certain parts of the network for private communication exchanges. For example, you might be the network administrator at a college where the payroll office is across campus from the personnel office. Yet these offices frequently need to share confidential information and common database files. These network locations could be designated as a private network using specialized encryption not available to the wider network.

Network Systems Corporation, Harris Computer Systems, CheckPoint Software Technologies, and KarlNet are examples of manufacturers that offer firewalls. Network Systems Corporation and KarlNet provide systems (Security Router and KarlBridge) that combine firewall and router capabilities.

VIRUS MONITORING

There are three varieties of software that can damage workstation or server files: viruses, Trojan horses, and worms.

- Viruses are algorithms that replicate themselves, spreading into executable files, into the system file allocation table, and into partition tables. They can result in corrupted files, deleted information, and systems that no longer boot.

- A Trojan horse is code that accompanies seemingly innocent software. But it can trigger damaging activity based on a date or event, such as April Fool's day. Trojan horses also damage data and programs.

- Worms are programs that look for "back doors"—vulnerable entry points into a computer system. Once the worm gains access, it may grow or duplicate files until the system can no longer function.

One method used to protect against this damaging software trio is to scan all files before they are placed on a file server, or on workstations that connect to a file server. Another method is to constantly monitor the server for viruses. For example, virus scanning NetWare Loadable Materials (NLMs) are available for Novell file servers.

Wide area networks and the Internet have caused some particularly complex problems because viruses may by attached to e-mail or FTP files.

Some firewalls can be equipped with virus scanning software. This is an especially good solution if your network is home to high volume e-mail or FTP traffic. The firewall can scan for viruses and block them from entering the network.

DISASTER RECOVERY

Disasters don't happen often, but they do happen. Lightening can strike a telephone line and follow it through a modem to a computer. If the computer is networked to a file server, it may follow the network cable into the server. This happened to one community college, destroying a computer lab, network equipment, and a file server. Roofs have collapsed in computer machine rooms, and floods and hurricanes have destroyed computer equipment. In one instance, vandals fired rifles through an outside window, destroying computer systems inside a business building.

The network manager is responsible for having contingency plans in place should disaster strike. The most basic disaster recovery step is to have an offsite location to store backup tapes. This location may be a bank vault, a branch office, or some other secure location away from your point of operations.

Another important step is to formulate a disaster recovery plan. The plan should outline both onsite and offsite recovery options. On a college campus or in a business park, other onsite departments or businesses may have similar equipment. For example, if your IBM RS/6000 order-entry server is damaged, you may be able to temporarily place applications on a neighbor's RS/6000. However, if the entire business park is destroyed by flooding, your disaster recovery plan should include the ability to continue operations offsite.

Your disaster recovery plan should take into account all of the following possibilities:

- A damaged tape system that prevents making backups and restores
- Operating system problems that cannot be fixed immediately
- One or more damaged CPUs
- Multiple disks that cannot function
- Downed telecommunications systems
- A series of damaged backup tapes
- Regional power outages that can last for days
- Extensive electrical damage
- Major portions of a network that have been damaged or destroyed
- Nonfunctioning UPS systems
- Flooded tape vaults
- Natural disasters

If you do not have the resources within your organization for disaster recovery, you should consider hiring a company that specializes in this area. Disaster recovery specialists have computers, backup systems, networks, and Internet access that you can use to keep your operation going after a disaster.

After you have formulated a disaster recovery plan, it should be reviewed by key people within the organization. This step will ensure the plan matches the business needs and goals of the organization. Some organizations have their external auditors review their disaster recovery plan as part of the regular audit.

The plan also should be tested to identify any areas of weakness or contingencies that have been missed. If your plan calls for help from a business neighbor or from a recovery specialist, go through a dry run as part of your test.

Companies have gone out of business because they were not prepared to face disasters that wiped out computer systems and networks.

NETWORK PRINT SERVICES

Before networks became a reality, there were two common ways to obtain printouts. One method was to send your printout to a central computer, such as a mainframe. The printout was sent to a printer directly connected to the mainframe, and you picked up the printout in a central operations area. The other method was to purchase a printer for every PC in your office area. Figure 8-5 illustrates these methods.

Networking has made possible printer sharing and printout distribution. Printer sharing is accomplished by installing **print servers** at key locations on the network. Network operating systems such as UNIX, Novell, and Microsoft NT support the use of print servers.

One way to establish a print server is to purchase software that turns a networked PC into a print server. Print requests are sent to that PC, which generates printouts on its direct-connected printers. This method has limitations in that the print server PC may also be doubling as someone's workstation. The workstation owner has to be prepared for interruptions as people come over for their printouts. Another disadvantage is that some PC-based print server software uses terminate-and-stay resident (TSR) programs (programs that stay in memory) in the server and the client. TSRs create memory contention, and if problems occur, they may "hang up" the host PC.

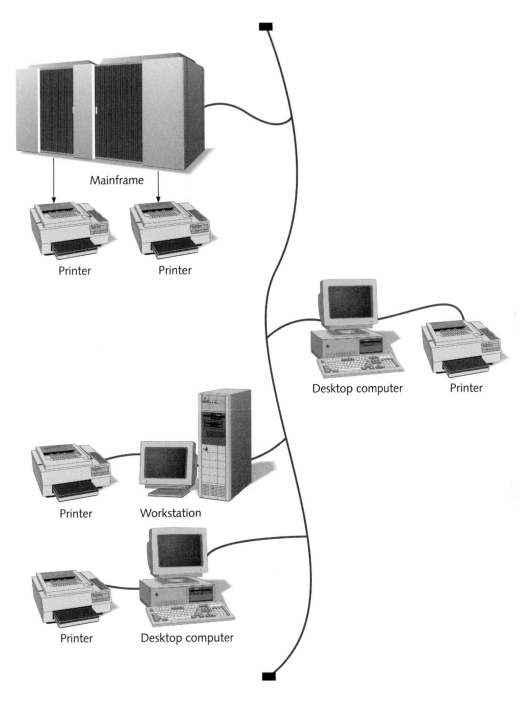

Figure 8-5

Printers directly connected to a mainframe and PCs

Mainframe

Printer   Printer

Desktop computer   Printer

Printer   Workstation

Printer   Desktop computer

A more reliable way to provide network printing is to use dedicated print servers. These are available in stand-alone units, or as cards that can be installed in the shared printer. Intel, Lantronics, and other manufacturers offer stand-alone devices (see Figure 8-6). Some print servers can support two or more printers. Manufacturers such as Hewlett-Packard offer printers with internal print server cards.

Figure 8-6

Stand-alone
print server

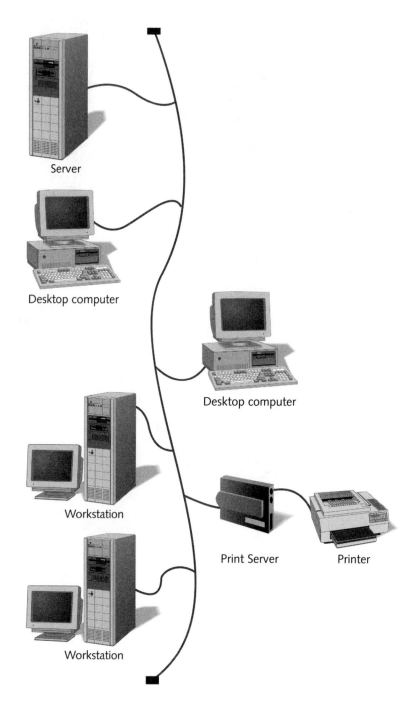

Server

Desktop computer

Desktop computer

Workstation

Print Server   Printer

Workstation

As is true for any node on the network, the print server has a unique Ethernet address. Print servers come with software that enables you to set up print functions and associate the print server with designated print queues.

DISK SHARING SERVICES

Network-aware operating systems such as Microsoft Windows, Microsoft NT, and UNIX allow the network administrator and network users to share disk volumes and directories. CD-ROM drives also can be shared on a network.

For example, you can share a subdirectory or all of the files on a disk drive from a single networked Microsoft Windows 95 workstation. You do this by selecting the *My Computer* icon. From there, you highlight a folder or subdirectory to share. Next select the *File* option from the toolbar and select *Properties* from the drop-down box. The properties option has a selection tab for file sharing. You can share files on your disk with selected users or with everyone on the network. This example shows how easy workstation disk sharing has become on networks. When the concept was introduced several years ago, it was necessary to perform extensive software setup on a server and at each workstation to share a disk.

Some network managers have installed arrays of shared CD-ROMs to enable their customers to run or load software from the network. This is accomplished by purchasing CD-ROM management software and the appropriate site licenses for the software that is shared. Some examples of shared CD-ROM software include dictionaries, encyclopedias, clip art libraries, and computer documentation. Products such as Microsoft Office are available with site licensing agreements, so they can be loaded from a shared CD-ROM or subdirectory.

SUMMARY

Responsibility for a network includes understanding the issues central to network management. For example, when you install network equipment, you need a way to monitor network activity using that equipment. Bridges, routers, and other devices should be SNMP-compliant for network monitoring.

Network security is another important management function. Security includes a wide range of issues. It involves establishing access rights to servers and to host computers. It includes providing reliable power and redundant hardware systems. Firewalls are important for protection against intruders. Virus monitoring and disaster recovery are important to ensure the long-term viability of your systems.

All the steps you take for network management need to achieve two important goals. The first goal is to protect the data on your network. This might include data such as research results, sales data, payroll data, publications, or personal spreadsheets. The second goal is to keep your network reliable. As soon as you install a network, demand for its services will escalate beyond your expectations. It will be your job to ensure that the network rarely fails and can grow to meet the demand.

KEY TERMS

Term/Acronym	Definition
Database Administrator (DBA)	This type of account exists on host and file server computers that house a database. The DBA has master security privileges for all levels of the database.
Data Encryption Standard	A network data encryption standard developed by the National Institute of Standards and Technology and IBM.
Defragmentation	Disk defragmentation is a process that rearranges data to fill in the empty spaces that develop on disks and make data easier to obtain.
Encryption Key	When data are encrypted on a network, some encryption methods use a password that must be known to both the sending and receiving nodes. The password acts as a key to unlock files.
File-By-File Backup	Most backups are performed to save data by file, rather than by binary image. File-by-file backups enable restores of single files, multiple files, subdirectories, directories, and complete volumes.
Image Backup	This type of backup uses a process that takes a "snapshot" of the entire contents of a disk or volume. Image backups are stored in binary format.
Network Management Station (NMS)	This workstation is a central device that gathers, tracks, and stores network performance data. It obtains the data from network equipment that runs agent software for collecting the data.
Network Agents	Repeaters, bridges, routers and other network devices become agents when they are equipped to gather network performance information.
Print Server	This device enables one or more people to send printouts to a network printer.
Power Filter	This device ensures that clean power is delivered to attached electrical equipment. It smooths out power "bumps" and delivers a constant level of power.

RAID	This stands for a Redundant Array of Inexpensive Disks, designed to provide data protection when a disk failure occurs.
Surge Protector	Lighting strikes, power plant difficulties, and other situations can result in temporary dramatic surges in electric power. The surge protector prevents these surges from damaging sensitive equipment, such as computer equipment.
System Administrator (SA)	A database system account type that has master security access to all databases on a server.
System Fault Tolerance	This involves building in duplicate portions of a system or designing systems to withstand hardware or software failures.
Uninterruptible Power Supply (UPS)	This device consists of a bank of rechargeable batteries that deliver power when the central source of power is down.
User Datagram Protocol (UDP)	The data transmitted from a network device, such as a router, to the network management station are encapsulated in this protocol.

REVIEW EXERCISES

1. Assume your file server is used to store personnel and payroll information that is frequently updated each day. How often would you defragment its disk? Why?

2. You are contacting vendors about purchasing a new router. Some vendors support SNMP and others support CMIP. Which vendor would you choose? Why?

3. What is MIB? How is it used?

4. Describe four areas to consider when you establish password protection on a network.

5. What is private-key data encryption?

6. What is the function of a power filter?

7. How is a system administrator different from a database administrator?

8. There are _____ levels of RAID. Please explain each level.

9. How does a firewall work? If you have a network that is connected to the Internet, where would you put a firewall?

10. How are viruses transmitted through the Internet?

11. When your backup drives are placed on a separate controller, this is called

    _____.

12. _____ is used to protect sensitive address information that may be sent through e-mail.

13. Assume you manage a network with one administrative server for business functions, such as accounting, human resources, payroll, and sales tracking. Develop a backup scheme for this server.

14. A _____ gathers data for the network management station.

15. Where is a component failure most likely to occur?

NETWORK MANAGEMENT: TAKING CONTROL

A good network manager is proactive instead of reactive. Anticipating your organization's demands on the network is an important step in meeting its needs. You will be a more effective manager when you keep close track of the existing network load in all types of situations. If you have successfully designed your network, the load will increase as more people grow to trust the computing resources you have helped to provide.

This chapter describes areas where network load occurs, and it presents ideas on how to monitor the load, such as tracking performance information.

Another way to be proactive is to implement network management tools. In this chapter we illustrate what network tools can do by describing two software packages for network management.

Most importantly, you will need to learn to be an effective planner in order to take control of your network. We conclude by describing five ways to plan into the future.

AFTER READING THIS CHAPTER YOU WILL BE ABLE TO:

- DESCRIBE THE SOURCES OF NETWORK LOAD
- DETERMINE HOW TO GATHER INFORMATION ON NETWORK LOAD
- DESCRIBE THE FUNCTIONS OF NETWORK MANAGEMENT SOFTWARE
- SHOW HOW PLANNING IMPACTS NETWORK MANAGEMENT

NETWORK LOAD

There is a saying in the computer world that "You can never have too much bandwidth." At every stage of growth and design, you must weigh the needs of network users against the ability of the network to handle the workload. Each new user and each new application places more demand on the network's capabilities. The network load can be divided into major categories, including the following:

- Workstation load

- Server load

- Host load

- Software load

- Client/server applications

- Network printing

- Configuration of the network management system

- Capacity management

- Intelligent network device load

Each of these areas is discussed in the sections that follow.

WORKSTATION LOAD

Managing the growth of a network involves keeping a record of when a new workstation is added to a network segment. More workstations mean more network traffic.

Not all workstations on a network are equal. For example, a Sun Microsystems' SPARCstation for scientific use will place more demand on a network than a Pentium-based PC with Microsoft Windows 95. A high speed 32-bit NIC with cache creates more network traffic than a slower 8-bit NIC with no cache.

The software drivers that a workstation uses to transmit to the network also affect network load. There are two types of drivers involved on workstations. One is the driver or "shell" used to communicate with network servers. For example, Novell uses ODI drivers (for networks using IPX and TCP/IP) or IPX/NETX drivers. The ODI drivers can produce more network load than the simpler IPX/NETX drivers. Workstations can also use a NIC driver for communicating on the network. Each NIC vendor writes drivers for their card. The network load created by NIC drivers varies by manufacturer.

Some organizations permit network users and departments to install their own workstations. The disadvantage of this practice is that the organization's network manager, especially with a large network, may not be able to track where growth is occurring. Also, with customers installing their own nodes, occasionally segment lengths are extended beyond the IEEE standards for guaranteed communications. Inappropriate cabling or connectors may be installed, or terminators may be removed from the end of the segment.

One solution to tracking workstation load is to keep an inventory of every workstation that is connected to the network. Some software packages automatically poll each network workstation (and other network devices) to create an automatic inventory. These packages can determine the type of workstation and information about the NIC used by the workstation. They also show the network location of each workstation. For example, Hewlett-Packard's OpenView and Sun's Solstice software are two packages with workstation monitoring capability. These packages are discussed later in this chapter.

SERVER LOAD

Like workstations, not all file servers on the network are equal. The file server elements that affect network load include the server operating system (NOS), the type of server, and how the server is used. For example, the server operating system has an influence on network load at several levels. One level is related to how often the NOS broadcasts its presence on the network. These broadcasts occur in the form of **Server Advertising Packets (SAP)**. The server also may **ping** (test for the presence of) nodes on the network to determine how to route data. A server does this by sending RIP (see Chapter 5) broadcasts. (We don't recommend using server routing because it creates unnecessary network traffic.) Another level is the network driver or shell used by the NOS to communicate with its workstations. A third level is the protocol used by the server. For example, NetWare uses IPX/SPX, and Microsoft NT uses NetBEUI. Both types of servers can generate more network traffic than a TCP/IP UNIX server.

The type of server is important to network load in terms of the server's capacity and speed. A single-processor server with one NIC will create a much lighter load than a quad-processor server with four NICs connected to the network. As is true for workstations, the speed of the server NICs and NIC drivers can influence network load.

How much a server is used is of particular importance. For instance, compare two types of servers: One is a NetWare server with a NOS license limit of 100 concurrent users and an average of 70 users. The other is a Microsoft NT server licensed for 400 users, which has an average of 325 users at one time. As you might guess, the Microsoft server will create more network traffic.

Network management requires planning before a server is installed on a network. First determine your baseline data for network performance. Before you permanently install the server and make it available, run some network tests to determine how much the server will increase network traffic. This will help you determine if you need to adjust the network load or install more bandwidth, such as through an FDDI ring or an ATM switch.

HOST LOAD

Hosts such as mainframes, minicomputers, and multi-user workstations create network load in the same way as servers. The capacity of the host operating system and of the attached NICs are important factors to weigh. Like the file server example, a mainframe that can host 500 concurrent users creates more network load than one that hosts 150 concurrent users. The number of NICs, their speed, and the NIC drivers also have an impact.

Host manufacturers may have some benchmark statistics that you can obtain to determine the load their products will create. Also, as you would do for a server, test the network load created by a host computer before you make it a permanent network resident. (As we discuss in Chapter 10, a protocol analyzer can be used to test network load.)

SOFTWARE LOAD

The software that travels on your network has a dramatic impact on load. Certain types of software are far more likely to increase network load than others. Again, compare two file servers: One server is used for word processing applications and spreadsheets. Another is used by architects for CAD applications. The word processing and spreadsheet files will not create as much network load as the CAD files. In both cases, the client workstation must make a request to the server to ship the files to the workstation. On the first server, it will send a word processing or spreadsheet application to run on the workstation. Next, it will send the data files to the workstation. The same process happens with the CAD application, but the files can be several times larger than the word processing files.

Some database systems create more load than others in networked applications. For example, compare an application written in Microsoft Access to one written in Microsoft SQL Server. Both application databases are 10-MB in size. Both have 10 users on average. Each time an Access user starts the application, the server sends the entire 10-MB database to the client workstation. When the SQL Server-based application is used, the database sends only the specific rows of information needed, such as 20 KB, not the entire database. Thus, the network with Access will experience far more load than the network with SQL Server.

CLIENT/SERVER APPLICATIONS

Client/server applications are designed to use processing resources where they can be accomplished most efficiently. In some instances the client workstation is the best processing candidate, such as for determining payroll calculations. In other instances the server database is the best candidate, such as for processing a large report from a predefined database view.

Unfortunately, not all client/server software is designed to make the most of available processing resources. Some applications, which send much of the processing work to the client, are known as **fat client** software. These systems can dramatically increase network traffic since large amounts of data have to be shipped to the client. True **thin client** systems are more desirable from the network load point of view. They ship less data across the network and are more efficient than fat client systems.

Client/server systems often enable computer users to have better access to data for creating reports. Some of these systems require the organization to maintain a reporting database on a separate server from the one used to update and process data. The data in the reporting database are updated from the main server on a regular basis, such as once a day. Since this update is shipped over the network, it can result in very heavy network traffic. Many organizations perform these updates at night to reduce the network impact.

When your organization decides to develop or purchase a new client/server system, it is important to determine how many people will be using it concurrently. Study the business or use patterns created by the system. For example, an electronic time card system will create high levels of traffic on the days when employees are completing their time cards.

The purchase of a new client/server system also may be accompanied by organization-wide upgrades or new purchases of workstations to serve as clients. This is another load factor to anticipate in order to be prepared for the increased network load.

NETWORK PRINTING

Print services increase the network load as they become more distributed throughout the network by using print servers. Each hardware-based print server counts as a network node and sends SAP polling information (to check for waiting print jobs) onto the network. Some print servers broadcast SAPs every two seconds and do not have an option to change the broadcast frequency. If you have a large number of these servers on your network, they may create a high network load.

Another load created by network printing is related to the types of files printed. Desktop publishing and complex graphics files are large and create more network load than smaller word processing files. As you plan for network growth, factor in the anticipated printing needs for each part of your organization.

CONFIGURATION OF THE NETWORK MANAGEMENT SYSTEM

Automated network management systems monitor portions of the network by using polling devices. They may poll workstations, servers, bridges, routers, and other equipment. The network manager has the option to establish different levels of polling. As network manger, you should check the vendor's recommendations on polling frequency. If you set up the software to poll continuously, this will cause very high network traffic. Experiment with polling levels to determine how frequently your software can poll without causing network problems.

CAPACITY MANAGEMENT

Growth on a network can occur at an explosive pace. Your best defense is to anticipate growth by keeping in touch with the evolving needs of network users. As you assess their needs, you will need to calculate the impact on existing resources. This process is called **capacity management**. Originally, computer systems capacity management focused only on keeping pace with demands for disk space. In network management, there are several areas that apply to capacity management. These areas include the following:

- Disk capacity
- CPU capacity
- Increases in network traffic
- Growth in number of users on the network
- New software applications
- New servers and hosts

Disk capacity remains a significant growth issue. One way to plan for the future is to keep statistics on disk usage growth. Establish spreadsheets or databases to show how your organization's disk space is presently allocated. Once you have baseline information, track the growth each month. Create formulas to show how specific areas are growing or shrinking over time. Use the table or graph functions in your spreadsheet or database software to display the information so it is easy to interpret. Tracking disk allocation growth in this manner will enable you to make projections on when to purchase new disks for servers and hosts.

The implementation of new software, such as client/server applications, has an impact on disk capacity planning as well as on network traffic. Work to understand the business needs of your organization so you will know how the software is to be used. This will enable you to determine if new disk drives must be purchased, and if network equipment needs to be added or upgraded.

As mentioned earlier, the addition of new servers and new hosts will very likely increase network traffic, as more users connect to the network. The process of buying new servers or hosts should include a determination of how many people will be using these systems. This also is the time to address network capacity issues for the new equipment. Will you need to change the existing network configuration? Will network equipment upgrades be required to handle the load? Will more offices require network connectivity?

CPU performance is another capacity planning issue. When a server or host is placed on the network, it may not take long for the demand on the computer to outpace the capacity of the CPU. Some organizations address this issue by purchasing equipment that can be expanded as needs grow. If the CPU is overloaded, they simply add one or more additional CPUs.

In most instances, network performance and the performance of computers attached to the network are viewed as interconnected. Growth in one area impacts growth in the other, and performance in one area affects performance in the other.

INTELLIGENT NETWORK DEVICE LOAD

As we discussed in Chapter 5, intelligent network devices, such as routers and hubs, create transmissions to poll the network. These transmissions are used to obtain information about changes, new equipment, the best transmission routes, and so on. For example, a router uses RIP broadcasts to poll the network. This yields important information. But it is up to you as the network manager to configure routers and other intelligent devices so they do not flood the network with requests for information. If your routers and hubs all are configured to poll with high frequency, the resulting network traffic can cause problems.

Increased network load also can result when there are multiple bridges on the network. If two or more bridges are configured as root bridges (see Chapter 5), the result is that too many BPDUs are broadcast. As network manager, you need to ensure that only one bridge is set up as the root. (See Table 9-1 for a summary of network load sources.)

Table 9-1

Summary of network load sources

Load Source	Factors Causing the Load
Workstations	NICs, network drivers, NOS shell
Servers	NICs, network drivers, NOS, SAPs, RIPs, server capacity, protocols in use
Hosts	NICs, network drivers, host operating system, capacity of host, protocols in use
Software	Size of files required, adaptation for network use
Client/server Applications	Network efficiency design, fat client vs. thin client, reporting design, user capacity
Network Printing	Number of print servers, SAP broadcasts, print file sizes
Network Management System	Data collection and polling configuration
Capacity Management	Addition of new servers, new software, more clients
Intelligent Network Devices	Polling frequencies, RIPs, BPDUs, configuration

COLLECTING BASELINE DATA

To determine how network demand is growing, you will need to establish baseline data on network performance. You can do this by collecting data about the network at a designated baseline starting point. It is useful to collect data at an anticipated peak period and at a period of normal activity. Continue to collect data for the peak and normal periods at regular intervals, such as once a week. Chart the data over time in graphs so you can observe how the load is changing.

There are several forms of data on network performance that can be useful to chart (see Table 9-2). These include network utilization, server utilization, error rates, number of packets transported, and the network transfer speeds. Network monitoring devices and network management packages can provide these statistics for you to track. We will discuss network monitoring devices in Chapter 10. Network management software is discussed later in this chapter.

Network utilization is calculated as the amount of bandwidth in use as a percentage of the total volume of transported data, measured in kilobytes. For example, the baseline network utilization might be 5 to 10 percent for normal activity periods and 30 percent for peak activity periods. If these figures climb to 40 percent for normal activity and 60 percent for peak activity, it may be time to consider segmenting the network.

One method for monitoring server utilization is to gather data on the number of *request being processed* packets. These packets are sent from the server to the requesting workstation when the server is too busy to process the request. An increase in the number of these packets reflects an increase in demand for that server. If the number of these packets increases dramatically, it may be time to add another NIC to the server or add more CPU power.

It is a good practice to identify the busiest servers and closely monitor the network load they create. As you increase a server's capacity to handle requests, you may want to segment the network to match the increasing load.

Network error rates include the number of packet collisions, incorrectly constructed packets, incomplete packets, and short packets ("runts"). An increase in error rates can mean that a bottleneck is developing because of network growth. It also can mean that there is a network problem, such as a defective terminator, to be corrected. If the error rates increase along with network utilization, this is an indication that the load is increasing.

The number of packets transported per second is a measure of network activity that supplements the network utilization statistics. Both numbers increase as the network load increases.

Network transfer speeds reflect how quickly a packet can reach its destination. If you have a 10-Mbps Ethernet network, this does not mean that packets are traveling at 10 Mbps. The normal transfer speed on the network will be considerably lower than optimum, because of time for recovery from collisions and other factors. Once you establish the baseline transfer speeds on your network, you will be able to tell when the network is congested or when there is a network problem. These conditions will be reflected in below normal transfer speeds for the network.

Table 9-2

Network performance
information
gathering

Network Performance Data
Network utilization
Server utilization
Error rates
Number of packets transmitted
Network transfer speed

As you gather performance statistics over time, trends will become more familiar to you, and it will become easier to distinguish network equipment problems from growth. The statistics will enable you to better diagnose server problems, NIC problems, and areas where bottlenecks are occurring.

MULTIPLE PROTOCOLS ON THE SAME NETWORK

Many network installations have a combination of file servers and host computers. A university might have an IBM mainframe computer, Microsoft NT servers, Novell NetWare servers, and other computers. A corporation might have a combination of IBM RS/6000 servers, NT servers, and DEC Alpha computers. In the first instance, the network would need to support TCP/IP, NetBEUI, IPX/SPX, and possibly SNA (for IBM communications). In the corporation example, the network would need to transport TCP/IP and NetBEUI (as illustrated in Figure 9-1.)

Figure 9-1

Corporate
network with
TCP/IP and
NetBEUI
protocols

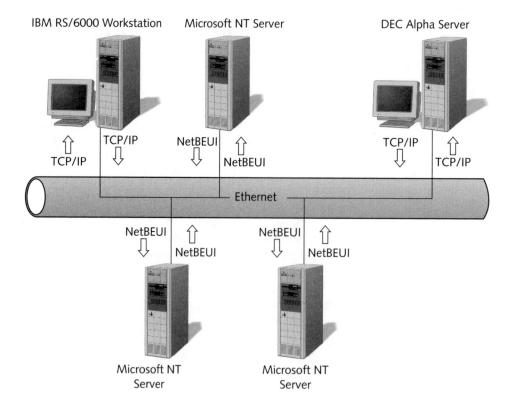

Multiple protocols can operate on the same network without performance degradation. If you have baseline data and regularly collect performance data, you will be able to track the network load on a network with multiple protocols. To track performance, you will need analysis tools that collect data on all the protocols you support. These tools are available through network management systems and the use of protocol analyzers. Network management tools are discussed in the next section of this chapter. Protocol analyzers are discussed in Chapter 10.

If there are routers on your network, it will be necessary to decide which protocols to route. This can be a network load issue, depending on where the protocols are routed. It also is a cost issue. You will need to purchase software for each protocol that is routed. The protocol routing software can be as expensive as the router. Another problem is associated with the use of NetBEUI on a router-based network. NetBEUI cannot be routed, so you will need to take this into account as you design the network. (NetBEUI must be bridged which creates increased load on router CPUs and router bridging tables.)

NETWORK MANAGEMENT TOOLS

There are several network management tools available that provide a range of services. For example, they can monitor network nodes such as repeaters, routers, bridges, hubs, workstations, servers, and hosts. If a router is down, the software graphically displays this condition and may sound an alarm to the network management station. Some management packages have the ability to reboot the router from the NMS. These packages can monitor network traffic and provide analysis of traffic based on the data collected by intelligent nodes, such as routers and hubs.

Some management packages are designed to be modular, so specific functions can be added as your network needs grow. Modules can be added that manage domain name services, user accounts, e-mail services, backup and restore services, file server configuration, printer services, and telecommunication services. Figure 9-2 illustrates how these modules are used within a main management module to compose an integrated network management software package.

Figure 9-2

Modular network management systems

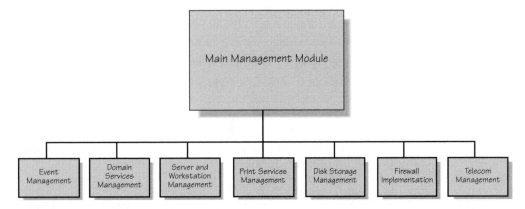

In the next section, we describe two network management packages: Hewlett-Packard's OpenView and Sun Microsystems' Solstice. Both packages offer a range of management services through optional modules, including some available from third-party vendors. We discuss these packages to illustrate how some of the management issues discussed in this chapter and in Chapter 8 can be concretely addressed. Both packages give the network manager a way to take control of network management.

HEWLETT-PACKARD OPENVIEW

OpenView is a modular product that provides network management, systems management, peripherals management, and telecommunications management. OpenView has a customer base of over 70,000 installations and runs under UNIX on workstations such as the Hewlett-Packard 9000 or a Sun SPARCstation. It has a graphical user interface (GUI) with support for Hewlett-Packard's X Windows, Sun's OpenWindows, or third party OSF/Motif's Window Manager. There also is a version of OpenView adapted for PC-based networks, which runs under Microsoft Windows on 80486 and Pentium workstations.

Network and System Management

The Network Node Manager is the main module for OpenView. This module supports TCP/IP and SNMP. It has a discovery capability that enables it to produce a graphical map of network nodes. After it has located nodes, it can monitor devices across the network. The software indicates the operational states of network devices by displaying them in different colors. For example, a device that is malfunctioning can be displayed in red.

Network Node Manager comes with an Event Browser that enables you to set up filters to capture network events. A filter can capture the source of the event (such as a router), the message, the time and date, and the severity of the problem. Event categories can be established so they are prioritized for the network manager. For example, a router that is "down" can be given a higher priority than a partitioned segment containing a single node.

Another capability is data collection of real-time and historical network information. For example, you can compare the present activity of a router with historical activity. This enables you to judge differences between normal and peak times.

On very large networks, up to 15 operators can be defined so the management load is distributed from the NMS. Each operator is assigned a view of the network that is related to his or her particular area to maintain. This capability might be used for a wide-area network where there are extensions of the network in remote parts of the same town, such as a college campus with satellite stations in high schools for evening classes.

Hewlett-Packard has a module for Network Node Manager called Node Manager for NetWare, that can be used to extend management to Novell NetWare-based networks. This software includes a NetWare Loadable Module (NLM) to run on the NetWare servers. The NLM monitors server performance including CPU load, number of users, disk usage, memory, and cache. By using SNMP traps, it can provide warning of problem events, such as too many users, security violations, CPU overload, disk volume dismounted, cache limit exceeded, and NLM unloaded.

The Node Manager for NetWare also provides central management of server administration. User accounts can be added or deleted, passwords can be changed, security rights can be modified, print queues can be managed, server commands can be executed remotely, and messages can be broadcast.

With the addition of the Station Manager software, NetWare client workstations can be monitored for problems. An inventory of all workstations can be taken to show processor types, memory mapping, network drivers in use, disk usage, and other information.

Another module that can be added to the Network Node Manager is the AdminCenter. The AdminCenter keeps a database of all objects on the network. Objects include systems (servers and network equipment), users, software, and peripherals. Through automatic discovery, this software can update the database at regular intervals to reflect changes. A history of objects is kept for later reference. One advantage of this software is the ability to perform **change management**. This is a record-keeping process used to track all changes on a network and all changes in software installations. If a network or software problem occurs, change management makes it possible for the network manager to review all recent changes. The problem then can be traced to a single change, such as installation of a new bridge. If the problem is related to a software upgrade, change management enables you to revert to using the previous version.

The OmniBack II module of OpenView is used for administration of organization-wide backups and restores. Backups can be arranged for different types of situations depending on the organization's needs. Backup "domains" are established for each type of backup. For example, one domain might be established for a group of servers. Another domain might be established for a specific workgroup of PC workstation users. The first domain might include a combination of incremental and full backups. In the second domain, specified PCs might be backed up each Wednesday and Friday evening. OmniBack II can be set up to use self-loading tape drives, so that backups occur at a specified time without human intervention.

OmniBack II can be scaled to very large network operations. Over 125 nodes can be backed up in one domain, using as many as 25 backup devices at the same time. Hewlett-Packard tests indicate that 25 GB can be backed up on a high-speed network.

The OpenView Software Distributor enables you to control installation of software across the network. Software can be distributed from one central repository ("depot"), from multiple depots, or from specified distribution points on a network. For example, assume your network is divided into workgroups. One workgroups uses Microsoft Office products. Another workgroup uses Borland products. With the Software Distributor, separate depots could be established for each workgroup to make the appropriate software available. One advantage to managed software distribution is that all users are working with the same version of software at the same time. This eliminates the difficulty of supporting multiple software versions and it creates more opportunities for sharing files.

Peripherals Management

OpenView has modules that enable you to manage key peripherals such as disk services and print services. One such module, OmniStorage provides client/server hierarchical storage management. OmniStorage spreads data across magnetic, optical, and tape storage facilities. For instance, in most businesses the current fiscal year's accounting data are accessed frequently and would be stored on the accounting server's hard drives. When the fiscal year is closed out, that data could be automatically compressed and migrated to an optical disk for future reference.

Software like OmniStorage can provide disk capacity management, by automatically storing data where it can be kept most economically. Data are migrated from expensive magnetic media to less-expensive tapes or CD-ROMs. In the process, critical hard drive space is freed for immediate production use.

Another peripherals management option is OpenSpool. This software provides centralized management of network print services. OpenSpool allows you to configure all network printers, print queues, printer forms, plotters, and font options from one place. Printer or print queue errors are trapped and displayed on print status screens. They also can be reported by e-mail.

With OpenSpool, specific print management functions are distributed to the responsible people. For example, the administrative assistant in a department may have the responsibility of managing print requests to that department's central laser printer. A view can be created so he or she is able to manage only the printouts directed to that printer. If a certain print request is printing one character per page by mistake, the administrative assistant can cancel the printout to conserve paper.

Telecommunications Management

Hewlett-Packard has created options for systems integrators and telecommunications equipment manufacturers to build telecommunications management software into OpenView. This enables network management and telecommunications management software to have the same look and feel in one package. Hewlett-Packard has taken this approach because network management and telecommunications management are closely related services and often are managed from the same information technology department.

SOLSTICE SUNNET MANAGER

Sun Microsystems's network management software is called Solstice. This software comes in two versions, based on the size of the network to be managed. Solstice Site Manager is used for small networks (100 nodes or less). For large multi-vendor networks, Sun offers the Solstice Domain Manager. Site Manager is scalable, so it can be converted to Domain Manager as the network becomes larger. Solstice runs under the Sun Solaris version of UNIX. It can be operated from a Sun SPARCstation or from a Pentium-based PC using Solaris. As with OpenView, Solstice has modules that can be added for specific management purposes.

Solstice is compatible with SNMP and with TCP/IP. It also comes with the option to add third-party software. For example, a module can be added to monitor Novell-based networks.

Network and System Management

Similar to OpenView, Solstice has the ability to learn all SNMP entities on the network. Since this can create extra network traffic, the process can be scheduled to occur regularly each night, so the network management display of individual network nodes is kept accurate. The display, called the Topology Map Display, shows servers, workstations, hubs, and other network elements.

Event Management

Advanced Event Management software comes with both Site Manager and Domain Manager versions. Event requests are built by the network manager to gather data from network elements, including repeaters, routers, bridges, servers, and hosts. Events can be defined to inform the network manager if equipment goes down, or to capture any other significant event. Some examples of events include a network segment with abnormally high traffic, a file server with high CPU usage, or a host that is sending too many short packets. (Note that the ability to monitor events is limited by the type of equipment on the network and the SNMP compliance of that equipment.)

Each event type can be given a priority by constructing a filter for an SNMP trap. For example, if you are trapping error conditions issued from a payroll server, you may be interested in monitoring print server traffic during the time payroll checks are being printed. A high priority could be given to errors indicating printing problems. An alarm can be set up to provide you with immediate notification when a printing problem occurs. If an alarm condition occurs, Solstice can display in red (or some other predefined color) a graphic image of the device that is having problems. Alarm reports can be generated to help diagnose network problems. For example, if you have narrowed a problem to a workstation NIC and a particular server NIC, the alarm report information will help provide detailed information about the errors occurring at both NICs.

Optivity

The display of network activity can supplemented by adding third-party software, such as Optivity from Bay Networks. There are three Optivity network management applications: Optivity LAN, Optivity Internetwork, and Optivity Design.

Optivity LAN is a set of management tools for managing LANs composed of hubs and frame switches. Optivity LAN can discover network entities that have the Network Management Modules (NMMs) installed on hubs, switches, and other intelligent network devices. Other entities, such as workstations and servers, can be manually added to the system.

Optivity LAN enables you to create graphical views of the network that can be divided into campuses or regions. For example, if your organization has an enterprise-wide network with installations in New York, Los Angeles, and St. Louis, Optivity can display separate views of each regional network. Folders can be created that show the resources in each view, such as hubs, routers, switches, subnets, LANs, and WANs.

Optivity LAN comes with an Enterprise Health Advisor, which traps predefined events in status panels. The status panels show colored icons for devices in critical status, warning status, caution status, acknowledge status, and operational status. The status levels are listed on a continuum, with critical status being most urgent and operational status being normal.

Another product, Optivity Internetwork, is a group of management tools designed for router-based networks. It also includes a network discovery capability and the Enterprise Health Advisor. Design and Analysis is a third tool that is used to help establish network growth trends and to design network additions.

ManageWise

Novell's ManageWise is another type of third-party software that can be used with Solstice. ManageWise is used to create a view of PC workstations connected to NetWare file servers. Another Novell tool, NetWare Management Agent, can be added to manage NetWare servers and workstations from the NMS. Management Agent is an SNMP agent installed on NetWare servers. It is connected to the network by means of an IP gateway.

Solstice AdminSuite

The AdminSuite is a tool set for administering Sun Solaris UNIX clients and hosts connected to the network. This tool is used for host management, workgroup management, account management, print services management, storage management, and software usage management. The host management portion of the software enables you to connect client systems to a host. For example, you may need to connect a diskless UNIX workstation to a host UNIX system for operation. AdminSuite is designed to automate the connection process to match the specific setups used by your organization.

Many operating systems enable you to establish workgroups for users who share software systems, such as an administrative office workgroup. People in a workgroup might share certain types of applications software and database information. The AdminSuite enables you to create workgroups and modify the users in each workgroup.

Account management automates the procedures for establishing user accounts. It enables the addition or deletion of users, creation of password policies, creation of log-in shells, and creation of home directories. For example, if you require that all users on a server have passwords over eight characters, AdminSuite can ensure that this requirement is automatically specified when an account is created.

Printer services such as creation of print queues, management of queues, and management of print servers can be handled through AdminSuite. Disk services also are handled through file system management. Storage can be divided into disk slices or UNIX disk partitions. Files are directed to the appropriate disk through the file system management. Solstice's software monitoring enables you to determine the usage levels, so you have information for capacity management decisions, such as when to purchase more disk storage.

Storage Protection

A Solstice add-on called DiskSuite provides insurance against disk failures for UNIX systems on the network. DiskSuite offers RAID protection for levels 0, 1, and 5. As added protection, it has journaling features. **Journals** are backup files that log new data transactions. If a transaction file is damaged or corrupted, the new transactions can be reconstructed from the journal files. Journals also can be mirrored for extra protection on critical volumes. With journaling, Sun estimates that data recovery can occur at a rate of 10 sec/GB. This eliminates the need to use *fsck* (the data recovery process) in UNIX, which can take 10 minutes or more per gigabyte.

FireWall

TCP/IP firewall protection is available with Solstice FireWall. FireWall enables you to create virtual private networks for security against intruders. The software also provides data encryption and IP address translation to keep internal network address information from the Internet. A Client Authentication component is used to control which individuals have access to applications on network clients and servers.

EFFECTIVE NETWORK MANAGEMENT

OpenView and Solstice have many other components that are not discussed in this chapter. The reason for presenting information on these management packages is to show that some functions of network management can be automated to make you a more effective network manager. For example, when you need to install four print servers in a location, your work will go faster if you have automated the queue setup.

Management software can help you view your network in a comprehensive fashion, so you can see beyond the individual parts. This enables you to plan for growth and address problem areas. Management software also helps you create smaller views of the network, so you can focus on individual situations, such as the existence of too many nodes on a segment.

As your network grows, so does the need for more people to help with network management tasks. This is another area where management software can help. Network management tasks can be delegated to night network operators, assistants with assigned network areas, and remote area network coordinators. Specific network views can be created for each person to reflect their area of responsibility.

PLANNING

The most powerful tool you have as a network manager is your ability to plan. Planning can be performed at all stages of network operation. The following are some planning areas that will help ensure that your network stays healthy:

- Know the business needs of your organization.

- Schedule network activities.

- Test new equipment.

- Know your performance statistics.

- Manage growth based on your resources.

Today's network manager has to stay current on the business needs of his or her organization. This involves developing an understanding of important cycles, such as the beginning of the fiscal year, sales cycles, payroll cycles, research commitments, and so on. It includes understanding workflow patterns, such as how forms are transmitted from office to office when someone is hired. And it includes involvement in new software and hardware purchases. The more you know about the business of your organization, the better you will be able to manage the network to accommodate current needs as well as growth for future needs.

When you know your organization's business needs, you are better able to plan network activities to minimize interruptions. For example, your planning might include establishing "system time," when you can take portions of the network down for repair without affecting critical business functions.

As you plan the installation of new equipment, include a phase for testing the equipment before it is installed and brought "live" onto the network. This will reduce "downtime" due to problems in equipment preparation, such as loading software and table entries on a new router. Part of the test might include monitoring the new equipment during system time, when there is low usage of the network. Also have a plan to "back out" an installation if necessary.

Your planning will be more effective if you know as much about your network as possible. One way to understand your network is to become familiar with performance statistics. These can help you know where growth is occurring and to plan upgrades before network performance is a problem. Many network management packages enable you to chart network statistics so you can view changes over time.

Companies use computer systems and their network as part of their strategy to stay ahead of the competition. Many companies have rapidly moved to client/server applications as part of their competitive edge. Some client/server applications have been implemented without first studying the impact on existing network resources. Planning for growth in software resources needs to be linked to limitations in the network's ability to handle the growth. New systems, new databases, and new production activities can bring a network to a halt unless matching growth is planned for the network.

SUMMARY

There are many load factors on any network. Workstations, file servers, and hosts all contribute to network load, as do software demands, particularly client/server implementations. Client/server development is still in its infancy, and not all developers use network resources effectively. Network print services are another load demand, especially as more print servers are added to the network. Even intelligent network devices and network management systems can increase the network load.

An effective way to track network load is to establish baseline data for network performance, so you will know when performance levels are changing.

Several vendors offer network management software for the network manager. Two examples, OpenView and Solstice, were described in this chapter. Both packages can automate management of small LANs and management of large enterprise-wide networks. An important function of these packages is the ability to trap error events and report them.

Planning affects the day-to-day administration of the network as well as future changes. The most effective network planners are those who understand the business needs of their organization and incorporate this understanding into their planning.

KEY TERMS

Term/Acronym	Definition
Capacity Management	This process involves calculating present capacity of network systems, including disk capacity, server capacity, CPU resources, and so on. After present capacity is known, projections are made to determine future equipment needs.
Change Management	This process tracks changes in the network and in systems attached to the network. Often change management is accomplished by entering changes in a database, with a description of the change, the date of the change, the reason for the change, and so on.
Fat Client	Some client/server software leaves most of the processing to the client rather than sharing processing resources. Such systems are called fat clients.
Journal	A backup file that keeps track of new transactions in a software system. If the main transaction file or a database is damaged, the journal files enable the newly entered transaction data to be recovered.

Ping	A network node can test for the presence of another node by sending a short query to that node. This process is called a ping.
Server Advertising Packets (SAP)	Network transmissions broadcast at regular intervals by a file server. The purpose of these transmissions is to show that the file server is functional and available to be accessed.
Thin Client	This term refers to client/server systems where processing resources are evenly allocated between client and server.

REVIEW EXERCISES

1. How does the server load impact a network?

2. Glendale College is planning to add a new client/server system (with new hardware), so that all of the 200 department chairs and administrative assistants can view the status of their budgets. How would you plan for the resulting impact on the network?

3. Describe five problem events you would trap and monitor using network management software.

4. How can change management help you as a network administrator? Provide two examples.

5. What is capacity planning? Why is it important for a network manager to perform capacity planning?

6. Why is Solstice's disk journaling feature useful? In what types of situations would you use it?

7. In what ways can software add to load on a network?

8. What are the advantages to using a product like Hewlett-Packard's Software Distributor?

9. You are the network manager for a large accounting firm. What steps would you take to learn the business needs of the firm?

10. Describe four baseline statistics you would obtain as manager of a network. Why would this be valuable information?

TROUBLESHOOTING NETWORKS

Troubleshooting problems on your network offers as much challenge as the initial network design. Network problems can be very difficult to trace. You may spend hours finding a defective transceiver or a workstation NIC that intermittently sends a network-wide broadcast storm. A network slowdown might be caused by one of 20 possible sources. Implementing the solution to your network problem often will take only a short time compared to the time you spend isolating it.

This chapter gives you several tools for network troubleshooting. These include developing overall troubleshooting approaches that will save you time. Obtaining the right troubleshooting equipment is important also. We present information on several types of troubleshooting equipment and the types of situations where it is used. Finally, we discuss the variety of problems that occur on networks and where to look for solutions.

**AFTER READING THIS
CHAPTER YOU WILL BE ABLE TO:**

- EXPLAIN BASIC NETWORK TROUBLESHOOTING APPROACHES

- ISOLATE A NETWORK PROBLEM

- DESCRIBE NETWORK TROUBLESHOOTING EQUIPMENT AND HOW IT IS USED

- DETERMINE THE TYPES OF PROBLEMS THAT OCCUR WITH NICS, SERVERS, REPEATERS, BRIDGES, ROUTERS AND OTHER NETWORK NODES

- DISCUSS HOW DESIGN ISSUES AFFECT NETWORK TROUBLESHOOTING

PROBLEM-SOLVING APPROACHES

Your best ally for solving network problems is to develop a set of approaches that are effective for the type of network you manage. Three broad guidelines are to know your network, know your users, and know the business processes of your organization (see Figure 10-1).

There are several steps that will help you know your network. As we mentioned in Chapter 9, one way is to gather baseline and ongoing performance statistics. These will help you understand what performance is normal for your network. They also will keep you aware of trouble spots as they develop. Another important step is to create diagrams of your network. You might create one diagram of the entire network and additional diagrams of subnets or of remote sites. Some network managers hang the network diagrams in their offices for quick reference. The process of setting up and using network management software also will help you know your network.

Sometimes the first report of a network problem will come from one of your network users. All of your users will have different levels of skill in reporting a problem. Users with more technical computer knowledge may be able to describe a problem better than those with less knowledge. Some users who call will be experiencing simple problems at their workstation, not network problems. Others will wait until a problem is severe before they call. The more you know your users, the better you will be able to assess the nature of the problems they are reporting. One approach is to train your users in problem reporting, so you start tracking down a problem with good clues.

In Chapter 9 we emphasized that understanding the business processes of your organization is important to network management. It also is important for troubleshooting network problems. For example, if you work for a publisher, there will be deadlines for completing projects, such as books. At these times, a large number of text and graphics print files are likely to be directed to networked laser and color printers. Your knowledge of what happens during these periods will help you take steps to prevent network problems. And should problems occur, you will have a better idea of how to address them.

INCREMENTAL PROBLEM SOLVING

Armed with knowledge of your network, users, and organization, you can take specific incremental steps to investigate and solve network problems. Some general steps to follow are shown in Table 10-1.

Table 10-1

Investigating network problems

Steps To Investigate Network Problems
Carefully listen to the problem report.
Obtain error messages or other details of the problem.
Check first for the simple solutions.
Determine if others are experiencing the problem.
Check to see what your management software indicates.
Check for any power outages.
Keep a log of reported problems.

If the problem is reported by a network user, listen carefully to his or her description. Even if he or she does not use the right terminology, the information still can be of value. Part of the challenge for you is to ask the right questions so you get as much information as possible.

An obvious, but sometimes overlooked step is to record the error message at the time it appears. If you try to recall the message from memory, you may lose some important information. For example, the error, "Network not responding" can lead you to a different set of troubleshooting steps than the message, "Network timeout error." These messages are similar and might be confused through recollection. The first message might be related to a damaged NIC. The second message could mean that your database server is down and the application is waiting to obtain data.

Another important step is to start with simple solutions. A printer may not be printing because the print server next to it is unplugged from the power or the cable is off. A repeater may be down because it is kept in a janitor's closet and the janitor has mistakenly unplugged the power. A new office employee may take a segment down by removing the cable from the wall connector in order to rearrange the office furniture. Or the new employee may use the wrong IP address as he or she configures the workstation software.

Determine if anyone else is experiencing the problem. For example, several people may report they cannot load a word processing software package. This may be due to a problem at the server they use to load the software. If only one person is experiencing this problem, however, it may point to trouble on one workstation.

If you have event monitoring on your network management software, check to see if any recent triggered events have been logged. Also check to determine if any devices are in a caution or warning status.

Power interruptions are a common source of network difficulties. Sometimes a bridge, router, hub, or other piece of equipment fails to boot properly following a power outage. Some power irregularities, such as a power sag or a small surge, go unnoticed. But the sag or surge may impact one or more network devices, even though no other equipment seems affected. If you manage a large campus-wide network, a localized power outage may take down only part of your network, leaving those who still have power perhaps (including the network manager) unaware there is a problem.

LOGGING PROBLEMS

One effective troubleshooting tool is to keep a log of all network problems and their solutions. Some network managers log problems in a database they have created for this purpose. Others build problem logging into **help desk** systems maintained by their organization. A help desk system is application software designed to keep information on computer systems, user questions, problem solutions, and other information that members of the organization can reference.

The advantage of tracking problems is that you soon accumulate a wealth of information on solutions. For example, you have the option to look up how you handled a problem you last addressed six months ago in order to jog your memory about the solution. The log of problems also can be used as a teaching tool and reference for other network support staff. Problems that repeatedly show up in the log may indicate that special attention is needed, such as replacing a router that has experienced five problems over two months.

TROUBLESHOOTING EQUIPMENT

It doesn't matter if your network is large or small, you will want to obtain network troubleshooting equipment to help find problems quickly. The investment in troubleshooting equipment is small when compared against lost productivity if the network has problems. There is a wide range of equipment that comes in various price categories. For example, your first test equipment for a small network may be an inexpensive voltmeter. If you manage a large network, you may decide to invest in an expensive protocol analyzer. Commonly used test equipment includes the following:

- Voltmeter, multimeter, and optical power meter
- Cable scanner
- Transceiver monitor
- MAU analyzer
- Time domain reflectometer
- Protocol analyzer
- Remote network monitoring

VOLTMETERS, MULTIMETERS, AND OPTICAL POWER METERS

A voltmeter enables you to test the voltage on network cable, to test power supplies, and to test signal strength on any network equipment. Instead of purchasing only a voltmeter, consider investing in a multimeter, which costs a little more. The multimeter will have both a voltmeter and an ohm meter. You will be able to test the cable resistance with the ohm meter to determine if it meets IEEE specifications.

The signal strength on a fiber optic cable run is measured by a an optical power meter. A separate light source is used to generate a wave that can be measured by the optical power meter.

CABLE SCANNERS

Cable scanners are designed to test the network cable plant, such as coaxial, twisted-pair, or fiber optic cable. To test the cable, a connector on a section of cable is attached to the scanner. The scanner "shoots" the cable by transmitting an electrical signal. It times the pulse to determine where the signal stops. This information is used to determine the cable length, which is shown on an LCD display or is printed out. Scanners are available to test cables at various speeds.

If the signal transmission is interrupted, the scanner is able to determine whether an open or short circuit exists. It reports the distance to the problem so you can trace the location.

Some scanners are designed to continuously check for cable problems and produce a report of the information they have collected. This feature is useful when you are working to locate an intermittent problem, such as an occasional short or a defective terminator resistor.

Cable scanners are relatively inexpensive and provide more information than a voltmeter or multimeter. For example, multimeters only indicate the presence of a short or open circuit. Scanners also show the location of problems and whether the cable is too long for IEEE specifications. A scanner also indicates if the cable has radio frequency interference or electromagnetic interference.

TRANSCEIVER MONITOR

Transceivers have low visibility on a network, but they play a critical role. These small devices are part of the **attachment unit interface (AUI)** for linking backbone cabling into network and computer equipment such as bridges, routers, hubs, and workstations. A defective transceiver can be hard to identify without the right equipment. The transceiver monitor can detect transceiver problems related to power, signal reception, and collision handling.

MAU ANALYZER

A MAU analyzer is used on token ring networks and provides information similar to a cable scanner. It generates a signal for the purpose of locating opens, shorts, and faulty cable connectors. Also, it can determine if the MAU is functioning properly.

TIME DOMAIN REFLECTOMETER

The time domain reflectometer (TDR) is similar to an oscilloscope. It can test line impedance, opens, shorts, electrical interference, cable distances, and connector and terminator problems. This device works by transmitting a signal and gathering information on the signal reflection that is returned. TDRs can duplicate the wave pattern of the signal to show impedance, signal strength, signal interference, distance, and other information. These devices provide more detailed information than cable scanners and are more expensive.

Some TDRs have a memory feature to capture several snapshots at different times, and to record the information in a printed report. This feature can help in locating intermittent cable problems or problems due to occasional interference.

Optical time domain reflectometers (OTDRs) are available for testing fiber optic cable. These devices transmit a light wave instead of an electrical impulse. The reflected signal is measured for distance and strength.

PROTOCOL ANALYZER

The most comprehensive network monitoring devices are protocol analyzers. These devices work in "promiscuous" mode to capture detailed information about the traffic moving across a network, including protocol and OSI layer information. Some protocol analyzers provide information derived from the OSI physical, data-link, and network layers. Others can analyze the upper OSI layers also.

Protocol layer analysis

From the physical layer, an analyzer can detect problems such as opens, shorts, and electrical interference. The analyzer may be attached to the network backbone or to a particular segmented portion of the network.

The data-link layer analysis produces information on data errors. This includes collisions, runt (incomplete) packets, corrupted packets, CRC errors (see Chapter 3), network bottlenecks, and broadcast storms. For example, assume you have received calls from users who cannot access your IBM mainframe. These users are located in a remote building on your business campus and connected to the network backbone by a bridge. All other IBM users at other campus locations are able to access the IBM. You attach the protocol analyzer to view transmissions from the remote building where users are having problems. The protocol analyzer shows a large number of runt and corrupted packets coming from the bridge in the remote building. This provides you with information to indicate that the bridge needs to be repaired or replaced.

At the network layer, a protocol analyzer enables you to view routing information contained in data packets. By viewing this information, you can analyze distances traveled by packets. For instance, in the business campus example, packets sent through the router in the remote building may be taking an unusually long network route to the mainframe. This indicates that you need to make some routing or cabling adjustments on the network. A first step would be to check the setup of the router in the remote building.

Some protocol analyzers can examine the transport, session, presentation, and application OSI layers. For example, you may have a user who is using the network version of Microsoft Word, which is loaded from a server that resides on an FDDI ring. The user reports that Word intermittently pauses during use. This symptom might indicate a problem at the user's workstation, such as a memory conflict, or it might indicate a problem on the network. Information obtained by monitoring the session layer via a protocol analyzer shows that transmissions between server and workstation are experiencing temporary interruptions. Additional data from other servers on the ring indicates that the server is intermittently disconnecting from the rest of the ring due to a malfunctioning NIC.

Analysis of protocols

Protocol analyzers contain software that is designed to interpret specific protocols. If you have a network using TCP/IP and IPX/SPX, you will need to purchase software options to monitor each of these protocols. As you add new protocols to the network, you can add software to the analyzer to monitor the new protocols.

Analyzers come with the option to create filters in order to capture specific information needed for troubleshooting problems. They also can store data captured over a given time range. As an example, you may be experiencing problems with a database backup because someone does not shut down their workstation at night. You can set up a filter to capture only data going to and from the database server at the time when backups are taken. In another example, you may have a print server that frequently hangs up. The print server is designed for TCP/IP- and IPX-originated printouts. A filter might be created to capture data addressed to that print server. The results might show that the print server hangs each time it receives an IPX transmission, indicating that the server should be reconfigured or replaced.

Some protocol analyzers can be programmed so that the filter signals an alarm event. If you suspect that an Internet intruder is trying to FTP a virus to one of your host computers, you can build a filter with an alarm so that you can capture the intruder's IP address.

Types of protocol analyzers

Protocol analyzers are available to monitor Ethernet, token ring, FDDI, ATM, ISDN, X.25, frame relay, and other types of networks. Some manufacturers have add-on modules and interfaces to expand the analyzer's capabilities as you build onto your network. For example, Tekelec's Chameleon has add-ons for all of the network types we have just mentioned, plus a module to test T1 communications.

The first protocol analyzers were available only as dedicated test instruments and looked similar to oscilloscopes. These types of analyzers remain in wide use and are preferred by many network managers. However, to use such an analyzer, you must transport the unit to the monitoring site and connect it to the network.

More recent protocol analyzers consist of software that runs on a PC workstation. For example, the Nitech NiteOwl analyzer is adapted for Microsoft Windows and can be placed on a desktop, portable, or laptop PC. The PC is transported to the monitoring site and connected via a NIC (which can be a PCMCIA interface). Other examples of PC-based analyzers are Compaq's Insight Manager, The Sniffer, and Novell's LANalyzer. Figure 10-2 shows a portable PC connected as a protocol analyzer.

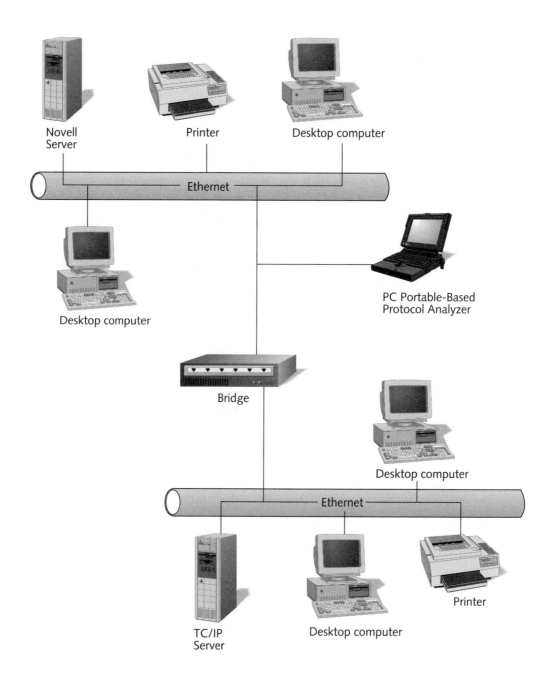

Figure 10-2

Portable PC
protocol
analyzer

REMOTE NETWORK MONITORING

A limitation of protocol analyzers is that they are a single node at a single location on the network. The information they collect is dependent on where they are placed. If you want to monitor the network in more than one place, you need to purchase several of these devices, at considerable expense.

A more effective and inexpensive way to monitor large networks is to have software acting as protocol analyzers on existing nodes throughout the network. To do this, Remote Network Monitoring (RMON) was conceived in the early 1990s by the Internet Engineering Task Force (IETF). The IETF designed an SNMP database called RMON MIB II for the purpose of gathering protocol analysis data by remote stations. The remote stations are agents or **probes**. Information gathered by the probes can be sent to a management station that compiles it into a database. RMON MIB II standards have been developed for Ethernet and token ring networks.

Similar to a dedicated protocol analyzer, the probe taps into the network in promiscuous mode, gathering information about network activity. Probes can be placed anywhere there is a need to continuously monitor the network. They even can be placed on the remote side of a T1 link or a dial-up link to gather information from each region of a WAN.

Probes can be devices dedicated to information gathering or they can be software placed on existing network nodes. Nodes that can double as RMON probes include: PC workstations, UNIX workstations, RISC processors, hubs, bridges, routers, and switches.

Figure 10-3 shows a network that uses existing RMON probes to gather information for the management station.

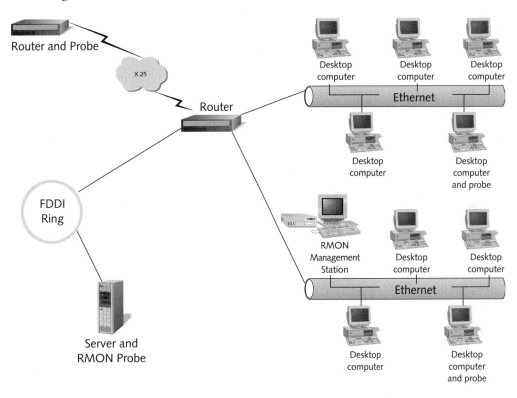

Figure 10-3

RMON probes and management station

When probe software is set up on an existing node, it is designed to continuously operate in the background, so it does not interfere with the node's main function. Since this is relatively new technology, the probe software can cause problems on a node with a high level of network or CPU activity, such as a server or a hub. The overhead from the probe software may cause the server or hub to slow down or to crash. Another disadvantage of placing probe software on a node is that someone may power-off the node. If you use this technology, you will need to weigh the benefit of using an existing node against the consequences of interfering with a node's primary function.

Some vendors have probe software that runs as a separate process on an existing system. If the probe software experiences a problem, it is designed to have no impact on the node's other functions.

Management stations

There are no standards for building software to interpret data collected by RMON probes. The effectiveness of the data depends on how well a vendor has written software applications on the management station to provide analysis of the MIB II data.

One highly effective solution is to purchase RMON management software that can be used with network management software such as OpenView or Solstice. An advantage of this approach is that OpenView and Solstice have utilities to integrate your own specialized management applications using languages such as C++.

Some network managers prefer stand-alone protocol analyzers to RMON for several reasons. Protocol analyzers support more analysis options and a full range of protocols. Protocol analyzers have a proven track record for solving network problems. RMON is a developing technology, with limitations in what it can track on multi-protocol networks. However, RMON MIB II is being incorporated into network monitoring software such as Novell's ManageWise and Microsoft's Network Monitor.

NETWORK PROBLEMS

NETWORK CABLING

Network cabling is the most common source of problems on a network. Cabling problems have many symptoms, such as disconnecting workstations, slow network services, a high level of packet errors, and unreliable data transmission. If you have reports of any of these problems, one place to start is by investigating the cable plant. There are several things to check related to cabling problems, including the following:

- Cable length
- Cable type
- Terminators
- Grounding
- Cable impedance
- An open or short
- RFI and EMI
- Connectors
- Distance between connections

Figure 10-4 summarizes cable troubleshooting.

Figure 10-4

Solving cable problems

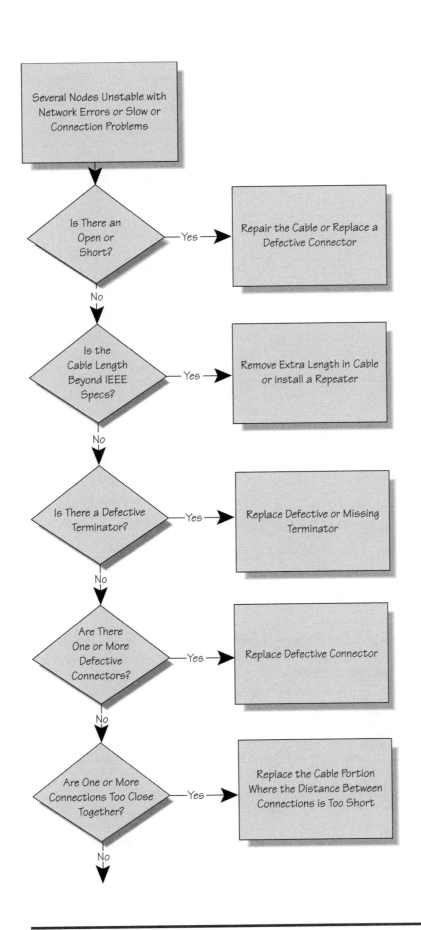

Figure 10-4

Continued

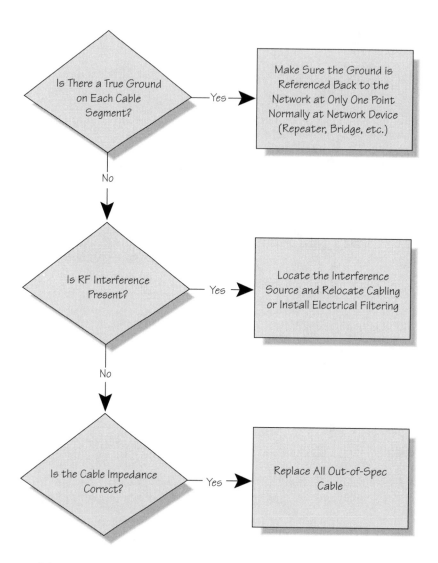

Cable length

According to the IEEE specifications, Ethernet and token ring networks must be able to send a packet to the most distant node in a given amount of time. If a network segment is extended beyond the IEEE specifications, there will be communication problems affecting all nodes on that segment.

If you use a protocol analyzer or RMON probe to analyze an overly long cable segment, it will show excessive packet collisions, especially late collisions. A late collision occurs when a node can put a majority of the packet on the cable but experiences a collision toward the end of the transmission of the packet. Another way to detect a segment that is too long is to use a cable scanner or TDR and shoot the distance of the cable.

Cable types

In places where users can install their own cabling, you may discover some nonstandard cabling. For example, network managers have found TV coaxial cable and antenna cable used instead of 50-ohm network cable. The labeling on the cable often will indicate it is the wrong type. A multimeter also will quickly show that the impedance is not 50 ohms.

Terminator

A segment with a defective or missing terminator responds like one that is too long. Workstations on the segment may disconnect, experience slow network response, or receive network error messages. If your cable scanner or TDR shows the segment distance is in spec, check the terminators. On an Ethernet network, the resistor in the terminator should be 50 ohms. If you don't have a multimeter to test the resistor, simply replace the terminator and see if the problem stops.

Grounding

Proper grounding is critical to packet transmission on the cable. Without it, the network packet transmissions will have many cyclic redundancy check (CRC) errors. As we mentioned in Chapter 3, Ethernet packets include this check to ensure the reliability of data transfer from the source node to the recipient node. A protocol analyzer can provide a report of CRC errors. A multimeter also can help determine if there is a grounding problem.

Grounding problems can be dangerous. In one instance, a network analyst at a university was asked to check on network problems in a lab. The ground for the segment on one side of the lab was a true ground. The segment on the other side had a floating ground. The analyst picked up both segments at once and received an electrical jolt that threw him to the floor.

Cable impedance

The IEEE specifications require 50 ohm impedance on Ethernet cable. Inexpensive cable may approach 50-ohms but be off just enough to cause data transmission problems. The symptoms are like those for a cable that is too long. A simple method to check the cable is to look at the part number printed on the cable. The part number should be RG-58 A/U. If the part number is not visible, check the cable with a TDR.

Opens and shorts

An intermittent open on a cable segment will prevent workstations on that segment from connecting to the network. A short may cause intermittent problems, network errors, and disconnection problems. A voltmeter, cable scanner, TDR, or protocol analyzer will help track down shorts and opens.

RFI and EMI

RFI and EMI can result in excessive "noise" or "jabber" on the cable. This happens when the cable is run too close to an electrical field, such as over fluorescent lights in the ceiling or through a machine shop with heavy electrical equipment. Use a TDR or a protocol analyzer to trace interference.

Connectors

A faulty connector can cause a short or open on the cable. If several workstations on a segment are experiencing problems, this may be due to a connector on a workstation close to the server. Shoot the cable from a point near the beginning of the segment. An open or short at a given location may indicate a failed connector. The best solution is to replace the connector.

Distance between connectors

Two adjacent workstations may have network communication problems if the distance between their connectors is too short. For example, on a thin coaxial Ethernet segment the minimum distance is 0.5 meters. Check to be certain that all workstations are separated by this distance or more.

ETHERNET TROUBLESHOOTING

In addition to checking for cable problems, there are several elements to check when an Ethernet network is experiencing difficulty. For example, as we mentioned in Chapter 3, there are different frame types, DIX and IEEE 802.3. Check to be sure that all servers and workstations are configured to use the correct frame type for your network.

If server Ethernet LANs are connected to a WAN, each LAN will have a unique network number. Servers, such as Novell NetWare, are configured to use the network number. Make sure that all servers on the same network use the same network number in the address configuration. Routers also must be configured with the correct network number.

Also on an Ethernet network, when your protocol analyzer detects late collisions or excessive CRC errors, check the repeaters, transceivers, and bridges for problems. See Figure 10-5 for Ethernet troubleshooting information.

TOKEN RING TROUBLESHOOTING

Cable problems are a good place to begin when troubleshooting a token ring network. If there are no detectable cabling problems and the entire network is down, check on whether **beaconing** is occurring. If the active monitor has a NIC that is functioning intermittently, you will need to remove that station from the hub so another active monitor can be designated. Replace the NIC and return the station to the hub. Also, check the standby monitor stations and their NICs to ensure all are functioning.

Another device to check is the MAU. A protocol analyzer can help you determine if the MAU is not working. Further, if the cable, connectors, and NICs show no problems, install a different MAU to determine if it is the source. If you attach a new station and problems occur, check to be certain the NIC is properly set for the network speed. (Token ring troubleshooting is summarized in Figure 10-6.)

TROUBLESHOOTING FIBER OPTIC CABLE

Fiber optic cable is used for network backbones and for high-speed network segments such as FDDI. Troubleshooting fiber optic cable presents some special problems, because the signal source is light and the medium is glass or plastic (usually glass). Fiber cable is especially susceptible to damage and should be examined for breaks or opens when problems occur. An OTDR is used to locate opens or measure power loss on a cable run. As we mentioned in Chapter 3, power loss is called **attenuation**. For example, network problems will result if attenuation is greater than 1.5 dB/km on an FDDI ring.

Fiber optic cable connections and terminations must be more precise than for metal cabling and take longer to install. Durable connections and terminations depend on whether the cable installer has the right tools and has been careful in his or her work. Improperly connected or terminated cable will cause problems. Dirty connectors also cause problems on fiber optic cable runs. Examine connections and terminations for dirt or for poor installation when you have problems on a fiber optic cable.

Another problem area is the angle of the bend around corners. This is called the **angular circumference**. The maximum angular circumference depends on the cable characteristics and the number of strands. Light will not transmit when the angular circumference is too great.

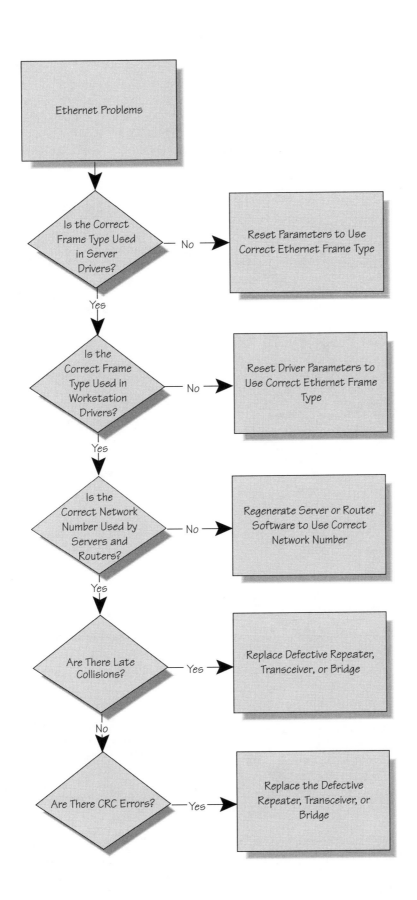

Figure 10-5

Troubleshooting Ethernet problems

Figure 10-6

Troubleshooting
token ring
problems

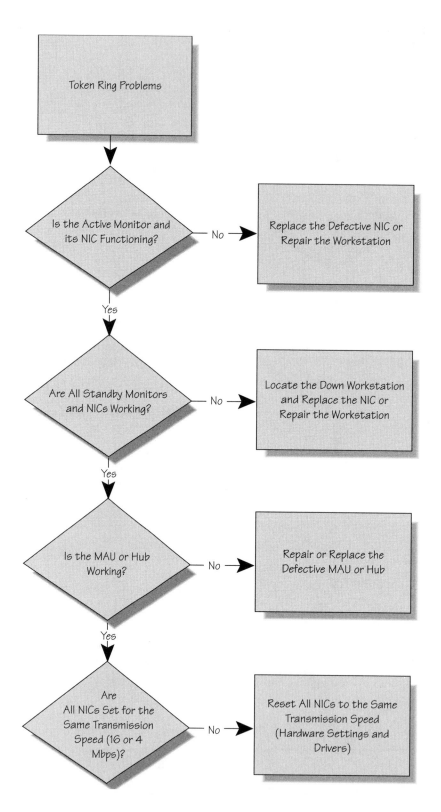

A last problem area can be the type of cable installed. Make sure that the appropriate cable is installed for the required distance of the cable run. Multi-mode fiber should not be used for distance runs that require single-mode cable, such as on a backbone. (Figure 10-7 shows troubleshooting steps for fiber optic cable.)

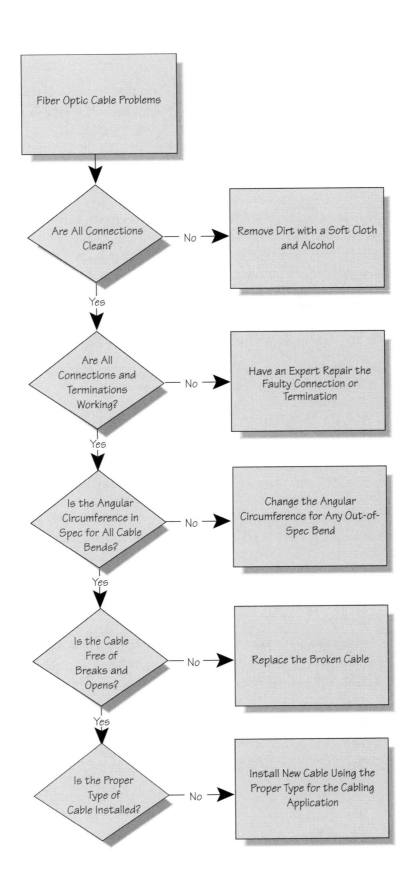

Figure 10-7

Troubleshooting fiber optic cabling problems

NIC PROBLEMS

NIC problems are common and can affect the entire network segment or network equipment such as a repeater or hub. Many NIC vendors include diagnostic software to help you determine if the NIC is working properly.

When you set up a NIC or if problems occur, check to be certain the vendor's network drivers are at the most current version level. Some vendors have updated drivers that can be downloaded from the Internet if you have an immediate need.

A NIC may have problems because it is set up to use the wrong frame type or the wrong cable type. For example, if a NIC does not connect to the network, check the cable type used. Some NICs can accept coaxial or twisted-pair cabling. Be certain the NIC setup information matches the cable connected to the NIC.

Occasionally, a NIC will malfunction and broadcast continuously. This situation can result in a network slowdown. A protocol analyzer will help you trace the problem to the offending NIC. With the protocol analyzer you can obtain the address of the NIC and trace its location. The easiest solution to try with a malfunctioning NIC is to reseat (remove and reinstall) the board in the device having problems. (Refer to Figure 10-8 for NIC problems.)

PRINT SERVERS

Print server problems are usually very apparent, because nothing appears at the printer after a print request is made. Print server capability has two components. The first component is at the printer end. The printer may be attached to a stand-alone hardware print server connected to the network, or it may have an internal print server card. Another option is to use a printer attached to an existing PC workstation and to have print server software on the workstation. This option is less frequently used because stand-alone print servers and print server cards are more reliable and competitively priced.

The second component of print services is the print server software on the file server or host. This software captures a printout and sends it to a printer queue that is "attached" (through software) to the print server (remote server) at the printer end. The queue is able to deliver the printout to the remote server because each remote server has a unique address. When printing problems occur, you will need to check the printer's print server and the print server software on the file server or host.

For a remote stand-alone print server or print server on a card, try the following steps (see Figure 10-9):

- Check that the network cable is attached to the print server and that the data cable is attached between the printer and print server.
- Check to be certain there is power to the printer and to the print server.
- Power the printer off and on. The problem may be a hung printer due to a control code sent to the printer. If the print server is a card in the printer, this action will reset it.
- Power the print server off and on. It may need to be reset due to a power problem or interference from the network.
- Check the configuration software for the print server to see if any parameters have been changed.
- Check to ensure that a queue has been defined for the print server and that the print server is attached to its defined file server print queue.

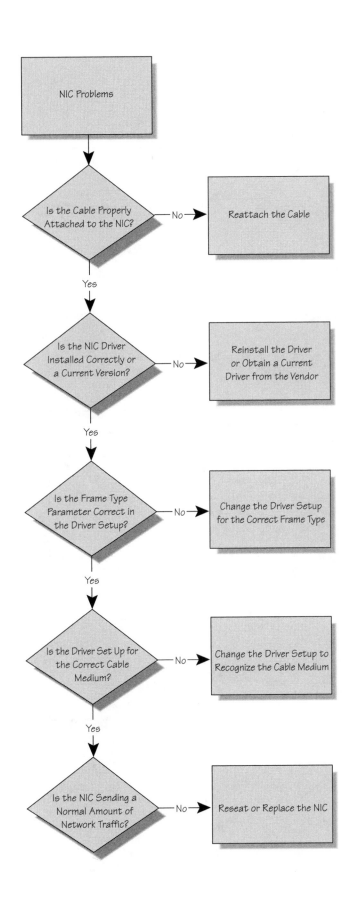

Figure 10-8

Troubleshooting
NICs

Figure 10-9

Troubleshooting
hardware print
servers

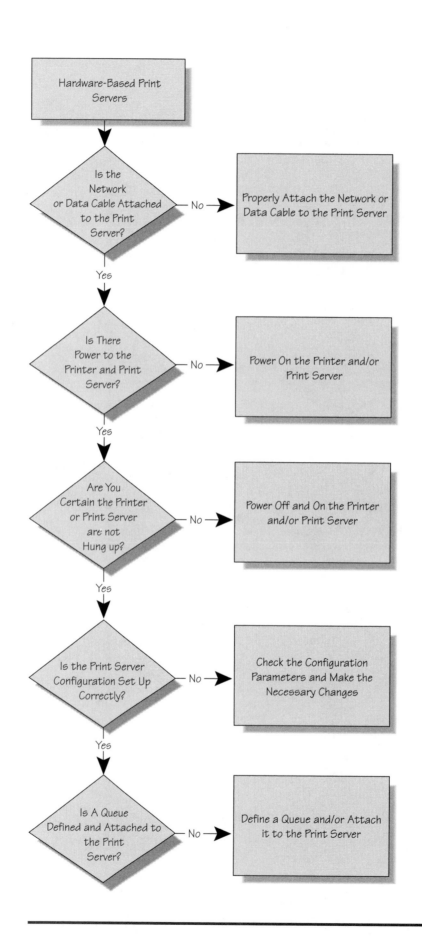

To troubleshoot problems with a software print server on the file server or host, try the following steps (see Figure 10-10):

- Check to be certain the print server has a print queue and is attached to the queue.

- Review the print server setup parameters to be certain they are accurate.

- Stop and then restart the print server software. It may have experienced an unrecoverable software error. If the print server is loaded as a NetWare NLM, unload the NLM and then reload it.

Figure 10-10

Troubleshooting print server software on the file server or host

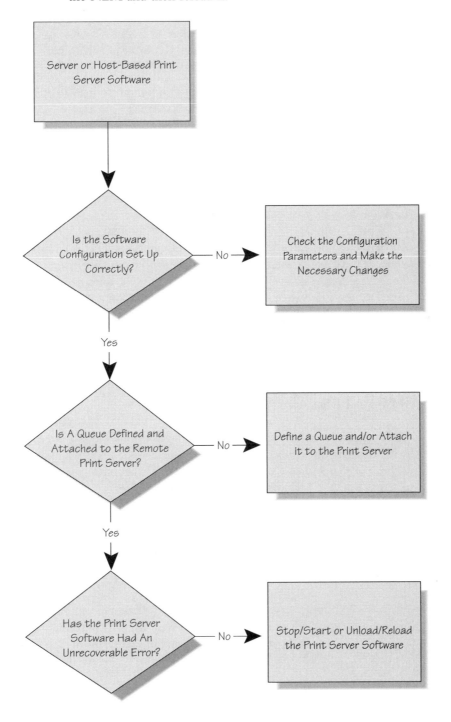

FILE SERVERS

File server operating systems can be tuned for network performance. For example, received packets are stored in server communication buffers until the server is ready to process the packet. A bottleneck or slow response will occur if the buffers are too small or if there are too few buffers to match the demand on the server. It may be necessary to reallocate or expand server memory to meet the need. Some vendors offer packages that automatically tune server parameters to meet changing demand. The tuning occurs automatically while the server is functioning.

The server NIC also can create bottlenecks and slow response. As demand increases on a server, it may be necessary to upgrade the NIC or to install additional NICs. Novell servers are easily configured to use several NICs.

Scaleable servers are an advantage when you anticipate growth in demand. Servers with scaleable CPUs can be upgraded when bottlenecks are created by an overloaded CPU. Microsoft NT version 3 supports up to four server CPUs. Microsoft NT version 4 is scaleable to eight server CPUs.

Refer to Figure 10-11 for a review of file server network performance issues.

GATEWAY

A malfunctioning gateway can have several symptoms. The most apparent symptom is that a node is missing. For example, if an SNA gateway to an IBM mainframe is down, the mainframe is no longer accessible to the network and will appear to be missing. The solution is to reboot the gateway or to replace it. The gateway on a Novell system may be a NIC in the server. If a Novell gateway is down, replace the NIC.

Malfunctioning gateways also can generate bad packets and high error rates on the network. A protocol analyzer or RMON probe can be used to trace the problem to the gateway.

REPEATERS

Some repeater problems are relatively simple to troubleshoot. For example, if network traffic is not going through a repeater, check to determine if a repeater segment is **partitioned**. Check the segment cable, connections, and NICs for problems. Correct any problems you find and reset the partitioned segment on the repeater.

If the entire repeater is down, check the power source and any fuses in the repeater.

Sometimes a malfunctioning repeater will send bad or corrupted packets. This can be determined by placing a protocol analyzer on the network and viewing the traffic into and out of the repeater. The easiest solution to this problem is to replace the repeater and return it to the vendor for repair.

Excessive collisions, network slowdowns, or a network bottleneck can be caused by an overloaded repeater. In this situation, you may need to make some design changes such as installing one or more bridges to segment sections of the network and prevent overloading.

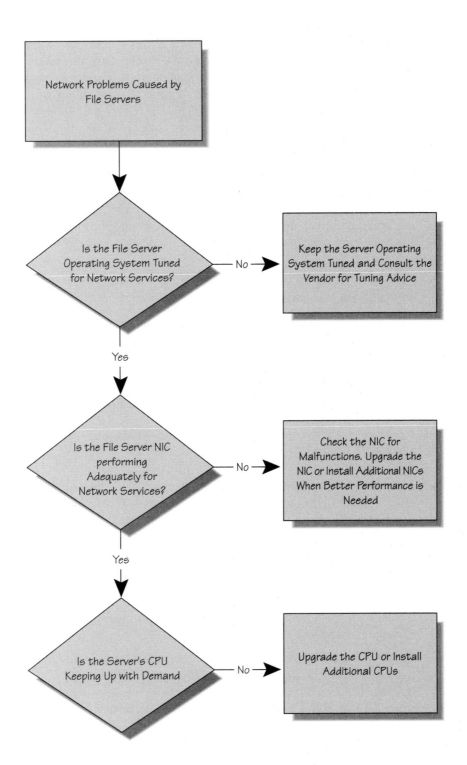

Figure 10-11

Troubleshooting file server performance problems on a network

BRIDGES

Symptoms of an overloaded bridge are similar to those of an overloaded repeater, including a high rate of network collisions, slowdowns, and bad packets. A protocol analyzer can help you determine if the problem is related to the bridge. To solve the problem you may need to install a router or hub in that part of the network. Also, check to be certain that a server or workstation NIC is not creating a broadcast storm and overloading the network.

A defective bridge can generate bad packets, excessive network traffic, and network slow-downs. Information about this situation can be gathered from a protocol analyzer or from RMON probe data. Check the bridge configuration and power supply. Try resetting the bridge to see if this cures the problem. If none of these things work, you may need to replace the bridge.

ROUTER PROBLEMS

As with other network equipment, malfunctioning routers produce bad packets, slow network response, and a high rate of collisions. When a router malfunctions, check the routing table and related areas. Check the following potential trouble spots:

- Is the routing software up-to-date?
- Is the power supply working properly?
- Is the router memory working?
- For PC-based routers, is the hard drive full or fragmented?
- For PC-based routers, are the hard drive and controller working?

The reported symptoms also may be due to an overloaded router. In this case, it may be necessary to redesign the network or to segment that portion of the network. Another solution may be to replace the router with an intelligent hub.

INTELLIGENT HUBS

Many hubs are designed in a modular fashion, so all of the hub may be working except a single board, such as a bridge module. If one module is defective, the hub isolates the problem and shuts it down. The board then can be removed and replaced with no interruption of service to other hub modules.

The symptoms of a defective module are similar to those for repeaters, bridges, and routers. These include bad packets, packet encapsulation errors, network errors, slow network response, and problem reports from users on a particular module.

Intelligent hubs can be monitored with the help of software on the hub or software at a network management station.

If there is a generalized failure of a hub, check fuses and the power supply. Also check the hub backplane to be sure it is working. If your network management software or protocol analyzer detect packet timing errors or excessive collisions, check the retiming module in the hub. Often this is a single board that can be replaced when it malfunctions.

REBOOTING NETWORK EQUIPMENT

Anytime you detect a problem with network equipment, try rebooting it. This technique works in many cases because most network equipment is CPU-based. As can happen on any CPU, some registers may get out of synchronization, register pointers may be lost, or a critical register may be empty. Rebooting the equipment forces the CPU registers to reset to a known state, and the equipment may be fully operational again.

IP OR NETWORK ADDRESS PROBLEMS

Information cannot be routed to its proper destination if there are addressing problems. The most common source of addressing problems is IP addressing on TCP/IP networks. For example, network problems can occur if two or more nodes are using the same IP address. This can result in extra network traffic and slow or no response at the nodes in conflict.

The assignment of IP addresses is often the responsibility of the network manager. You can avoid conflicts by maintaining an IP address database showing the address assigned to each node. IP address conflicts can be traced by means of a protocol analyzer or an RMON probe.

MAIL SYSTEMS

Network traffic and bottlenecks sometimes are caused by mail systems that go awry. For example, in the early versions of a popular mail system, there were instances where a single message was transmitted thousands of times to a single destination. The problem was corrected by a software fix.

Defective mail systems can create severe network problems. Make certain your mail server or servers are set up in the most efficient way and that the software is kept up to date. Another source of mail system problems can occur when there are several mail servers and mail systems. Addressing and forwarding problems can develop wherein some mail goes into an endless loop between servers. This problem might happen on a college campus where academic users have VAX mail, administrative users have Microsoft Mail or Exchange, and physical plant users have their own server with CC:MAIL.

ISOLATING NETWORK PROBLEMS

The amount of difficulty you may experience in isolating a network problem is related to the size of your network, its complexity, and the type of network. Small token ring networks are relatively easy to troubleshoot because of their star configuration. If a beaconing network cannot resolve its problem without your help, there is usually a downed node. Management software, a TDR, or a protocol analyzer can be used to locate the node and isolate it for repair. The network continues running after the node is removed.

Problems are more difficult to isolate on an Ethernet network, particularly if they are intermittent. A defective NIC, repeater, bridge, router or other piece of equipment can result in similar network symptoms, such as network slowdowns. Network troubleshooting equipment, such as a protocol analyzer, is very effective for resolving problems. SNMP-compliant equipment also helps, especially on complex networks, so you can use network management software to isolate problems. (See Figure 10-12 for tips on solving network problems.)

Figure 10-12

Solving network
problems

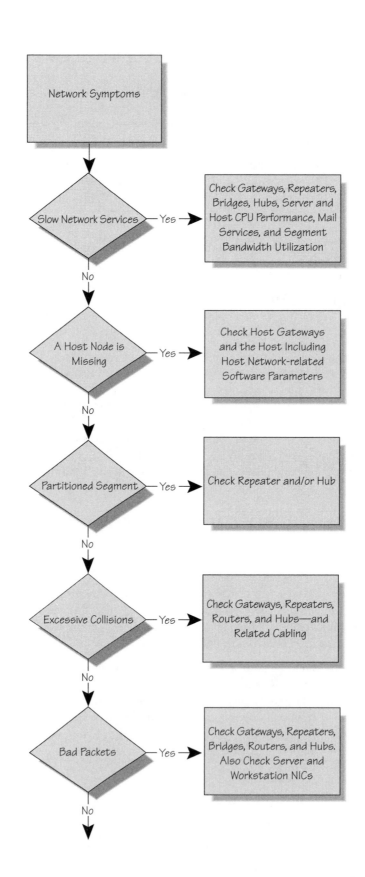

Figure 10-12

Continued

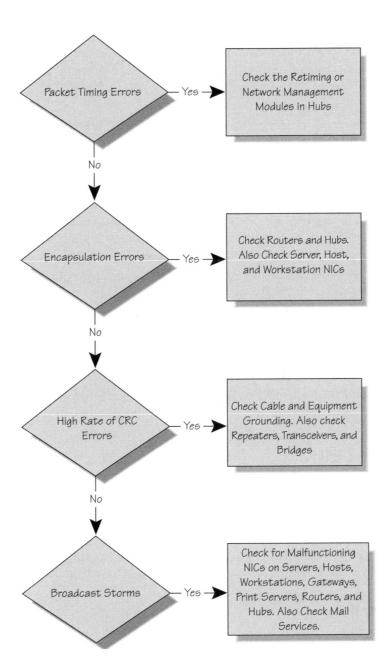

When you plan a network, plan to purchase troubleshooting equipment and management software. They will save hours spent in isolating problems.

ELIMINATING PROBLEMS THROUGH DESIGN

Often the best solution to problems is found in network design. If you begin the design with a knowledge of your users and their business, you will be able to avoid bottlenecks and excessive traffic problems from the beginning. For example, a business campus may use ID card readers in the cafeteria and gym areas. The server for the card readers may be located in the cafeteria's main office. If your network design includes the ability to segment this area from the rest of the network, business functions will not be slowed due to the high traffic from the card readers.

After a network is in place, you will need to make design modifications to solve problems. For instance, traffic on a subnet may be greater than you anticipated, making it necessary to divide it into two subnets. Your network management software and performance statistics will help as you face these decisions.

SUMMARY

The first step in troubleshooting a network problem is to come equipped with a set of strategies. These include knowledge of your networking environment, developing skills to obtain information on problems, and starting with the most immediate solutions. There is no reason to haul out your protocol analyzer when you can determine through a telephone conversation that a print server is not working because it is unplugged.

Appropriate troubleshooting equipment is vital to the network manager. In this chapter we have discussed several kinds of equipment, ranging from the inexpensive to the expensive. For simple networks, a multimeter or cable scanner may be all that is needed. Larger networks will require TDRs or protocol analyzers to trace problems. RMON probes are an alternative that will be appealing to managers of large networks spanning multiple locations or regions.

Also in this chapter we have presented suggestions for troubleshooting problems on all kinds of network equipment, such as cabling, NICs, servers, gateways, repeaters, bridges, routers, and hubs. Many problems have the same symptoms, which can make troubleshooting a difficult process. The right troubleshooting equipment and your knowledge of the network environment are crucial when difficult problems appear.

KEY TERMS

Term/Acronym	Definition
Angular Circumference	The measurement of the maximum amount of bend in fiber optic cable.
Attachment Unit Interface (AUI)	This interface is used to connect Ethernet, fiber optic, and other backbone cabling to hubs, routers, and other network equipment.
Attenuation	The power loss on fiber optic cable as measured in decibels.
Beaconing	A token ring network goes into a beaconing state when an error condition is detected. The error condition is signaled when a node sends a beacon frame to broadcast that there is a problem. The network remains in this state until the problem is resolved.
Help Desk	This application software is used to keep data on hardware and software problems, along with information on how the problems have been solved. The help desk software is tied into a database that can be used for reference.
Partition	An Ethernet network device will shut down (partition) a segment that it determines is malfunctioning
Probes	These may be stand-alone or existing network devices equipped with software to gather information about network performance. They are used to collect data for an RMON MIB II database.

REVIEW EXERCISES

1. Why is help desk software useful in network troubleshooting?

2. The angle of bend on fiber optic cable is called _____?

3. What is a TDR? How does it work? What is the difference between a TDR and an OTDR?

4. What steps would you take to resolve beaconing on a token ring network?

5. Why does rebooting equipment sometimes resolve problems?

6. Assume that a new PC workstation has just been added to an Ethernet network. However, the NIC does not detect the network and will not communicate. What steps would you take to troubleshoot this problem?

7. You are manager of an Ethernet network and are receiving reports that users in an office area cannot access a Sequent host computer used for administrative processing. Your knowledge of the network tells you that there is a repeater between these users and the Sequent. What network problems would you look for in this situation?

8. Five users on a token ring network have called to report they cannot reach their Novell file server. How would you troubleshoot these problem reports?

9. Compare the advantages of using a traditional protocol analyzer to the advantages of using RMON probes for gathering information about a network.

10. Your protocol analyzer indicates there are packet-timing errors on your network. Where would you look first to solve this problem?

11. What is the maximum attenuation permitted on an FDDI ring? How is attenuation measured?

12. What tests can you perform using a cable scanner?

13. What are CRC errors? Name two possible sources of CRC errors on a network.

14. Why is it important to ensure that every node on a TCP/IP network has a unique IP address?

15. Assume that a user reports a problem with his or her network printer. The printer has an internal print server card. The card supports IPX and TCP/IP routed printouts. All printouts through the Novell file server work without problems, but printouts from an IBM mainframe hang up the printer. What steps would you take to troubleshoot this dilemma?

16. You are the network manager for a college that has one main campus and four regional campuses throughout the state. Each regional campus is fully networked and connected to the main campus network. How would you monitor network activity for the entire WAN?

17. Describe how two different mail systems might cause network problems on a large business campus.

18. You are hired to audit an Ethernet network for a company located in a four-story building. The company is experiencing network communication problems. The network is entirely coaxial-based. As you examine the network, you find some sections of cable that have 54-ohm impedance. Describe why this might be a problem.

19. What would you look for first when asked to solve a network problem?

20. How would you trace an open on an FDDI ring? How would you trace it on an Ethernet cable segment?

FUTURE NETWORKING:
NEW TECHNOLOGIES AND SONET

The 1990s have launched many significant changes in computing that will affect us all in the next two decades. These changes are possible because networks have connected more people to more computers than ever before. Through networks, more software is available, with greater promise for true productivity increases. The act of bringing more software to the desktop has brought more demand on software companies to make systems easier to use. For example, early spreadsheet software required technical knowledge of how to set up a spreadsheet, how to write formulas, and how to write macros. Now spreadsheet software, such as Microsoft Excel, is available with "wizards" to step users through creating a spreadsheet. And keystroke-recording features automatically create macros.

AFTER READING THIS
CHAPTER YOU WILL BE ABLE TO:

- EXPLAIN HOW DEVELOPMENTS IN CLIENT/SERVER AND WEB SOFTWARE APPLICATIONS WILL AFFECT FUTURE NETWORKS

- DESCRIBE THE NETWORKING IMPACT OF ELECTRONIC IMAGING, ELECTRONIC DATA INTERCHANGE, AND ELECTRONIC FORMS

- EXPLAIN HOW VOICE-BASED ELECTRONIC MAIL WILL AFFECT NETWORKS

- DESCRIBE THE CAPABILITIES OF SONET

- EXPLAIN HOW SONET WORKS

Networks, PC workstations, and software are interrelated in that advances in one area create pressure for advances in the other two. For instance, as software systems develop more features, they require more memory and more disk space on the PC workstation. When these files are transmitted across a network they create more traffic and require higher network speeds. Combined voice, video, and data applications place even more demand on networks.

This chapter describes some of the dramatic developments that are affecting network services. These include client/server software advances, electronic imaging, electronic forms, the Internet, and the virtual university. SONET is recognized as the networking technology most likely to provide the huge bandwidth that will be necessary to accommodate these developments. This chapter provides an explanation of SONET and how its future appears linked with that of Asynchronous Transfer Mode (ATM).

CLIENT/SERVER SOFTWARE

Client/server applications began appearing in the late 1980s as a means to provide more information to users than previously achieved from traditional mainframe or file server-based application systems. Mainframe solutions have not been successful in fully meeting the reporting and data query needs of users. File server systems have not been efficient in handling large databases of information. Client/server applications are designed to fill the gaps left by mainframe and file server approaches.

Client/server applications have focused on quickly bringing data to customers. Users are able to build queries and reports to meet their information needs without writing complex computer code. These applications are made possible by a combination of technological tools that include the following:

- Relational databases
- Graphical user interfaces (GUI)
- Rapid application development tools (RAD)
- Powerful reporting tools
- More powerful PC workstations
- Networks

Relational databases have made it possible to store large amounts of data on a server. These databases can be designed for fast access to data for updating, query, or reporting. Modern relational databases can store voice and video information as well as data. They also provide **open access** paths (standard guidelines for reaching data) so that a variety of reporting and development tools can access the data. (Two common data access routes are Open Database Connectivity (ODBC) and X/Open XA.) This connectivity has created an active market for companies that offer RAD development tools and GUI reporting tools.

Ninety percent of client/server applications are developed in the GUI environment with RAD development tools. The GUI environment is easy for the customer to use, and the RAD tools are easier for programmers to work with than older development methods. More powerful PC workstations have made it possible to use GUI and to access large amounts of data held in relational databases.

Networks provide the link to the applications and to the data. Many client/server systems are designed to be three-tiered, meaning that there are three critical pieces (see Figure 11-1). One piece is the PC client workstation, which contains the GUI presentation logic. Another piece is the application server, which stores client/server applications and reports (business process logic) used by the client. The third piece is the database server, which provides data-related services, including security.

Figure 11-1

Three-tiered
client/server
system

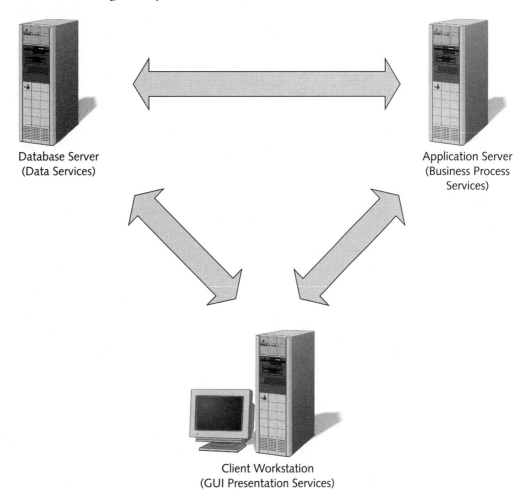

Database Server
(Data Services)

Application Server
(Business Process
Services)

Client Workstation
(GUI Presentation Services)

The network demands from client/server applications will continue to grow. GUI reporting tools make it possible for more clients to write their own database queries quickly. As more clients transport more ad hoc report data, network demands increase. This is particularly true when that data is video or voice information.

RAD tools are reducing application development cycles, so developers can place more applications with more functionality on the network. Since the applications are developed in GUI format, they attract new customers who did not use computers in the past. This introduces more people to network computing, resulting in more network traffic.

Organizations that have a large investment in client/server technology are quickly moving to implement high-speed networks, such as ATM. New demands to transmit voice and video data, as well as large database queries, require the bandwidth (and low latency for video) capabilities of ATM.

ELECTRONIC IMAGING

Storing **electronic images** is another byproduct of relational database technology and client/server applications. Organizations are switching from placing information on microfiche to storing the same information as an electronic image in a database. Contracts, canceled checks, time cards, and other "hard copy" data are scanned into the computer as electronic images. The images are stored in a database for future reference or duplication. When this information ages, it is archived on CD-ROM for later access.

ELECTRONIC FORMS

As a complement to electronic imaging, organizations are replacing paper forms with electronic forms. Organizations have forms for all types of purposes. These include job applications, W4 tax forms, purchase orders, invoices, interdepartmental requisitions, personnel hiring forms, forms for reporting grades, and so on. When a paper form is completed, often it needs to be carried to one or more offices for signatures, date stamps, and filing. Forms are time-consuming and reduce productivity.

An electronic form contains the same information as a paper form, but it is housed in a computer. The user calls up the form he or she needs, and completes the blanks on the screen. When the form is completed, it is sent electronically to the next person who must review it, such as a signature authority. After the electronic signature is completed, the form is sent electronically to the next destination, or filed in a database.

Electronic forms are built into client/server applications to eliminate "paper flow." One prominent client/server software vendor has eliminated over 50 % of their paper forms by substituting electronic forms.

WEB APPLICATIONS

Many client/server developers are moving to interface their products with the World Wide Web (tools that provide a common GUI) on the Internet. RAD software manufacturers such as PowerSoft, Microsoft, Computer Associates, and Borland offer development tools to build Web applications.

Web server applications have the advantage in that they reduce the need for a powerful PC client workstation. Instead of running on the client, applications and report functions run from a Web server (see Figure 11-2). This reduces network traffic between client, application server, and database server. But this is offset by rapidly increasing numbers of clients that are connecting to Web servers. And there is high volume network traffic between the Web and database servers.

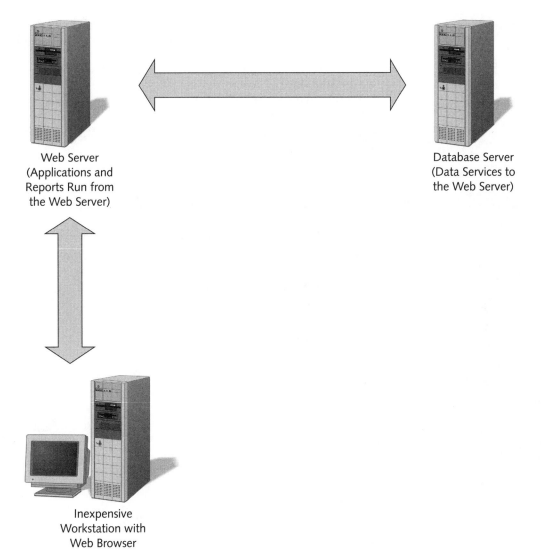

Figure 11-2

Web-based
application
systems

Web Server
(Applications and
Reports Run from
the Web Server)

Database Server
(Data Services to
the Web Server)

Inexpensive
Workstation with
Web Browser

Web applications are promising in that they reduce expenses for workstations. But they shift the expense to creating additional network and server resources to handle the load. For example, as more applications run from the Web, more Web servers are needed, and more connections need to be set up to Web servers.

Traffic between Web application servers and database servers also needs to be considered. One way to handle increased traffic between servers is to place them on high-speed networks, such as on fast Ethernet or ATM.

THE INTERNET

The Web has had a dramatic impact on Internet communications. Millions of people regularly access the Web for private and business information. In a very short time, the Internet has shifted from an education-centered enterprise to a business-centered enterprise. Books, magazines, videos, electronic equipment, software, and other consumer goods are easily ordered through the Web. Many businesses have a Web page to advertise their services.

Universities and colleges have Web pages to provide information about their educational services. Many high schools, cities, and private individuals have created Web pages too.

Growth in the Web presents some special challenges to Internet providers. Public and private Internet providers face the challenge of constantly upgrading modem pools, hubs, routers, and other equipment. If equipment is not upgraded, Web traffic becomes bottle-necked. The demand created by the Web alone will accelerate development of new networking hardware and software to keep pace with new Web developments, such as voice and video communications.

ELECTRONIC DATA INTERCHANGE

One Web-related business application that is likely to grow is **electronic data interchange (EDI)**. EDI is the process of using electronic means to transmit business data, rather than sending computer tapes or diskettes. For example, many companies use EDI to send purchase orders to their vendors, and the vendors send back electronic invoices. Data are exchanged through dial-up connections and modems (see Figure 11-3). EDI is also used to make automatic payroll deposits. Some companies and universities use EDI to send payroll information to banks or bank clearinghouses.

Figure 11-3

Electronic data interchange through modems

Desktop computer   Modem   Modem   Desktop computer

Using the Web for EDI is a step up from modem-to-modem wire transfers, since many organizations have ready Internet access with easy-to-use GUI interfaces. As Web security is improved, the Web will be a viable provider of EDI services.

VIRTUAL UNIVERSITY

A significant future Web presence will be the **virtual university**. With voice, video, and data capabilities, the Web promises to be a great way to offer classes for long-distance learning (see Figure 11-4). The advantage for students is that they can access classes, resources, and professors from just about anywhere. The advantage for universities is that they can save on buildings and equipment; and professors who used to commute to satellite campuses can instead provide instruction through the Web, without leaving town.

Opportunities exist for high schools as well to implement extended studies and summer school courses by means of the Internet. Basic math, English, and history courses could be offered. GED and self-improvement courses could be offered as well. Even credit card payments can be made through the Web.

Figure 11-4

Virtual
university on
the Internet

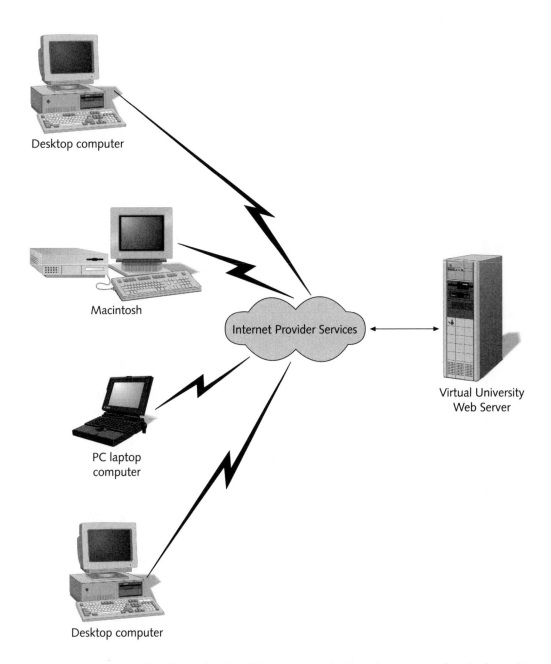

Desktop computer

Macintosh

Internet Provider Services

Virtual University
Web Server

PC laptop
computer

Desktop computer

Some universities and colleges already offer courses and selected programs of study through the Internet. One university, for example, offers a master's degree in telecommunications. As more universities and colleges develop programs, the need for high-speed network communications will grow so that homes, schools, and businesses can all be linked.

CONNECTING FROM HOME

The traditional method for connecting to the Internet has been by using a modem. Through his or her modem, the user dials up the modem of his or her Internet provider. As networking technology advances, this means of networking is rapidly changing. Telephone and cable TV companies are providing network access through cable TV and telephone line, by installing more fiber optic cable from city to city. Home users throughout the country will have direct cable access to the Internet by means of a wall outlet, providing greater incentive to access the Web. There will also be an impact on telephone, music, TV, and computer devices as these are combined into single electronic units.

ELECTRONIC MAIL

Electronic mail systems used from home and from work have implemented **voice messaging** capabilities. Voice messages can be sent on LANs, WANs, or through the Internet. For example, at work you may use voice messaging through Microsoft Mail or Microsoft Exchange, and at home you may use voice messaging through CompuServe Mail.

Electronic voice mail translates into a higher volume of network traffic because voice files are very large. It also is possible to attach large files to electronic mail, such as spreadsheets, databases, and word processing files, which are another source of high network traffic.

NETWORKS OF THE FUTURE

Networks of the future will need to find ways to accommodate high-volume traffic generated by client/server, Web, imaging, electronic forms, electronic mail, and other applications. Networking equipment will need to provide very high bandwidths to handle emerging applications.

Besides high bandwidth, it will be necessary to have reliable 24-hour service, with virtually no downtime. Our dependence on networks has become as great as that on telephone systems. Network problems will have to become "self-healing" in that alternate data routes will have to be immediately available.

At present, **synchronized optical network (SONET)** communications has the center stage as the networking technology of the future. If you are designing a network that will require high-speed communications, design it to use ATM (see Chapter 3) now, with the ability to adapt to SONET in the near future.

SONET

SONET is becoming the de facto standard for the very high-speed communications used by corporations, universities, telephone companies, and others. The Alliance for Telecommunications Industry Solutions (ATIS) developed the standard, which is endorsed by ANSI.

A significant advantage of SONET is that it is nonproprietary, so point-to-point network equipment can be purchased from a variety of vendors. SONET can connect to interfaces for ATM, SMDS, ISDN, PBX, routers, and other equipment.

SONET high-speed communications require single-mode fiber optic cable. Currently, signals can be transmitted over very long distances at speeds of up to 2.488 Gbps. SONET is designed to support future speeds of 13.271 Gbps and possibly beyond.

As demand for information grows, the network can be adapted to handle the load, if it is built to be SONET-compliant. For example, video conferencing to multiple points will be possible. Virtual reality applications will be supported. Both kinds of support will mean a wide range of possibilities for Web and client/server applications. It will create new opportunities for the virtual university and long-distance learning. SONET can be used also to transport high-fidelity music, radio broadcasts, and supercomputer images (such as detailed maps or topographics).

Since telephone and cable companies are adopting SONET, very high-speed communications will be brought into businesses and homes across the country. Internet communications and international data networks will be affected.

TRANSMISSION SPEED

SONET operates at a base level of 51.84 Mbps. This level is called Synchronous Transport Signal Level 1 (STS-1). From here, the signal can be incrementally multiplexed to higher speeds as needed for a particular type of service. The currently available range of speeds is given in Table 11-1.

Table 11-1

Existing SONET transmission rates

STS Level	Transmission Rate (Mbps)
STS-1	51.84
STS-3	155.52
STS-9	466.56
STS-12	622.08
STS-18	933.12
STS-24	1,244
STS-36	1,866
STS-48	2,488

Future SONET transmission speeds are anticipated to reach STS level 256 at 13.271 Gbps. These capabilities far exceed what is presently available with T1 or T3 telecommunications at 1.544 Mbps and 44.7 Mbps.

NETWORK ARCHITECTURE

SONET travels in a ring topology that is designed to provide three options for recovery from failure. One option is unidirectional path switching. With this option there is one fiber optic ring. The data signal is transmitted in both directions around the ring. The receiving node determines which signal to accept. If there is a break in one path, the signal on the alternative path still reaches the destination node. The data sent along the alternative path include a warning to the node that only one path is open.

Automatic protection switching is another form of recovery for a network failure. If a failure is detected at some point on the SONET network, the data are directed to an alternate switching node and are redirected to the assigned destination.

The third method of recovery provides the greatest level of redundancy. Bidirectional line switching requires a dual ring topology, so there are always two paths to a node (see Figure 11-5).

The data are sent to both rings, but in opposite directions. If there is a break along one path, the data on the second path will still get through. Pacific Bell uses bidirectional line switching and advertises protection switching within 50 milliseconds of transmission failure. Based on this fast recovery capability, their objective is to keep service available "99.999%" of the time.

Figure 11-5

SONET bidirectional line switching with dual rings

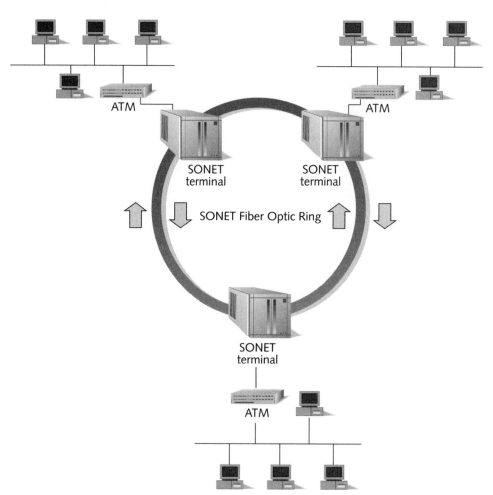

SONET FRAME

The STS-1 frame is the basic building block of the SONET frame. The STS-1 frame size is 90 bytes. It consists of **virtual tributaries (VTs)** as needed by the application (such as for voice, data, or video). Each VT is a separate envelope of data. The VT determines how a carrier signal is mapped into the SONET frame. For example, VTs are presently defined to map T1 (VT1.5) and T3 (VT6) communications. The VT design enables it to transport asynchronous signals as well as synchronous.

Besides carrying multiple VTs, the STS-1 frame contains a preface of overhead bits. The overhead bits contain error-detecting and other transport maintenance information for the frame. Figure 11-6 shows the STS-1 frame structure.

Figure 11-6

STS-1 SONET frame

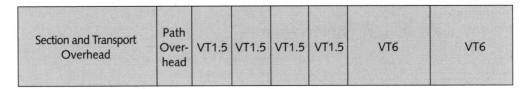

Section and Transport Overhead	Path Over-head	VT1.5	VT1.5	VT1.5	VT1.5	VT6	VT6

←──────────────────────── 90 bytes ────────────────────────→

There are four protocol layers used in SONET. The first is the photonic layer. This layer is similar to the physical layer of the OSI model. It handles transportation and conversion of the transported signals. The transmitted electrical signals are changed into optical signals to place onto the fiber optic cable, and the received optical signals are changed back to electrical signals.

The second layer is called the section layer. This layer encapsulates data, ensures that data are sent in the correct order, ensures the timing of each frame, and checks for transmission errors.

Next is the line layer. The line layer monitors for problems and handles recovery switching if a problem is detected. It also is responsible for multiplexing the signal and for ensuring that the entire frame reaches its destination.

The path layer provides signal mapping into the VTs. For example, it might map an ATM signal into one VT and an SMDS signal into another VT. Also, it ensures the success of the VT path from source to destination.

SONET HARDWARE

Several different types of hardware components make up a SONET network. SONET components are called elements. One element is the signal regenerator. This device operates as a receiver/transmitter. It can boost a received signal to extend it over very long distances. The CPE is the device used at the customer's end to interface his or her network with the SONET service provider. A wideband digital cross-connect is used to terminate the SONET signals and cross-connect VT level signals from optical to electrical media. Another SONET element is the broadband digital cross-connect. This device is used like a hub to route signal traffic, while interfacing incoming and outgoing signals to match different SONET routes on the network.

An add-drop multiplexer (ADM) is used to translate SONET signals to other network signals, such as ATM. The ADM also can translate back to SONET, such as translating an ATM signal to a SONET signal. Further, it can add a lower-speed signal, such as an ATM signal, to a higher-speed signal, such as an optical SONET signal. Similarly, it can drop the lower-speed signal off at the next site, for instance at another ATM site. Through the ADM, a signal from one site is placed (added) onto the SONET network. When the destination site is reached, the signal is dropped off at that destination. If an ADM site is not a dropoff point for a particular signal, the signal continues through the ADM toward its destination.

AN EXPERIMENT INTO THE FUTURE

Fifteen California Bay area organizations are participating in a project to link Internet services through ATM to SONET. The group members include the following:

- Apple Computer
- Digital Equipment Corporation
- Hewlett-Packard
- International Computer Science Institute
- Lawrence Berkeley Laboratory
- Lawrence Livermore National Laboratory
- NASA Ames Research Center
- Pacific Bell
- Sandia National laboratories
- Silicon Graphics
- SRI International
- Stanford University
- Sun Microsystems
- University of California, Berkeley
- Xerox Palo Alto Research Center

These members have an ATM-based network with SONET capability provided through Pacific Bell. The network is called BAGNet. An assumption of the project is that SONET and ATM are the high-speed communications vehicles of the future. One of the goals is to provide IP-based Internet services through ATM and on through SONET. To accomplish the goal, they are working to map IP onto ATM.

Through projects like the BAGNet initiative, we are moving closer to making national and international high-bandwidth networking a reality.

SUMMARY

Future networks will have to be capable of handling more data and larger files than ever before. Client/server software will continue to push networks for better response and the ability to carry large amounts of data. Electronic mail, electronic imaging, and wider use of electronic forms will create additional demands on bandwidth.

Another area of tremendous growth is the Internet and Web-based applications. The Internet is home to millions of users, with more Web pages appearing each day.

Enterprise-wide networks of the future will have to be able to provide nearly unlimited bandwidth to handle the expectations for growth in computer applications. SONET and ATM are presently the likely candidates to supply high-speed networks for the future (which means we will move from packet-based to cell-based networks). Many telecommunications providers are preparing SONET networks to bring high-speed communications to all parts of the country.

KEY TERMS

Term/Acronym	Definition
Electronic Data Interchange (EDI)	This process is used to transfer information, such as purchase orders, in electronic form over dedicated lines, telephone line modems, or other communications paths.
Electronic Imaging	Maps, contracts, photographs, forms, and other paper-based images can be duplicated as electronic images on a computer.
Open Access	Standard rules or guidelines for reaching data in a database to create queries, reports, or data updates.
Synchronous Optical Network (SONET)	A very high-speed data communications standard that operates over fiber optic cable.
Virtual Tributary	A means of enveloping unique data in separate paths within a SONET frame, so that multiple forms of data can be rapidly transported.
Virtual University	This phrase refers to the idea of offering classes long distance through electronic means, such as the Internet.
Voice Messaging	Electronic messages with voice reproduction that can be sent through networks such as the Internet.

REVIEW EXERCISES

1. _____ tools help programmers develop software applications more quickly than in the past.

2. What are the protocol layers in SONET?

3. How does SONET provide protected data communications?

4. What is electronic data interchange? How is it being used today?

5. What kind of network traffic is a relational database likely to create?

6. What is an ADM's function on a SONET network?

7. What types of network problems will be caused by the virtual university? Is the virtual university a realistic concept?

8. Experiment with the Internet and a browser, such as Netscape, Internet Explorer, or Mosaic. Find some statistics on present Internet use. Report any speed or access problems as part of your Internet research.

9. Contact your local cable TV provider. Do they plan to offer networking access in the near future? If so, how will they do it?

10. What services are provided by your local telephone company? Do they have ISDN? Do they plan to offer networking services at some point?

11. What device is used to transmit SONET signals over long distances?

12. Check with your college or university administrative offices. Are they using electronic forms? If so, what forms are electronic and how are they transmitted?

GLOSSARY

A

Addressing Network equipment is identified by means of a unique "address." No two network computers, printers, or other network equipment will have the same address assigned to them.

Angular Circumference The measurement of the maximum amount of bend in fiber optic cable.

ARCNET This proprietary transport method is similar to token ring. ARCNET has a limited geographic range and transmits data at much slower speeds than token ring.

Asynchronous Transfer Mode (ATM) A transport method that uses multiple channels and switching to send voice, video, and data transmissions on the same network. ATM data transfer stresses efficient, high-speed data throughput.

Attachment Unit Interface (AUI) This interface is used to connect Ethernet, fiber optic, and other backbone cabling to hubs, routers, and other network equipment.

Attenuation The power loss on fiber optic cable as measured in decibels.

B

Backplane Modular equipment has a main circuit board or backplane with plug-in connectors for the modular boards. The main circuit board provides connections between the modular boards, power to the modular boards, and grounding.

Baseband A network cable with only one channel to transmit data.

Beaconing A token ring network goes into a beaconing state when an error condition is detected. The error condition is signaled when a node sends a beacon frame to broadcast that there is a problem. The network remains in this state until the problem is resolved.

BNC T Connector This coaxial connector is in the shape of a T. The top ends are connected to the cable (or one may be connected to a terminator). The bottom of the T goes to the network node.

Broadband This type of cable has several channels for transmitting data simultaneously.

Broadcast Storm This situation occurs when a network segment is saturated with more packets than can be effectively handled.

Bus Topology This type of network is configured so that nodes are connected to a segment of cable in the logical shape of a line, with a terminator at each end.

C

Cable Scanner This testing instrument is used to measure cable length on a network.

CablePlant All the combined cable wire that runs in a building or on a campus.

Cabling The communication wire used to connect equipment in a network. The cable provides a medium for the electrical signal that carries information from one networked computer to another.

Call Control Signal This signal is used to initiate communication between two nodes using a switched virtual circuit on a frame relay network. The signal also is used to disconnect communication between the nodes.

Capacity Management This process involves calculating present capacity of network systems, including disk capacity, server capacity, CPU resources, and other factors. After present capacity is known, projections are made to determine future equipment needs.

Cascade A bridging technique where each bridge is connected to two networks.

Cell ATM data are encoded into units called cells for transmission on the network.

Change Management This process tracks changes in the network and in systems attached to the network. Often change management is accomplished by entering changes in a database, with a description of the change, the date of the change, and the reason for the change.

Channel Service Unit (CSU) This device provides an interface between a router communications port and a communications line, such as T1.

Client A computer that is used to access a file server, mainframe, minicomputer, or other computer that allows access to multiple users. The client may use the accessed computer (host) in order to process data. Other software and data may be transferred from the main computer to the client for processing.

Client/Server Applications Many software applications are being written based on networking capabilities. In client/server systems, processing of data may occur at the workstation (client) or at the host or server.

Collision At times, packets collide on an Ethernet network, particularly when network traffic is high. A packet collision serves as an indication that broadcasting should stop until the collision situation has passed.

Connectivity The ability to connect a variety of devices to a network. Network connectivity is based on factors such as the network protocol, the type of cabling, and the speed of the network.

Cost This value is used to determine the most efficient pathways on a network. It is calculated based on line speed and distance to the root bridge.

D

Data Communications Equipment (DCE) A network device that performs packet switching.

Data Encryption The process of creating computer algorithms that encode and decode data so that they are protected from interception by others.

Data Encryption Standard A network data encryption standard developed by the National Institute of Standards and Technology and IBM.

Data Packet The unit of information that is sent from one network node to the next. A computer on the network forms data into small distinct units. The data-filled units are sent one at a time to the receiving computer.

Data Service Unit (DSU) This unit is used along with a CSU for communications over a T1 line. The DSU converts data to be sent over the line, and it converts data received from the line into a readable digital format.

Data Terminal Equipment (DTE) Terminals, workstations, and host computers that operate on a packet-switching network are called DTEs.

Database Administrator (DBA) This type of account exists on host and file server computers that house a database. The DBA has master security privileges for all levels of the database.

Datagram TCP/IP breaks data into these smaller units, which can be transmitted in streams on the network.

Defragmentation Disk defragmentation is a process that rearranges data to fill in the empty spaces that develop on disks.

Dotted Decimal Notation System The most common IP address scheme, where address references are separated by periods.

E

Echo Canceler This device is used to eliminate signal reflection in the cabling of a network. Echo cancelers are used on ISDN networks.

Electro-Magnetic Interference (EMI) Magnetic force fields are generated by many electrical devices. These force fields can cause interference with electric signals in nearby computer cabling.

Electronic Data Interchange (EDI) This process is used to transfer information, such as purchase orders, in electronic form over dedicated lines, telephone line modems, or other communications paths.

Electronic Imaging Maps, contracts, photographs, forms, and other paper-based images can be duplicated as electronic images on a computer.

Encryption Key When data are encrypted on a network, some encryption methods use a password that must be known to both the sending and receiving nodes. The password acts as a key to unlock files.

Ethernet This network transport system uses the CSMA/CD access method for packet transmission in LAN applications. Ethernet is typically implemented in a bus or star topology.

F

Fat Client Some client/server software leaves most of the processing to the client rather than sharing processing resources. Such systems are called fat clients.

Fat Pipe High-speed fiber optic or copper cable (fast Ethernet or 100 Mbps) used to link network equipment on a backbone.

Fiber Distributed Data Interface (FDDI) A transport system that uses token passing to implement high-speed data transfer. FDDI networks can support voice and video transmissions in addition to data.

File Server A computer with an operating system that enables multiple users to access it and share software applications and data files.

File Transfer Protocol (FTP) Software designed to transfer data files from one computer system to another, such as from an MVS system to a UNIX system.

File-By-File Backup Most backups are performed to save data by file, rather than by binary image. File-by-file backups enable restores of single files, multiple files, subdirectories, directories, and complete volumes.

Filtering This is the ability of a bridge to determine that a packet should be directed to its originating LAN and not forwarded to a connecting or different LAN.

Firewall These devices (and software) protect networks and file servers from unauthorized access. They also help reduce unwanted network traffic.

Flooding When a bridge cannot determine the destination of a packet, it may forward the packet to all known networks.

G

Graphical User Interface (GUI) An interface that uses pictures and graphics to represent operations on the computer.

H

Hello BPDU Packets transmitted by a root bridge at a specified interval. The packets acknowledge to other bridges that the root bridge is working.

Help Desk This application software is used to keep data on hardware and software problems, along with information on how the problems have been solved. The help desk software is tied into a database that can be used for reference.

HIPPI This transport method is designed for use with peripherals that need very high data speeds, such as supercomputer disk drives. HIPPI is capable of transmitting very large data packets along a single channel.

Hop Each time a packet travels through a router, it has gone one hop. The number of hops is tracked by some protocols to determine if a packet should be discarded as lost or aged.

Host This type of computer has an operating system that allows multiple computers to access it at the same time. Programs and information may be processed at the host, or they may be downloaded to the accessing computer (client) for processing.

Hot Swap Some network equipment allows you to replace defective boards without powering down the equipment. These hot swaps are a form of fault tolerance.

I

Image Backup This type of backup uses a process that takes a "snapshot" of the entire contents of a disk or volume. Image backups are stored in binary format.

Internetwork Packet Exchange (IPX) This protocol is used by Novell NetWare and provides best-effort delivery of data packets. This protocol uses a variation of the data transfer algorithm known as routing information protocol.

J

Journal A backup file that keeps track of new transactions in a software system. If the main transaction file or a database is damaged, the journal files enable the newly entered transaction data to be recovered.

L

Layered Architecture In the network model, this means that data packets travel up and down defined communication levels, such as those described in the OSI model. Each level or layer adds information to or extracts information from the data packet.

Line-Of-Sight Transmissions Relatively short-distance radio signal transmissions that travel from point to point along the Earth's surface.

Local Area Network (LAN) A series of interconnected computers, printers, and other computer equipment that share hardware and software resources. The service area is usually limited to a given floor, office area, or building.

M

Media Access Control (MAC) A sublayer of the OSI data-link layer. It uses network addressing for transmitting and receiving data. It also schedules transmissions on shared access mediums, such as Ethernet.

Media Filter Electronic interference is eliminated on twisted-pair cabling by using a media filter.

Metropolitan Area Network (MAN) A network that reaches throughout a large area, such as a city or a large college campus.

Multi-Port Bridges These bridges can link several individual segments into one network.

N

NetWare A commonly used file server operating system that provides file services, print services, and access security to network workstations through the IPX protocol.

NetWare Core Protocol (NCP) Novell file servers use this configuration of drivers to communicate with nodes and other file servers on a network.

Network A communication system that enables many users to share computer resources such as personal computers, application software, data/voice/video information, host computers, printers, and fax capabilities.

Network Agents Repeaters, bridges, routers and other network devices become agents when they are equipped to gather network performance information.

Network File System (NFS) This network file transfer protocol ships files as streams of records.

Network Interface Card (NIC) This electrical circuit board is used by computers, printers, and other equipment so they are able to connect to a network and transfer data.

Network Management Station (NMS) This workstation is a central device that gathers, tracks, and stores network performance data. It obtains the data from network equipment that runs agent software for collecting the data.

Network Shell Each workstation on a Novell network is equipped with drivers that are called the network shell. These drivers enable the workstation to communicate with file servers and other workstations.

Network Speed The speed at which network architecture permits packets to travel on the cable.

Network Traffic The amount and frequency of data transported over a network. Many network monitoring tools measure network traffic in terms of a percentage of full use of the network bandwidth.

Node Any device or entity connected to a network is a node. Network-connected personal computers, file servers, printers, and mainframes are individual nodes.

O

Open Access Standard rules or guidelines for reaching data in a database to create queries, reports, or data updates.

P

Packet Switching A simultaneous parallel conversation of data along separate paths in the same switch.

Partition An Ethernet network device will shut down (partition) a segment that it determines is malfunctioning

Peer Protocol In the OSI model, this is used by nodes to communicate within one layer.

Peer-to-Peer Communication In this type of communication, any computer can communicate with other computers on an equal or peer-like basis.

Ping A network node can test for the presence of another node by sending a short query to that node. This process is called a ping.

Power Budget The minimum power level required to transmit a light wave successfully along fiber optic cable.

Power Filter This device ensures that clean power is delivered to attached electrical equipment. It smooths out power "bumps" and delivers a constant level of power.

Primitive A command used by a layer in the OSI model to communicate with an adjacent layer.

Print Server This device enables one or more people to send printouts to a network printer.

Probes   These may be stand-alone or existing network devices equipped with software to gather information about network performance. They are used to collect data for an RMON MIB II database.

Propagation Velocity (Vp)   One means to show how fast data packets travel is to express their speed in terms of a percentage of the speed of light, which is the propagation velocity.

Protocol   An established guideline that determines how networked data are formatted into a packet, how they are transmitted, and how they are interpreted at the receiving end.

R

Radio Frequency Interference (RFI)   Electronic devices operate at frequencies that cause them to emit radio waves. These radio waves can cause interference on computer cabling and other communication equipment.

Redundancy   Alternate network routes or alternate equipment are built into some networks to ensure that packets reach their destination in the event of equipment failure. For example, when one bridge fails, packets can be redirected to a different bridge on their way to the destination node.

Redundant Array of Inexpensive Disks (RAID)   Designed to provide data protection when a disk failure occurs.

Ring Topology   The configuration of a network in the shape of a continuous ring or circle, with nodes connected around the ring.

S

Security   The ability to protect data from unauthorized access, such as tapping into network traffic.

Segment   A network can be divided into smaller units, called segments. A segment on an Ethernet network is terminated at each end and supports up to 30 nodes (reserving one node for a repeater or hub connection).

Segmenting   In this process, the network manager isolates a portion of the network to reduce bottlenecks and to reduce the impact of a network malfunction on other portions of the network.

Sequenced Packet Exchange (SPX)   This protocol is packet-oriented and relies on sequence numbers or acknowledgments (provided by the packet) for data transmission.

Server Advertising Packets   Network transmissions broadcast at regular intervals by a file server. The purpose of these transmissions is to show that the file server is functional and available to be accessed.

Source Routing   A technique used by token ring bridges to forward packets to a network.

Spanning Tree Algorithm   This algorithm is used to ensure packets are not transmitted in an endless loop. It also enables packets to be sent along the most cost-effective network path.

Spread Spectrum   This is a wide-bandwidth electronic signal transmission frequency.

Spread Spectrum Technology (SST) This technology is used by wireless networks in place of cable to allow network nodes to communicate. Network data are transmitted by means of high-frequency radio signals.

Star Topology In this topology, a network is configured with a central hub and cable segments radiating from the hub to the nodes.

Stripping In this process, data are removed from a token ring or FDDI network by the sending node.

Subnet Many networks are really composed of several smaller networks that combine to make a larger network. The smaller networks are subnets.

Surge Protector Lighting strikes, power plant difficulties, and other situations can result in temporary dramatic surges in electric power. The surge protector prevents these surges from damaging sensitive equipment, such as computer equipment.

Switching Fabric The switching method used by a hub.

Synchronous Optical Network (SONET) A very high-speed data communications standard that operates over fiber optic cable.

System Administrator A database system account type that has master security access to all databases on a server.

System Fault Tolerance This involves building in duplicate portions of a system or designing systems to withstand hardware or software failures.

System Redundancy A network system that has built-in measures to prevent failure is said to be redundant. System redundancy might include alternate network paths, fail-safe network equipment, and algorithms to handle network errors.

Systems Network Architecture (SNA) This communications protocol is used by IBM for communications between IBM mainframe computers and terminals.

T

Telecommuting Some employers offer a program to allow employees to work from home or from a remote computing site. The employee uses telephone lines or wireless communications to access the host computers at a central work site.

Terminal Emulator Some mainframes and minicomputers are designed to communicate with terminals instead of PC workstations. A terminal emulator software program is run on a workstation to make it act like a terminal.

Thin Client This term refers to client/server systems where processing resources are evenly allocated between client and server.

Token Ring This network transport method passes a token from node to node. The token is used to coordinate transmission of data, because only the node possessing the token can send data.

Topology The layout or physical design of a network is its topology. Networks are built with different physical designs, including a star shape, a circle, and a straight line.

Transmission Control Protocol/Internet Protocol (TCP/IP) Two combined protocols. TCP is a reliable connection-oriented data transfer method that uses connectionless routing, which is provided by IP.

Transmission Rate The speed at which data are transported on a network. On some networks the speed may be as low as 1 megabits per second (Mbps), and on others it may be over 100 Mbps.

U

Uninterruptible Power Supply (UPS) This device consists of a bank of rechargeable batteries that deliver power when the central source of power is down.

User Datagram Protocol (UDP) This TCP/IP protocol defines how to construct datagrams and transmit them on the network.

V

Virtual Circuit A logical communication path established by the OSI network layer for sending and receiving data.

Virtual Tributary A means of enveloping unique data in separate paths within a SONET frame, so that multiple forms of data can be rapidly transported.

Virtual University This phrase refers to the idea of offering classes long distance through electronic means, such as the Internet.

Voice Messaging Electronic messages with voice reproduction that can be sent through networks such as the Internet.

W

Wide Area Network (WAN) A far reaching system of networks. WANs can extend across state lines and across continents. They make it possible for thousands of users to send data to one another.

Wiring Closet This small room or closet provides a place for network equipment and central network wiring, such as punch-downs and patch panels.

Workgroup   To a network-aware operating system such as Microsoft Windows, Microsoft NT, or Novell NetWare, a workgroup is a logical grouping of computer users for the purpose of sharing files, executables, and other computer functions.

Workstation   Any computer that has its own CPU. The workstation may be used as a stand-alone computer for word processing, spreadsheet creation, or other software applications. It also may be used to access another computer such as a file server or a mainframe computer.

X

Xerox Network System (XNS)   XNS was developed to provide a means for nodes to communicate on Ethernet networks. The IPX protocol is modeled after XNS. XNS packet construction is similar to the IEEE 802.3 format.

INDEX